# Captured by the City

# Captured by the City:
# Perspectives in Urban Culture Studies

Edited by

## Blagovesta M. Momchedjikova

**CAMBRIDGE
SCHOLARS**

P U B L I S H I N G

Captured by the City:
Perspectives in Urban Culture Studies,
Edited by Blagovesta M. Momchedjikova

This book first published 2013

Cambridge Scholars Publishing

12 Back Chapman Street, Newcastle upon Tyne, NE6 2XX, UK

British Library Cataloguing in Publication Data
A catalogue record for this book is available from the British Library

ISBN (10): 1-4438-4289-3, ISBN (13): 978-1-4438-4289-1

To my wonderful parents—
Prof. Dr. Mihail Blagoev Momchedjikov
and Dipl. Eng. Toshka Atanassova Momchedjikova—
two serious engineers with a soft spot for cities.
They have taught me all about living in cities and loving it.

"When a man rides a long time through wild regions he feels the desire for a city."
—Italo Calvino, *Invisible Cities*

# TABLE OF CONTENTS

## Part II. City Identities: in Transit and Situ

## Part III. Performing the City: Voices and Practices

# LIST OF ILLUSTRATIONS

# ACKNOWLEDGEMENTS

First and foremost, I would like to thank the contributors to this volume—Inés Rae, Lois Ascher, David Michalski, Tara H. Milbrandt, Matthew A. Postal, Nathalie Boucher, Margarita Kompelmahler, Tolonda M. Tolbert, J. Emmanuel Raymundo, Michelle Lee Dent, Samuel Neural, Keisha-Gaye Anderson, Joe Trotta, Ronald Dorris, E. Jerry Persaud, Matthew Hawkins, Marta Rabikowska, Melanie Sovern, Rafaela Santos— for their remarkable commitment during the hot summer months of 2012. I met many of these same contributors at the annual Mid-Atlantic Popular/American Culture Association (MAPACA) conferences over the years, when they presented at the Urban Culture Area, which I have been so fortunate to chair for the past ten years. I owe a lot to this organization and its leaders: Tom Kitts, Lois Ascher, the late Loretta Lorence, Gary Earl Ross, Pam Detrixhe, Tracey Bowen, Marilyn Stern, Scott Henderson, Jason Davids Scott, who have allowed me to be in the company of such stellar scholars and artists.

It is the Urban Culture Area presentations, writing workshops, post-conference dinners, phone and skype conversations, questionnaires, and emails that planted the idea about a permanent center for Urban Culture research and exchange in my head. The idea then flourished among seven of us: Samuel Neural (Anthropology), Tara Milbrandt (Sociology), David Michalski (Cultural Studies), Inés Rae (Photographic Studies), Joe Trotta (Linguistics), Godefroy Desrosier-Lauzon (History), and myself (Performance Studies), and we began to call ourselves, as per Godefroy's suggestion, an 'Urban Culture Collective'. And that is how this book was born. Since all seven of us came from different disciplines but shared a fascination with cities, Tara suggested that the book showcase precisely that: how different disciplines approach the city, and I cannot thank her enough for that. She was also kind enough to let me name this volume after her original research on street photographers, and thus we have *Captured by the City*. Thank you, Tara, as well as Sam and David, who spent many, many hours on the phone with me, helping me sort through a ton of logistics along the steep and sometimes thorny path towards successfully completing this book. And, thank you, Cambridge Scholars Publishing, for trusting in this volume.

I would like to extend my warmest thanks also to The Expository Writing Program at New York University, directed by Prof. Pat C. Hoy II, where I have been teaching for the past fifteen years. That place has nurtured me as a thinker, teacher, and writer. Here, I have been able to grow personally and professionally, testing ideas, conducting research, exploring the city, and even publishing my work on the *Panorama of the City of New York* and Flushing Meadows Corona Park in the textbook for essay writing students. Special thanks go also to Prof. Darlene Forrest and Prof. Randy Martin, the co-directors of the Tisch School of the Arts writing initiative that I am a part of. They have always encouraged me to integrate my love of the city into my teaching. I am also grateful to my wonderful colleagues and students, who continue to enrich my perspective of the city through theirs.

And since I have mentioned the *Panorama*, I would like also to thank the Queens Museum of Art and the many fantastic individuals there who continue to indulge me in my city scale model obsession: the museum director Tom Finkelpearl (who continuously taps into my knowledge of the *Panorama*), the director of exhibitions Hitomi Iwasaki (who invited me to plan an exhibition on panoramas with her), the director of education Lauren Schloss (who hired me to give public tours of the model), the director of external affairs David Strauss (who commissioned me to write the script for the *Panorama* media show), the manager of the New New Yorkers program outreach Jose Rodriguez (who arranged for me to teach a class about the *Panorama* for immigrants). Certainly, special thanks go to Prof. Barbara Kirshenblatt-Gimblett from New York University, who sensed the magic of the *Panorama* and expertly guided my doctoral dissertation on it; to Prof. May Joseph from Pratt Institute, who encouraged me to write about the poetics of cities and let me share my knowledge with the students in her institution through a class on the Culture of Cities; and to my very special friends, attorney-at-law Nathan Waxman and his wife Karen L. Dean: they taught me that 'urban aesthetics' is not a choice; it's a way of life.

Further, I would like to thank David Michalski, the editor-in-chief of *Streetnotes,* for granting me the privilege to edit a special issue out of his journal—*Urban Feel.* Through it, I realized that every person's feelings about the city are unique and complex; and that Urban Culture is not just a theme—it is a field. Putting *Urban Feel* together in 2010 prepared me for the scope of work that I would later engage in with *Captured by the City: Perspectives in Urban Culture Studies.*

Last but not least, many, many thanks to my family and friends for supporting me in the process of putting this book together, and to David Michalski and Ingrid Nunez for making it look the way it should!

# INTRODUCTION

## URBAN CULTURE STUDIES

### BLAGOVESTA M. MOMCHEDJIKOVA

## What is Urban Culture Studies?

Cities are living organisms: they grow, change, or sometimes disappear. They are fascinatingly porous: letting those who want in and those who want—out. They can embrace but they can also reject. They can be robust and healthy but they can also be sick. They can be obliviously happy but also depressingly sad. Many and intricate are the processes—planned or accidental—that sustain, speed up, or slow down the pulse of the city, infinitely affecting city dwellers, who may or may not have precipitated these processes. Urban Culture Studies aims at sensing and studying that pulse of the city: at times irregular, always complex, and never disingenuous.

Urban Culture Studies is, simply put, an amalgamation of disciplines, approaches, and methodologies, whose common interest lies in the city, any city—mundane, fragmented, and monotone, yet simultaneously also extraordinary, coherent, and polyphonic. It engages the colorful and contradictory urban form—the physical environment (a building, a neighborhood, a park) and its reverberations into other physical or non-physical worlds (a memory, a feeling, a sound)—from a variety of traditional perspectives: sociological, anthropological, historical, linguistic, photographic, while also relying on the inter-disciplinary conversations already begun by the newer cultural, visual, performance, and popular culture studies.

Unlike the established discipline of Urban Studies, for example, which deals with the city as an object, and which is reserved for the more exclusive group of urban planners, policy makers, and architects, the currently forming discipline of Urban Culture Studies embraces the city as a dynamic encounter, an artistic endeavor, an event, a practice, a performance, an interplay, and is open to academics from a variety of fields, artists, and practitioners alike. Ultimately, it attempts to carve its own, unique field of inquiry: based on the plurality of perspectives on the city, which complement each other, and in their plurality grant us a better understanding of cities—why do we dream about them, flock to them, develop them, negotiate them, leave them, or return to them—and the complex, contradictory lives we live in them.

## Why Now?

The city has preoccupied generations of thinkers, poets, planners, and policy makers. From Georg Simmel to Richard Sennet, Walter Benjamin to Michel deCerteau, Baron Hausmann to Robert Moses, Italo Calvino to Yi-fu Tuan, Jane Jacobs to Sharon Zukin, the city has been considered a legitimate place: be it with its problems or with its wonders, but almost always with its unmatched experiences. The proliferation of social media in the last decade, however, has posed a particular challenge to how we think about place and thus, about cities and ourselves in them. Facebook, Twitter, and Skype allow us to inhabit many disparate places at the same time. Now deCerteau's famous walk, which connected the "here" and "there" on the city street has become a mouse click, which has collapsed "here" into "there": they are simply one and the same thing.

Whether we borrow the term "hybrid place" from geographer Andrew Blum or "non-place" from anthropologist Marc Auge, to describe this state of virtual living in many places at the same time, one thing is clear—while euphorically friending, texting, or chatting, we are less and less present to the only one place that can provide us with tangible sensations and experiences: the immediate and urgent *here*. We browse the world wide web more so than scout the city streets, disconnected from the live city yet LinkedIn. The city has thus become a service provider for posts, blogs, tweets—a loser to these, perhaps safer, virtual representations. And we, consuming sites, updating profiles, i-touching cold electronics away, boast multiple selves. Unchained by the challenges of real-life urbanity, these selves wander our cities like ghosts—hybrid selves, non-selves?

Urban Culture Studies allows us to approach the diffusion of place and resulting diffusion of self as processes of reversible nature. With its emphasis on the tangible connections among people, places, and interactions, it offers a holistic and humanitarian approach to urban self and urban place, which can help re-position us in the world of global information towards the revival of both self and place. In such re-positioning, we can recover our experience of place and self precisely due to the interplay between physical and virtual place, physical and virtual self, not in spite of it. As a combination of disciplines and methodologies, it fosters not interface but face-to-face exchanges and communities—the true antidotes to the alienating effects of virtual consumerism. And that too, contributes to making our cities healthier.

## Why Captured by the City?

But as we expand into new locations and selves thanks to never-ending technological innovations, natural and man-made disasters continue to redraw the landscape of cities—uprooting people, erasing places—all over the world. Such oppositional developments affect how we experience, preserve, and remember cities and ourselves in them. Equipped with memory sticks and zip drives, we transmit and store our memories in bytes, as if our electronic devices are indeed responsible for one of the most distinctly human experiences: that of remembering. To engage in the act of remembering means to summon up a visceral, tangible experience of a person, a site, an object, an event, or the combination of some or all of these, as well as the feelings that they provoked. Such acts of remembering locate us in time and place and thus create personal as well as cultural identity: they make us into who we really are.

These acts of remembering, however, are slowly fleeing from us because we live the virtual life more so than the real one yet at the end of the day we bring back no tangible evidence from that virtual existence, and thus no memories. And that is how *Captured by the City: Perspectives in Urban Culture Studies* came to be. It is an effort to remind us that although we prefer to embrace the internet, the real city still embraces us: it still collects rent, heat, electric, gas, water, cable, garbage, bus, subway charges from us; it still fuels our desires, hopes, disappointments; it still perplexes, surprises, fascinates us. This book is a serious reminder that we are still caught in the real city's web of ideas, connections, and contradictions, right *here*.

Ultimately, *Captured by the City* aims to re-enact for its readers, as it did for its contributors, the art of being present to the city, which is a prerequisite to remembering, enjoying, imagining, and planning the city. This is the book's main goal, and its main asset. Being present suggests that one is *here,* and that one is here *now*—that one is consciously connected to her immediate surroundings, processing what is happening to her in the context of these very surroundings. This collection also hopes to inspire its readers to wake up to the present and to engage in their own art of being present, which helps restore the value of real human connections and communities in the face of numbing virtual consumption—a genuine advancement of the discipline of Urban Culture Studies.

## How is This Collection Put Together?

Made up of eighteen essays, this collection represents the possibilities for critical reading, thinking, and writing that Urban Culture Studies, as a discipline, opens up. Thematically, the essays in the volume cover a wide range—the preservation of place in memory; the successful daily use of public spaces; the relationship between personal, communal, and cultural identity; gentrification, urban development, and disaster; immigration, travel, and the displacement of self; staging belonging through everyday or scheduled performances, language, and sound. Stylistically, the texts represent a mix of genres—historical or ethnographic studies of public sites and events; poetic accounts of personal geographies through cities; explorations of highly orchestrated or improvised events in designated urban areas. Taken together, the texts re-enact the basic principle of the discipline of Urban Culture Studies—inter-connectivity.

The three-part structure of the volume—Places, People, and Performances—with six essays in each part—is, to an extent, arbitrary, as places, people, and performances (scheduled, spontaneous, or mundane) are always interconnected and interdependent: you cannot consider one without the others. Still, there are some governing factors such as priorities and perspectives within each text that allow for the texts to be grouped in this particular way, and that provoke dynamic connections within each part. At the same time, dynamic connections across all three parts are also expected and hoped for. In living urban environments, it is like that as well: everything is always connected to everything else: it is these connections in the city that we hope to illuminate through our studies, foster through the combination of our different perspectives, and cause through the life of each text in this volume next to another.

Unique to this collection is the two-paragraph, formal introductory section to each essay. While the first paragraph outlines the author's discipline, methodology, and particular engagement with the urban in general, the second details the essay's particular project. The purpose of these reflective paragraphs is twofold: to both position every contributor within a particular field of inquiry (say, Sociology, Anthropology, History, Visual Studies) as well as on the broader, overlapping spectrum of Urban Culture. It is these two paragraphs that explicitly connect all essays to each other and to the larger project of this book: to establish the legitimacy and urgency of the new Urban Culture Studies discipline. While there are many important books out there, which offer fascinating inter-disciplinary studies within the same discipline, thus broadening the scope of that particular discipline, *Captured by the City* offers a cross-disciplinary (photographic, sociological, historical, architectural, anthropological, linguistic, theatrical, etc.) examination of the common urban theme, thus broadening the scope of Urban Culture Studies as a field in itself.

## Places, People, Performances

*Part One: City Places: In Memory, History, and Real-time* deals with the preservation, development, and improvement of place. Ines Rae asks us to consider how the memory of place gets constructed: comparing photographs of Preston, England, with the memories that they produce, she ponders if memory belongs to people, places, images, or stories. Lois Ascher proposes that in the face of destruction, memory resides in museums, like the one that former residents of Boston's West End (a notorious victim to urban development) created. For David Michalski, however, urban memories exist in fragmentation and collage, as do his of Buffalo, New York—his hometown. Still, though fragmented, any act of remembering allows us to claim the city, as does any practice in the city. One such practice is street-postering, which Tara Milbrandt observes as it divides the city of Toronto and its residents when a ban threatens it. Another is park construction, which Matthew Postal shows can be rather successful in New York City when the interests of policy makers and park goers coincide. But to create useful public places, Nathalie Boucher cautions, we have to heed to our contemporary needs of public place not to what history instructs us, and thus she finds unexpected liveliness in many "doomed" public sites in downtown Los Angeles.

*Part Two: City Identities: In Transit and Situ* explores what happens to the urban self in the face of economic, geographic, and social change. Margarita Kompelmahler observes the struggles of Soviet immigrants in the Twin Cities, Minnesota, to preserve their former national identity through customs such as social dance, while also trying to remain publicly invisible in their adopted home. The opposite is the case in Tolonda Tolbert's study of the "Gatekeepers"—a certain gathering of men from Afro-Caribbean descent, who openly guard their community against the forces of gentrification on a particular block in Brooklyn, New York. J. Emmanuel Raymundo shows us how in moments of urban crisis (as evidenced by disaster and cinematic representation), certain identities quickly disappear—African Americans from hurricane-ridden New Orleans at the dawn of $21^{st}$ century, and Asian Americans from the apocalyptic movie *San Francisco* (1936). Temporary (and temporal) disappearance and dislocation, and the subsequent remake of self is what Michelle Dent experiences during her teaching assignment in Abu Dhabi;

what Steve, a Mohawk ironworker from Montreal in New York City narrates in Samuel Neural's ethnography; and what Keisha Gaye-Anderson goes through as a young Jamaican woman who wants to succeed in The Big Apple.

*Part Three: Performing the City: Voices and Practices* studies the interactions between people and places, as evidenced in everyday or scheduled activities, and how these contribute to one's sense of belonging to the city. Joe Trotta considers how place breeds certain linguistic expressions, and how urban dialects form and develop as a result of inhabiting particular places. This is furthered in Ronald Dorris' study of the musicality of speech that the residents of New Orleans possess, and how it formed historically. For E. Jerry Persaud, that's the case with hip hop music, which both reflects and perpetuates the inner-city ghetto: as a physical place, a state of mind, a lifestyle, a lexicon, and a flow. Mathew Hawkins and Marta Rabikowska show how cities provoke artistic creation as they pioneer their film practices in a bar in Plumstead, England, in an effort to discover the larger community of that particular area, to which they also want to belong. Melanie Sovern, too, studies how theatrical improvisation and street performance allow a particular theater troupe to engage with and celebrate New York City. Finally, Rafaela Santos' self-portrait stares at us, as we read the heartfelt stories of a black Latina from the Bronx, New York, who is determined to break the cycle of poverty she grew up in, and leave her mark on the city against all odds.

# Goals

*Captured by the City: New Perspectives in Urban Culture Studies* is a reader, a textbook, and a navigation tool for those intrigued by everything urban, those curious to understand the range of possibilities that this recently formed field presents, and those dedicated to its further development and expansion. As a collection of different disciplines, subjects, tools, methodologies, approaches, and writing styles, this book can be useful to teachers and students, scholars and artists, regardless of their particular affiliations because it demonstrates not the advancement of a single discipline but how different disciplines intersect to form a new field of study—Urban Culture Studies, which is, by its very nature, cross-disciplinary. As such, *Captured by the City* is foundational: it is a new rubric, which helps its readers approach the multi-faceted city from a variety of angles, and see it the way Urban Culture Studies does: through all its parts.

Teachers can use this volume to teach the city from a myriad of perspectives, and from several perspectives at the same time. By critically addressing the complexities of cities, teachers can educate students how to be better readers, thinkers, and writers, and how to improve the future of cities. *Captured by the City* can be a useful textbook for those who are dedicated to teaching Urban Culture Studies; it can also be of interest to the many different disciplines that it represents: Sociology, Anthropology, History, Linguistics, Architectural History, Urban Studies, American Studies, African-American Studies, Caribbean Studies, Postcolonial Studies, Critical Media Studies, Photographic Studies, Film Studies, English, Comparative Literature, Documentary Poetics, Writing, Cultural Studies, Theater Studies, Dance Studies, Performance Studies, Feminist Ethnography, Race and Cultural Criminology. Students can use this volume to learn to see the city as a dynamic entity, which is so rich that in order to grasp it fully, one needs to embrace a multitude of approaches and disciplines. That can lead students to critically think about their own roles in the daily performance of the city. Further, it can offer students models of inquiry and inter-connectivity, help identify opportunities for research, and present different approaches to writing about the city.

Ultimately, *Captured by the City: New Perspectives in Urban Culture Studies* aims to create a lively exchange of viewpoints among scholars, teachers, artists, and students. It strives to prepare the ground for the founding of a Center for Urban Culture Studies in the nearest future, where the lively exchange of viewpoints will continue through workshops, classes, symposia, publications, and performances. I enjoyed putting this volume together immensely and I invite you to share in my joy as you flip through the essays and learn more about the often mysterious interplay among built environments, people's interactions, and infrastructure in cities. I hope that you will understand why and how all of us in this book are intrigued, obsessed, puzzled, fascinated, and, well, fully captured by the city, and that, in turn, will make you wonder about your own relationship with the city.

# PART I

## CITY PLACES:
## IN MEMORY, HISTORY, AND REAL-TIME

.

# CHAPTER ONE

## REMEMBERING THE CITY:
## MEMORY-IMAGES

## INÉS RAE

The research is located within the discipline of photographic studies. It is an investigation into the relation of the photographic work to the world depicted, and the balance achieved between the neutral document, mirroring reality, and the latent criticism of that reality. Through a photographic practice that uses methods of visual ethnography, alongside an interest in the complexity of the relationship between urban representations, memory, place, and identity, it is possible to piece together the particularities of lived experience.

The current project, *Memory City*, documents a series of personal memories volunteered by inhabitants of Preston and an attempt to explore the relationship between personal memory and public space. It opens up a dialogue between the city's population to encourage them to claim ownership over their public space by experiencing it as a dynamic site where private memories and a public present interact. One of the goals of the project is to explore people's, shared and differing, senses of belonging and document the emotional histories that exist in the living memories of a city's inhabitants; to enable a narration of the city "from below" in order to expose the dynamic, personal qualities of urban change.

We live in a "memorious" world where every step and every movement we make encounters memorialized objects, spaces and relations. The streets we walk along and the roads we drive upon are filled with engravings of past practices. The grooves in the pavement where millions of feet have worn down the surface, the variety of street furniture designs memorializing different industrial and social fashions: our environments are scarred by historical memories. What kinds of memory engravings *have been* inscribed on those places but also what kind of engravings *are being* inscribed upon those places? In this essay I look at some of the memory-talk and memory-images that the people in the *Memory City* project used to define the place of their memories in the urban spaces of Preston's past. Preston, one of the UK's newest cities, has often found itself in the shadow of larger cities in the North West of the UK, namely Manchester and Liverpool. The *Memory City* project chose Preston for its research in order to encourage the exploration of Preston as a subject for photographic studies and to generally focus more attention on the city.

The memory of a city space is one characterized by its mutability, both on an individual level and in a wider spectrum. At a basic level, it might be said that people perceive at least two cities: one architectural, and one more nebulous city, a city of the mind, of association, superstition and boundary. As Gary Bridge and Sophie Watson have commented, "[c]ities are not simply material or lived spaces—they are also spaces of the imagination and spaces of association," two factors which are in continual correspondence with one another (Bridge and Watson 2003: 7). Beyond this, there are further possible grounds for mutation. One is the contrast between the individual and the whole within the city space. Another is the impact of earlier memories upon any particular memory in question. A third is the manner in which memory (in more general terms here) colludes in the way the city of the present is perceived. After all, if cities are, as Bridge and Watson suggest, places of the imagination, then they are not simply day dreams; they are on-going, permanent dreams (or imaginaries), dreams which flow in and out of one another in the process of producing an entire mythology of personal, and group space.

The association between cities and dreams here is not without precedent. Steve Pile, in reference to both Benjamin and Freud, has suggested that

> ... elements of the city resemble dream elements—for not only can sites in cities be visited many times and the meanings of the locality change upon the "orientation" of the visit, but also cities bring together elements from different places and urban spaces are produced through the intersection of

crosscutting social relations, which combine to produce meaningful places. (Pile 2003: 85)

This proposition, in some ways, appears to fit in with some of the areas of research carried out, in terms of people's memories of Preston. Pat Woods, who was originally from Wigan, but eventually moved to Preston in 1979, provides an example of the way in which a city can "incorporate" other places, something, which is indeed connected to "the intersection of crosscutting social relations." When asked if there was a sense of community in the area to which she moved, Pat responds with the following comments:

> Yes, it was actually because we used to baby-sit for each other and, err, a lot of people hadn't been brought up in Preston like we were, so it was a kind of ex-pats commune if you like. So, because we didn't have any family near us we stuck together. Although there were one or two Prestonians in the group, they were mainly people who'd moved up like ourselves. (Selective Transcript 02:28)

The way in which Pat remembers her place of residence is fundamentally torn. On one level, it is an area of Preston bound together by "community spirit," which is in turn linked both concretely and sensuously to the town itself. However, from another angle, it is also (certainly in terms of Pat's Memory) sensuously *apart* from the town. The sense of community is one contingent upon this shared other existence; it is a community both inside Preston, and yet simultaneously grounded in multiple other locations. These other locations, for Pat, bleed into the overall experience of city space. This intersection produces a place of a certain meaning for Pat, yet one, which is certainly a place of liminal, mutable meaning.

"Dreaming" the city (and probably dreaming in itself) then, is also linked with the transgression of boundaries. The memory of a certain place, at a certain time, is stained with the memory of another place; one which is constantly looked back to (not necessarily out of choice), checked and verified in the affirmation of a certain way of life. There is then, a double transgression: firstly there is a basic, physical, transgression of space (from Wigan to Preston, in Pat's case). Secondly, there is an invasion by the place (Wigan) upon the memory, something which influences the way in which the "current" situation is perceived, and space is navigated. Concrete moves into memory (or imagination), which proceeds to translate, or transfer, its foundation back to its original state.

This method of remembrance strikes a pattern with another constituent of Preston who was interviewed. John Browne, who moved to Preston when he was "about twelve," describes his sense of living in the city through a poem by Stevie Smith:

> What's the one, Not Waving but Drowning, I've [unintelligible] yes, she said he must have wandered out, he must have gone too far out and he says no he didn't go too far out he's been too far out all his life, so yes I did feel different, yes. (John Browne Transcript 11)

It is useful to quote here the section of the original poem to which John alludes:

> Nobody heard him, the dead man,
> But still he lay moaning:
> I was much further out than you thought
> Not waving but drowning. (Smith 1999: 198)

John's emphasis upon these last two lines provides an illuminating way of examining his, and perhaps Pat's, experience of the city. In some ways, John is an "outsider." Although he may appear to be integrated within city life, he is always "further out," always slightly removed from the center. However, it is not that simple. Both Pat's and John's memories of being in Preston are not merely of being "outsiders," of being situated in an objective stance, from which one might wave. They are also memories in which the subjects view themselves as being submerged within the city, drowning within its territorial confines and yet still reaching out and gasping for their previous existences, their previous material and intellectual conditions. Again, the transition from one place to another is a mutable, capricious, and self-reflexive process. However, these transitions are ones which have a definite foundation; they are not simply examples of a dream, imagination, or oscillating memory which has lost the ability to retain an adequate grip on what might be deemed "real." They are direct consequences of an initial material act (in this case migration). Or to put it rather more eloquently, as Marx and Engels once stated: "the production of ideas, of conceptions, of consciousness, is at first directly interwoven with the material activity and the material intercourse of men [and women], the language of real life" (Engels and Marx 1977: 46).

The above notion (one which is roughly correspondent to the overall idea of base and superstructure) poses a difficult question when looking into people's perceptions of cities. People's sensuous experience of the city, it might be said, is something, which is at odds with the actual physical, architectural space of the city. A personal perception of the city is therefore limited in its inclusion of the city as whole. The contrast between experiencing the city as a whole, or as a more secularized space is something, which Jonathan Raban has looked at in his book, *Soft City:*

> When I first came to London, I moved about much more freely than I do now; I took the liberties of a tourist and measured the distances by miles rather than the relationship of the known to the unknown. […] It is the visitor that goes everywhere; to the resident a river or a railway track, even if it is bridged every few hundred yards, may be as absolute a boundary as a snake pit or an ocean. (Raban 1988: 167)

Raban's argument here relies on a further proposition that inhabitants of a city come to construct their own personal boundaries of a city, a "private city [which] emerges from his [or her] personal symbols and taboos" (169). To some extent, these ideas fit in with another resident of Preston who was interviewed. Joyce Hilton, a resident of Preston all her life talks specifically about memories involving entertainment. She talks about the fact that residents had a certain cinema in their "area'" to which they would go, where "everybody knew each-other" (JH Transcript 6). This testifies to a certain system of local boundaries, to which Joyce adhered. However, once inside these boundaries, there is a further development, on a smaller level. Joyce goes on to talk about the inside of the cinema, in which there would be "factions," corresponding to the larger surrounding area in which the cinema lay: "we were from the Fishwick area, whilst some people would come from Ribbleton Avenue, you know, the other side of the cinema, and another lot lived down Blackpool Road" (Ibid.).

Joyce's description of the cinema displays an automatic equation between the "areas" of the cinema, and the surrounding area of Preston. The inside of the cinema is a living simulacrum of its, as Raban would term, "soft" environs. However, although this is a personal memory, it is nevertheless one remembered in terms of a group construction. The system of representation, which Joyce describes, is no doubt strikingly similar to the way in which Raban describes similar situations, as "talismans, more important even than the house or the street, magical guarantees of a certain kind of identity" (Raban 1988: 168). The city (and its representation) is also measured purely in terms of known and unknown. Identity, though, is something, which extends to each particular faction, thereby affirming a joint "soft" experience of the city. The imperatives not to transcend these boundaries then, rest on an implicit, mutual understanding between groups of certain people; the mysticism, as Raban might discern, in this case is almost tribal.

In some sense, this can simply be put down to an affirmation of a certain way of life, or identity. As Chris Weedon, along with many others, has pointed out, "Like the structure of meaning in language, identity is relational. It is defined in a relation of difference to what it is not" (Weedon 2004: 19). This appears to be the case; the particular groups to which Joyce refers are all defined in terms of their differential nature. In terms of the cinema, Joyce went on to say that if someone was to sit in the "wrong" area, "people would say "what are you doing here," you know, and you'd feel uncomfortable" (JH Transcript 6). Joyce also talks about going to a different dance hall than the hall to which her area would normally attend. In this different dance hall she would be "looked down on" (Ibid.). Indeed, another person interviewed in Preston went as far to describe some areas as "the darker parts of Preston" (Neil Cartright Transcript 4), presumably referring to the poorer sections of the city. People's sense of an area is also specifically linked with economic factors then.

To go back to Marx and Engel's statement quoted earlier, if people's consciousness, ideas and so on are formed as a result of the material interactions between one another, then this seems an interesting example. Instead of being formed purely from longevity, association and superstition (mainly as a result of the city's architectural make-up), the "soft city" depicted here is one which arises out of economic issues, of one's individual economic factions, and of class in its more broad sense. Each area is bound by a close knit economic loyalty. The experience, however, is still one of mysticism and ritual, shown most aptly for the factions to which Joyce refers in her description of the cinema. This mysticism is more of an economic, material strain though, one in which taboos (similar to the way in which early divisions of labor would operate) and symbols keep the economic system afloat. This is, of course, a slightly different route to arrive at this particular conclusion than what Raban, and indeed others, might employ. The focus upon an individual experience of the city is one which has always been present, however, this focus can only go so far before it runs into abstractions, comments which are limited only to one individual, and which, therefore, can only serve a limited purpose. Joyce's, and others, perception of the city is perhaps something grounded within the past; close knit, microcosmic communities within the city might be something which can be said to have been outlived. However, this does not stop one reading the city's mutable nature, and people's memories of this, as a dream, as a series of intersections, cross-sections and invasions which appear incomprehensible, yet which all have a material foundation. The city is a place where one must use signs in order to grapple with the enormity of the situation. This does not mean, however, that these signs cannot be added to a wider scheme, a memory and imagination, which extend far further than atomized instances.

Photographs, despite their representational realism and apparent immediacy do not necessarily provide straightforward access to the scenes or experiences they record. The possibility that photographs capture un-experienced events creates a parallel between the workings of the camera and the structure of memory.

As I have been working with both stories and images, I thought it appropriate to reflect on the Bergsonian sense of the "virtual" character of memory. In *Mind-Energy*, Bergson writes:

> Every clear description of a psychical state is made up of images, and we are saying that the recollection of an image is not an image ... The memory seems to be to the perception what the image reflected in the mirror is to the object in front of it. The object can be touched as well as seen; acts on us as well as we on it; is pregnant with possible actions; it is *actual*. The image is *virtual*, and though it resembles the object, it is incapable of doing what the object does. Our actual existence, then whilst it is unrolled in time, duplicates itself all along with a virtual existence, a mirror-image. (Bergson 2007: 147)

I am not suggesting that this somehow captures the core or essence of Bergson's entire approach to memory, time or duration. Since a part of this work on memory concerns the relationships between images and memories, it is a useful, if controversial, starting point; "controversial," because, at least in the negative sense, Bergson got this *almost* right. "Almost," because it would appear that the recollection of an image is not a *re*-collection of an image. At a personal, individual level it is, instead, the reconstruction of a series of sensations, a collection of contextual inferences, and a pattern of social and personal markers that focus the so-called memory of the image in a series of times, places and circumstances—some of which are, indeed, "virtual."

To clarify this, I have chosen three fragments of memory from the *Memory City* project. In each case, there is a voiced articulation associated with a generic or personal image. The images do not re-present or duplicate what is remembered. Instead, the relationships between image and account point to curious features of the communication of memories.

Memory 1

I met my wife at the bus station. We were both drunk after a night out and I knocked her over and she fell on the floor and hit her head. She seemed a bit confused and I wasn't sure if it was because of concussion or because she was drunk. I put her in a taxi. I saw her 3 months later and she didn't recognize me until I said, "How's your head?" and then she remembered who I was. We've been married 20 yrs. I keep waiting for her to bump her head again and say, "Who the hell are you?"

Fig. 1-1. Preston Bus Station.

In this example, we have a generic image of the inside of Preston bus station. The person is being asked about the redevelopment of Preston town center and about their memories of its soon-to-be-replaced bus station. What this person does not do is remember the bus station itself. What he remembers is a personally significant array of events about his marriage—which he recounts in very loving and humble terms. The bus station is not a remembered image; it is used to spark a range of brightly impressed sensations and significances.

Of particular interest is that his memory makes reference to four different temporal frames: the temporality of the event ("I met my wife at the bus station"); the temporality of the interval ("I saw her three months later"); the temporality of accumulation ("we've been married twenty years") and the temporality of duration ("I keep waiting for her to bump her head again"). I want to suggest that memories enfold regimes of time into lived experience and that their social "situatedness"—in this case in the interpersonal dialogue of an interview—is, in part, a matter of realizing these temporal regimes as modes of social experience. That memory supports the multi-temporal character of social experience.

Memory 2

I was a student at the Harris Art School in Avenham Lane, Preston from 1959 to 1961. We were sent out sketching in Preston, and we usually did a minimum of work. I remember when we were told to go to the docks to sketch, we hid underneath some empty goods wagons, peering out between the wheels, until we saw our tutor's legs go past. Then knowing that the coast was clear, we simply explored the docks for a while. He never did find us.

Fig. 1-2. Harris Art School.

There are similar observations in the second example: there is, again, the temporality of the interval ("from 1959 to 1961"); and there is also, the temporality of the event ("when we were told to go to the docks"). I want to use this example to illustrate a different point; the discontinuity between image and memory.

What is interesting here is how the photographic image around which the conversation is taking place does not capture the narrative for which it stands as the documentary instance. The image here (Fig.1-2) was brought to me after the conversation from which the accompanying extract is taken occurred. Here, we have a posed, stage-managed photograph of a drawing class out for a day in the park. Yet the memory of this image takes place elsewhere. It is not in this scene, this captured place at all but in a different memory-scape altogether.

On the one hand, I could say that this photographic image is the spark that ignites several personal significances. Following Ricoeur's homage to Edward Casey, I could say, that this person "does not simply remember [herself], seeing, experiencing, learning; rather, [she] recalls the situations in the world in which [she] has seen, experienced, learned" (Ricoeur 2006: 36). On the other hand, in contrast to Ricoeur's notion of memories as "discrete forms with more or less discernible borders" (22), it seems that neither the borders of the memory nor the borders of the image are at all easy to discern. Where are the borders of this image if what it refers to is not in the image? Like the photographic image or "souvenir" (Ibid.) the borders of any remembered "situation in the world" ("memoire") are porous and unstable. The image and the memory are not at all the same—either photographically or cognitively.

Memory 3

R: I was more interested in going on walks around the river [...] and swimming in the river at night, which was very exciting; cold and miserable and horrid, but it was nice to be able to say to your friends the day after "I was swimming in the river last night at 10 o'clock." In actual fact it was terrible, you know, and you were muddy and cold and dirty, but it sounded good.
I: So who would you have gone to swim with in the river?
R: Girlfriends, but you'd meet the lads down there as well, yeah, yeah.
I: So was that quite a big thing?
R: If one of your friends was very fast, which one was, she'd go off with a boy, you know, for ten minutes and we never asked what they did, ever, we didn't want to know. But it wasn't rife, you know, mostly you didn't.

There is another issue at stake here. The image in this example (Fig. 1-3) was again brought to me after the conversation that occurred when asked what she used to get up to in Preston when she was younger. In response she talks about swimming in the river at night, meeting girlfriends—and boys. She remembers a "very fast" friend. The photograph—in contrast to the intimate, exciting narrative that invokes cold, dirt, mud and misery, camaraderie and illicit liaisons—evokes solitude, even meditation.

Its staging and point of view—its disappearance leftwards, her framing between the dark riverbank and the overhanging tree (protective or menacing, depending on how you want to interpret it) give the image a suspended and even dream-like quality. There is something here about the ways that personal stories and snapshot images reveal an interaction between grounded bodily experience and ethereal imagination in the recollection and social exhibition of personal memories.

Fig. 1-3. Girl by the Lake.

It is not necessarily the story that is always grounded whilst the image is suspended. It is also the case that the snapshot image can work as a fixed and solid framework for a dream-like story in which things are apparent, then non-apparent and then apparent again. Sometimes it is the story that is dream-like rather than the image.

It is not that memories are the conscious of subconscious phantasies. In the interpersonal exhibition and communication of memories there appears to be a semi-structured "in-betweenness" to memory work: an amalgam of the concrete, the visceral, the tangible and the ephemeral, the intangible and disembodied qualities of everyday experience. To put it tentatively, memory communication, at least at an interpersonal level, appears either as a glue that binds together these qualities or as a solvent that dissolves their taken-for-granted unity.

> ... *memories are selective for place*: they seek out particular places as their natural habitats. Why this propensity? Partly because places furnish convenient points of attachment for memories; but also because places provide situations in which remembered actions can deploy themselves. Or more precisely, places are *congealed scenes* for remembered contents; and as such they serve to situate what we remember. (Casey 2000: 189)

Casey's idea of memories as "congealed scenes" for remembered contents seemed a promising way of addressing the intersections between personal memories and Preston's city places. What I actually found was that there is a distinctly uncongealed quality to these intersections. Rather than seeing place in terms of congealed layers of remembrance, it may be more appropriate to understand places as points of ignition for multi-modal memory narratives.

# Bibliography

Bergson, H. (2007). *Mind-Energy*, London: Palgrave Macmillan.

Bridge, G. & Watson, S. (2003). "City Imaginaries" in *A Companion to the City*, ed. G. Bridge and S. Watson. Malden and Oxford: Blackwell Publishers.

Casey, E. (2000). *Remembering: A Phenomenological Study*, Bloomington: Indiana University Press.

Ehrenreich, B. (1989). *Fear of Falling: The Inner Life of the Middle Class*, London: Pantheon Books.

Engels, F & Marx, K. (1977) *The German Ideology*, ed. CJ Arthur. London: Lawrence and Wishart.

Halbwachs, M. (1980). *The Collective Memory*. New York and London: Harper and Row.

Pile, S. (2003). "Sleepwalking in the Modern City: Walter Benjamin and Sigmund Freud in The World of Dreams" in *A Companion to the City*, ed. G. Bridge and S. Watson. Malden and Oxford: Blackwell Publishers.

Raban, J. (1988). *Soft City*. London: Harvill.

Rae, I. (2009). *Memory City*. A collaborative research project since 2009. http://www.memorycity.org

Ricoeur, P. (2006). *Memory, History, Forgetting*. Chicago: University of Chicago Press.

Smith, S. (1999). "Not Waving but Drowning" in *The Harvill Book of Twentieth Century Poetry in English*, ed. M. Schmidt. London: Harvill.

Warhol, A. (1964). *Empire*, 485 min silent.

Weedon, C. (2004). *Identity and Culture: Narratives of Difference and Belonging*. Maidenhead: Open University Press.

# CHAPTER TWO

# PRESERVING COMMUNITY: BOSTON'S WEST END

# LOIS ASCHER

While this project should be placed within the interdisciplinary humanistic contexts of history, urban studies, the civic, it is best viewed as a memorial essay on a vanished community, the physical aspects of which were sacrificed to the questionable growth of urban progress. Through the use of memory as instrument it sets itself against the language of traditional urban renewal theory most often based on the "paternalism" of government institutions. It seeks from the reader the recognition that to become a nation, which celebrates urbanity we must create a consciousness inclusive of *all* peoples.

Through the method of document investigation combined with oral history the essay demonstrates the power of memory to reconstruct our urban environments. It works to alter the methodology of urban "renewal" from one exclusive to bricks and mortar to the inclusion of those urban populations most affected by government initiatives. In narrating the story of those urban pioneers with the courage to move forward, literally out of ashes to recreate community, it reminds us that urban life *can* be built on the determination of those most affected by it.

# A Love Letter, Warning, Memory

First and foremost this essay is a love letter. It is a love letter to those West Enders who have opened their hearts and their memories to me, sharing their past and helping me to remember mine. In that way more than any other have I come to experience what a terrible loss the urban renewal of the West End was—not just for its residents but for all of us who aspire to live lives cocooned within a community of human beings who care about one another, an urban village.

Next, this essay is a warning, not just about the destructive nature of carelessly governed urban renewal but also of what happens to a nation when it destroys "places worth caring about" along with the people who live there. If the public urban realm is, as James Howard Kunstler says it is "the physical manifestation of the common good" (2004), then its destruction in the name of profit and profiteering is an attack on everyone. It is only when we come to understand that those who share our communal spaces are "neighbors not foreigners" (Nunley 2012: 1), that the destruction of our human and geographic environments will stop.

Finally, this essay is a memory of a memory. Because the memories of the original West Enders who long for community are really our own, and will be lost if we destroy the roots that bind us to one another cutting us off from "memorable times that [we] treasure in our hearts forever and ever" (Cloonan 2011: 7).

# Dedication

To Jim, Bruno, Bruce and Ritchie whose generosity and kindness have taught me that it *is* possible to maintain grace of character despite encountering the worst kinds of human catastrophes. It has been a privilege to know you and to work with you.[1]

---

[1] The last names of interviewees Jim Campano, Bruce Guarino, Duane Lucia, Bruno Roberto, will be listed after each quote unless they are named within the text. All of them come from personal interviews conducted with the author and from whom I have permission to quote.

... somehow the struggle of the West End residents went unopposed by the majority of Boston ... [who did not recognize] ... that the trash building up in the streets was not because this place was a slum but because the city withdrew garbage collection as part of its policy to justify tearing down the community. They wouldn't have bought the story that the demolition was for the best because they would have had understanding and compassion for the people who lived there as neighbors and not foreigners. (Nunley 2012: 1)

... we were a melting pot in Boston. (Jim Campano)

They left reluctantly, angrily, heart-brokenly. No one left willingly. "It was like being shoved out of your womb" (Campano). They still remember. Even after 50 years, they meet and reminisce. They share photographs and stories in a quarterly newspaper, *The West Ender*. It is perhaps the most famous example of urban renewal gone wrong, repeatedly written about by sociologists and urban activists like Jane Jacobs and Herbert Gans. But for the people of the West End, this was not an academic problem; it was the destruction of their way of life.

"It was like a fire" one former resident, Bruce Guarino, says. Only it was worse than a fire. Most fires are not deliberately set. This destruction was deliberate. It was about tax money and bankers' profits. It was about real estate deals and tony high-rise condominiums. It was about destroying a slum that wasn't a slum, a classic example of what Jane Jacobs refers to as a paternalistic approach to "slum" dwelling (Jacobs 1992: 271).

Don't repair your tenement apartments, landlords were told 8 years before the actual demolition took place. And they didn't. So the area deteriorated, creating its own rational for a destruction that broke people's hearts and ruined people's lives. According to one survivor, Bruno Roberto, some even died of broken hearts as the deliberate and callous devastation that followed the wrecking ball created vacant lots out of what had been homes and anonymous high rises out of what was once a neighborhood.

The West End's destruction touched the lives of both the average citizen and those who rose to prominence in a culture that has always built itself on the dreams of immigrants: "I wish I could go back to my roots. I can't. They're gone," says Leonard Nimoy ("West End Memories" 2012), in a backstage interview after giving the 2012 commencement address at Boston University. Mr. Spock of *Star Trek* fame is also a West Ender. He continues: "The buildings are all torn down ... the street configuration has changed so much." As Nimoy talks about his character, it becomes evident that his portrayal of Spock drew deeply on cherished West End memories among neighbors for whom the trauma of immigration was mended through living in a community which accepted and cared for them: "Spock ... was a character with a rich and dynamic inner life," Nimoy. "He was the embodiment of the outsider, like the immigrants who surrounded me. How do you find your way as the alien in a foreign culture? Where does your identity and dignity come from?" And then, further:

> My folks came to the United States as ... aliens, and they became citizens. I was born in Boston a citizen; I went to Hollywood, and I became an alien. (Nimoy "West End Memories" 2012)

"If you lived here you'd be home now," say the signs on the elegant new high rise construction built to replace the low rise apartment buildings, once the homes of a diverse ethnic and racial mix of working class people. I passed that sign and its menacing looking buildings for years without understanding what lay behind their origin. In "Thoreau Place," one of these groupings (who says that irony is dead), home for West Enders no longer existed. There was only sterile structure with empty street corridors where once there had been street life. Automobiles now reside invisibly in multi-level garages that mirror the residences of their owners, another barrier to community building in the newly formed West End neighborhood.

Unlike the new "neighborhood," in the old neighborhood everybody really did know your name. When asked in a film interview what his fondest memory of the West End was, Jim Campano, founder of the newsletter and the museum, spoke of its welcoming aspects.

> You felt completely comfortable there ... we were a melting pot in Boston and Boston is a segregated city but ... as soon as you came into the West End you were accepted. (*Only a Memory Now* 2010)

And the village really did help to raise its children. Youths who dared to misbehave were physically disciplined by neighbors who reminded them that their "parents would thank them" (Roberto). If you became ill, food would appear in various ethnic guises, and "your grandmother could walk down the street at 3 o'clock in the morning without fear" (Roberto).

If there *was* a fight, it resulted from neighborhood, not racial, divisions. West Enders stuck together, ignoring ethnic differences, in contrast with other districts in which the busing crisis soon to follow created violent competition for that little piece of dignity claimed by meeting a simple need for education. And racial harmony continued after the neighborhood's demise, as 500 West Enders gathered in memory of an African American, former West End boxer (Guarino). Sadly, this existing harmony was dismissed by government bureaucrats, intent on razing the community to gain alleged tax benefits for the City of Boston, warning that Boston would become a "black ghetto if we didn't take the neighborhood down" (*Only a Memory Now* 2010), a fear used so frequently by eminent domain supporters that urban renewal was often referred to as "black removal."

Windows and doors were left unlocked. There were no alarm systems; instead, there were neighbors who looked out for you. When your mother washed the floors in the summer she left doors and windows open and went off for a family day at a beach while they dried (Roberto, discussion). There was no fear of robbery. One policeman reportedly went his entire career without making a single arrest. There was no need. Protection was generated by a community whose lives were lived on the street.

The quality of "personal safety and security on the street among ... strangers" in the West End of Boston *is* what made it a "successful city district" (Jacobs 1992: 30). Before urban "renewal" (another irony), the West End's comfortable diversity was not a matter of "accident" but a deliberately sought after community, the kind, which grows out of a vital street life reinforced by "the presence of people who use many facilities in common" (150). Writing on diversity as a necessary component in a viable and engaging urban environment, Jane Jacobs stresses the importance of people appearing on city streets at varying times "hour by hour through the day" (152), preventing the formation of a "ring of stagnation, decay, vacancies" (155), making places like the West End so desirable that Jim Campano says that even those with a great deal of money "Brahmins with trust funds that lived in the West End—old time Yankees," elected to stay (*Only a Memory Now* 2010).

Unlike wealthier suburban neighborhoods where people closet themselves in backyards filled with the clutter of suburban life—personal playgrounds and swimming pools, stainless steel grills and enormous decks—those in densely populated urban neighborhoods rely on public playgrounds, streets, and spaces between store fronts to socialize. The streets have to "serve as a secondary social center for adults, as well as a primary one for youngsters" (Gans 1992: 18). They hang out on corners and out of windows. "Climbing the Greasy Pole" and pinning dollar bills on the Madonna during street festivals replace invitation only backyard barbecues. While on-street activity grows out of apartment living, it also builds those connections felt so powerfully by people in the West End, generating an urban sanctuary more compelling than the numerous upscale gated communities patrolled by self-appointed, dangerous, neighborhood watch commandos who populate too many of America's paranoid suburbs.

There was awareness that they didn't have a lot of material goods: "Material wealth was not a priority and therefore minimized the feelings of envy and jealousy" (Lombardi-Sacco 2010: 8). However, West Enders knew what they *did* have was priceless: "This neighborhood was a working class enormously diverse community built on respect, appreciation of the basic necessities and commitment to the wellbeing and welfare of each other" (Ibid.).

Unfortunately, however, despite this small enclave of communal good will in its West End, the city of Boston was deteriorating around them (O'Connor 1992: 60). Taxes were climbing while city income was being reduced by factors such as businesses relocating outside the city in pursuit of lower taxes and numbers of non-profit institutions in a city filled with universities and hospitals. Predatory suburban shopping malls were luring "quality shoppers" (67), away from the main downtown shopping district as once fashionable addresses like those in the Back Bay, were being transformed into rooming houses for educational institutions. The concern over urban blight grew into a contagion, driven by the twin engines of greed and indifference, a reform structured on the backs of those deemed least adept at self-defense. Sadly, government initiatives of "urban renewal" *became* the engine through which developers and city officials profited by targeting poorer neighborhoods. Viewing the West End district as a "dangerous slum area" (63), one Boston banker said: "There's only one way you can cure the West End, and that is to wipe it out" (64).

At first, West End residents were promised new living quarters in low rent housing to be constructed *in the West End* (61, italics mine). The Housing Authority guaranteed that "Families displaced by the West End Project" (62), would be given "top priority" to get into public housing" (Ibid.) in accordance with a 1951 law that promised any resident ousted by eminent domain the right to "move back into the property when it was done before it was put up for rent *if they could afford it*" (Bagley 1992: 2, italics mine). As the project developed, references to housing became scarce until official eviction notices delivered in the spring of 1958 contained no mention of affordable public housing. According to former City Solicitor and West End resident, Frank Privitera, "the city's promises were illusory" (1-2). Jim Campano recalls that when evicted from the West End, his mother's apartment cost $29.00 a month. After "renewal," the cheapest apartment she could find was $600 a month. West End as home became a forbidden entity.

Instead of humanly scaled, low rise buildings and narrow streets filled with a vibrant street life, a Boston lawyer turned developer with close political ties to city hall and Boston's mayor, erected five residential complexes. Each, slated to contain a "23-story tower building accompanied by a 16-story concrete slab apartment building and a row of 3-story town houses" (O'Connor 1992: 66-7), was designed to return middle class families to the city. Gone were smells and sounds that signified "home" to West Enders: the smell of a linoleum store, of "tasty sauce filling our home with wonderful scents ... when company came" (Campbell 2012: 3). As former resident Tony Taro reminisces: "A short walk down [South Margin] Street brought you to ... Silvestri's Bakery [and]...the aroma of hot fresh baked bread ... and Norman Street hosted Mrs. Miller's variety store with those big jars of pickles on the counter ... The one thing all of these businesses had in common was that they treated their customers with respect, and would know almost everybody by their first name" (Taro 2010: 3). Gone as well, was signaling one another by knocking on pipes, a noise which nobody minded because everybody was engaged in one another's lives in the same way that a large loving family tolerates sound generated in the act of living lives together as a community. Alas, the pristine new high-rise buildings with their concrete skins and expensive square footage no longer allowed space for aromatic or auditory nostalgia.

Turns out everyone wanted to do remember when. (Jim Campano)

I trust you realize how distinctive what you have done is—I don't think a newspaper ... ever came out of a slum clearance project nor that these would evoke interest and participation from those who displaced the cleared. (Herbert Gans, posted at West End Museum, 2012)

Surprisingly, however, unlike other victims of urban renewal, the literal disappearance of the West End neighborhood did not completely extinguish the community. Magically, the bonds forged over decades withstood the destruction of the buildings, while new memories were created as West Enders "updated one another on their children and grandchildren" (Bagley 2007: 2), through the pages of the newsletter. Ultimately, the power of memory helped generate a 4,000 square foot store front museum formally dedicated to the history of the neighborhood, one of the only museums in America, says Duane Lucia, its executive director, to address the subject of urban renewal in depth. Its immediate genesis was an exhibit by the Bostonian Society, *The Last Tenement,* currently the museum's permanent exhibit (Lucia). Of the two remaining spaces, the main archive room holds temporary revolving exhibitions, while the Privitera Family Gallery features exhibitions changed bi-monthly (Lucia). In this manner, the museum aids the newsletter in knitting together the connections so brutally severed by the taking of the West End community, a focus complemented by its mission to "collect, preserve, and interpret the history and culture of the West End of Boston" (Lucia). Indeed, as the mortar was setting at 150 Staniford Street #7, the West End neighborhood was reshaping itself into a gathering place, which stands at the nexus of past, present and future. As it has grown, West End voices (Lucia) re-emerge, as in artist Evelyn Berde's recent show, *Leaving the River*, which conflates the simultaneous loss of her brother to drowning with the loss of community.

The museum archives a rich oral history, preserving it for future generations to understand first-hand how decisions made by government cocooned in concrete offices alter the destinies of citizen and city alike. The voices—sometimes funny, sometimes sad, on occasion tragic, and always poignant—are appropriately quartered among artifacts, which recreate the life of a community, still cherished decades after its physical disappearance. They remind us that the immigrants who helped build America did not live solely in the storied mansions of Beacon Hill and the regal Back Bay, but in working class neighborhoods of places like the West End, residing in barber shops, diners, tobacco shops, tattoo parlors and burlesque halls. Most completely they emerged from a sidewalk community, which reflected the varied and vibrant tapestry that make up the richness of human existence.

Thus, the revitalization of neighborhood ties in the West End reinforced truths expounded by Jane Jacobs in her crusade against indifferent and powerful government. Because the West End community did NOT disappear when the wrecking balls appeared. It merely went underground, re-emerging decades later through the determination of individuals like Jim Campano, proving that community ties and individual needs can be stronger than bureaucratic initiatives. From a reunion of 150 people who attended camp together as children came the first newsletter, providing a venue to revisit memories that had for years lain dormant, cloaked in isolation. "I am writing this letter to you with tears in my eyes," wrote one respondent (Neustadt 1992: 94). "For 30 years I have felt like I have had no past ... reading the newsletter I see I was not alone" (Ibid.). As interest in reconnection grew, so grew the museum's presence, invoking the essence of the earlier neighborhood.

When one enters the museum, he is immediately surrounded by a palpable nostalgia. Here are no precious objet d'arts as are present in most museums. Instead, there is the lovingly rescued detritus of the daily life of a neighborhood rich in racial and ethnic diversity. Scooters, ingeniously constructed out of wooden boxes and colored bottle caps stand close by a vintage couch; an antique Singer Sewing Machine has a piece of curbing as its neighbor. Disparate artifacts rescued from the demolition, shelter underneath a flag also rescued from a destroyed local ethnic church. Photographs are everywhere, integrating objects with the lives of a still beloved community. If one spends more than ½ an hour here he is likely to encounter any number of people—both former West Enders and others—who drop in for a visit. Letters written to the *The West Ender,* reminisce over their travel "down the beautiful memory lanes, streets, alleyways … I'm very thankful I grew up in such a diversified, caring neighborhood," writes Shirley Berry, one former resident:

> It was a great way to start life … We learned to live and respect each other's customs and religions, something that kids need today. (Berry 2010: 8)

The museum also functions as a neighborhood resource, maintaining and preserving archives and oral histories while documenting an area whose existence has been crucial to Boston's growth from town to city since Colonial times (Lucia). Recently mounted exhibits focus on such disparate elements as the West End's role as Boston's transportation hub—its canal system, rope making, bridges—its role as immigrant haven and even as a center for the art of burlesque. From Charles Bulfinch, architect, to Leonard Nimoy, actor, and Sumner Redstone of Viacom, entrepreneur, the West End's native sons and daughters remind us that more individuals than Abraham Lincoln progressed from humble beginnings to greatness.

## Moving Forward While Looking Back

> I've channeled my anger. We have to stop being at each other's throats.
> (Jim Campano)

It is perhaps difficult for outsiders to believe in the existence of this dedication to a way of life in a place where economic struggles persistently plagued the search for one's daily bread. But according to Bruce Guarino, West Ender and museum tour guide, their community WAS a utopia in its "flavor … ethnicity and … liveliness" (*Only a Memory Now* 2010). It was a utopia in the real sense of the word: nowhere. Because after the wrecking balls smashed through the neighborhood, collapsing small and negotiable streets into large thoroughfares, hardscaped into traffic ridden concrete carcasses, the West End *was* nowhere. City Hall Plaza, one of the many "brutalist concrete monstrosities to house government" (Ibid.), has replaced Scollay Square. The seven primary schools and most of their children have disappeared, along with grocery stores, pharmacies, bakeries and other building blocks of neighborhoods, sacrificed along with Joe and Nemo's Diner, a piece of Americana lost forever. On-street parking is forbidden in the new West End, contributing to the demise of street life. Yet the street, as James Howard Kunstler reminds us, *is* the public realm in America because "we don't have ... thousand year old cathedral plazas and market squares" (Kunstler 2004). In his recent TED talk on urban space and suburban life, Kunstler critiques the American landscape as an environment "filled with places not worth caring about," which generate despair (Ibid.). The public realm he reminds us, is the "physical manifestation of the common good," which, when destroyed, "automatically degrade[s] the ... character of ... [our] communal life" (Ibid.). The graceful mix of public and private space in the original West End fits Kunstler's descriptions because it invoked a lasting recognition of "common good" through communal living. That is, in fact, how the West End earned the epithet, "The best little neighborhood this side of heaven."

Despite its physical disappearance miraculously—uniquely—the community remains, held together by museum and memory, invoked through the quarterly newsletter. What Bruce Guarino calls the "bygone era gone forever ... only a memory now" (*Only a Memory Now* 2010), has been restored at least in part, transformed by those unwilling to concede defeat to the forces of bureaucratic elitism. It has been rescued by people who possess memories of a neighborhood "so alive it was incredible ..." (Ibid.), as expressed in the poem "from these times":

> I am from quiet times, from Elvis to Eisenhower, the Cold War and the
>     Korean War.
> I am from Catherine and Michael. From empty the icebox to clean the
>     room.
> I am from splendid Sunday dinners, tasty sauce filling our home with
>     wonderful scents ...
> I am from the trolley and the bus, whose long rides to school kept me
>     dreaming with the glistening stars ...
> I am from amazing times, from hide and seek to stickball and volley ball.
> I am from memorable times that I treasure in my heart forever and ever.
>                                                     (Cloonan 2011: 7)

This neighborhood, which for a time lived only in the hearts of the people from the West End is once again a living breathing presence in the city of Boston. Its original vibrancy is recreated through museum exhibits and programming as diverse as the neighborhood itself once was: from a rope-making workshop for children, to an exhibition on the "Vintage Costumes of Burlesque." Echoing the settlement houses that once aided immigrants in adapting to American life, the West End Museum aids current citizens in understanding what it means to live in a civic community whose government recognizes the importance of *all* its citizens, not just those with access to the halls of power.

The museum, however, has another important role to play in continuing the crusade against the use of urban renewal initiatives to orphan people in large metropolitan areas. Those too young to remember, consider the events with disbelief, in part because it *was* so unbelievable. The story reads like a sensationalized media piece: government lying to residents while deliberately creating a slum out of a desirable working class neighborhood; government refusing to collect garbage, then showcasing the rubbish in newspaper photographs; children "ripped out of their homes"; elderly, who "lost their little womb, their support and a lot of whom died" (Campano). The plight of this "grieving population" is "kept alive" (Campano), so that the rest of us can come to understand the results of indifferent urban planning on affected populations. Thus do these activities of "West End storytellers" become "acts of communal resilience," to teach us the terrible lessons that come out of the erroneous beliefs "that the future can be built as if there had not been a past" (Murray 2012). In this way, future societies may come to recognize that urban renewal choices impact more than infrastructure and buildings. As Jim Campano, the museum's founder, tells urban planning students at the end of his talks with them: "Your decisions affect people's lives" (Campano).

# Bibliography

Bagley, S. H. (2007). "'Greatest neighborhood' remembered in West End Museum created by folks transplanted to Somerville" in *Wicked Local Somerville*.http://www.wickedlocal.com/somerville/town_info/history/

Belmont, V. (2004). "West End Residents Struggle to Raise Neighborhood's Profile." *City in Transition*. Emerson College. http://journalism.emerson.edu/changingboston/west_end/loyalties.htm

Berry, S. R. (2008). Letter. *The West Ender*. Vol. 26. No. 1: 8.

*Boston's West End: "Only a Memory Now."* (2010). Produced and written by J. Cleveland, P. Dassau, C. Pratt and R. Smith. Wentworth Institute of Technology.

Campbell, R. (2012). "Boston's Old West End Persists as a 'Palace'" in *Boston Globe.*

Cloonan, C. (2011). "I am From These Times" in *The West Ender.* Vol. 27. No.3:7.

Fisher, S. M. and C. Hughes, eds. (1992). *The Last Tenement: Confronting Community and Urban Renewal in Boston's West End.* Boston: The Bostonian Society.

Fried, M. (1992). "Grief and Adaptation: The Impact of Relocation in Boston's West End" in Ibid., 80-93.

Gans, H. J. (1982). *The Urban Villagers: Group and Class in the Life of Italian-Americans.* New York: The Free Press.

—. (1992)."The Urban Village Revisited: The World of the West End Just Before its Destruction" in *The Last Tenement: Confronting Community and Urban Renewal in Boston's West End*, ed. S. Fisher and C. Hughes, 14-21.

Jacobs, J. (1992). *The Death and Life of Great American Cities.* New York: Vintage Books.

Kunstler, J. H. (2001). "Boston: Overcoming History and Modernism" in *The City in Mind: Meditations on the Urban Condition.* New York: The Free Press.

—. (2004)."The Tragedy of Suburbia." TED Talk. Monterey, California.

Lombardi-Sacco, P. (2010). "Memories of the West End" in *The West Ender.* Vol. 26, No. 3:8.

Murray, H. (2012). "Pulverizing the Past" in *Architecture Boston.* Boston Society of Architects. Vol. 15. No. 3. http://www.architects.org/architectureboston/articles/pulverizing-past

Neustadt, K. (1992)."'It is Indeed a Strange and Wonderful Emotion You Arouse': Memory, History, and the 'Old West End," in *The Last Tenement: Confronting Community and Urban Renewal in Boston's West End*, ed. S. Fisher and C. Hughes, 94-105.

Nimoy, L. (2012). "West End Memories." *Radio Boston* WBUR. Boston.

Nunley, J. O. (2012). "Shadows of a City." Unpublished paper. Wentworth Institute of Technology.

O'Connor, T. H. (1992). "The Urban Renewal Chronicle: The Politics of Urban Renewal in Boston" in *The Last Tenement: Confronting Community and Urban Renewal in Boston's West End*, ed. Fisher and Hughes, 60-71.

Taro, T. (2010)."A Walk Down South Margin Street" in *The West Ender.* Vol. 26, No.3: 3-7.

# CHAPTER THREE

# BUFFALO:
# NOTEBOOK ON MY RETURN

# DAVID MICHALSKI


This project can be best placed within the broad discipline of humanist
social science. It draws on the techniques of folklore, auto-ethnography
and investigatory poetics to probe the urban experience as it lays its claim
to the mind. It attempts to reconstruct, through documents and first person
memories, the emotional pull, which leads us to identify with cities. At the
same time, through its juxtaposition of divergent voices and forms of
historical consciousness, it disrupts the smooth packaging of city histories,
as they are often found in popular geographical and historical texts.

Investigatory poetics uses the methods of documentary collage to
highlight and contrast the various sounds, words and concepts that make
up events and places. The urban theorist can use this method as a means to
reassemble the multivalent character of the urban life world. The act of
composing the city anew from various sources, shown here in notebook or
scrapbook form, allows the composer (and her or his reader) to question
the way the city stages relations between the self and social history. It also
reveals how the city bundles memories, emotions and psychic investment
in the process of plotting its own history.

*Buffalo: Notebook on My Return* is an ode to the city of Buffalo, New York. Part memoir and part research notebook, it seeks to disclose a poetics of memory and place-making central to the way we imagine cities. It is written in the form of a scrapbook assembled from personal anecdotes and public artifacts uncovered in archives and libraries to present a means of remembering both the city and self.

I am not alone in my feelings for this city. In the last fifty years about half of its residents left, many fleeing the negative consequences of deindustrialization, an economics of decline, and the cycle of disruptions and violence that accompanies such a social collapse. This same out-migration, however, has given birth to an imaginary Buffalo, one driven by emotion and nostalgia. Today, the city's history and memories are woven together across an uneven and distorted screen.

Projecting Buffalonia in this poetic collage form is therapeutic for me. I moved away from Buffalo nearly twenty years ago and my effort to remember it here is rooted in an effort to recollect my own dislocated communal and familial connections. But this poem can also be read as an investigation of nostalgia as such, one that aims to reflect on the kind of knowing that is activated by this uniquely human sense. "Buffalo: Notebook on My Return" is not simply about salvaging my experiences. It's an examination of the relations between urban geography, history and memory, a study of how the stories of a city's past interact to produce a kind of magnetism.

Through its reconstruction of the city, this ode to Buffalo works to deconstruct the forces animating such reminiscence. It places the glow of civic pride alongside the shame of bigotry and chauvinism, and juxtaposes the trauma caused by a loss of community beside the desire for resiliency and hope. In doing so, it seeks to show how the making of the urban historical imagination is always freighted with the emotions and struggles evoked by memory, a burden that, once unfolded, reveals a profound love for city living, one that transcends the parochial to open an examination of the dynamics of urban culture.

Rather than providing a document of loyalty to Buffalo, that is, a document of loyalty to *place*, within an economy that demands this same heartfelt pride and allegiance as a form of spatial regulation, I hope the emotional tensions exposed here signal a deeper bond between people and their cities, one that gives rise to and animates our captivation with the urban form in a new way, an inclination to see ourselves not only as witnesses to a city's history, but as intimate participants in the city's larger social story.

The city lies on the shores of a torrent.
Air clear, marked only
by the rustling of clouds.

The city was built on the delta of Beaver Creek.
The air made golden,
by the sun soaked pollen.

The city rose on the beaches of a northern sea.
Where the blue sky is speckled
by bleached white shells.

The city began under the boughs of the white pine.
Air thick with fog and smoke,
anticipatory of the city to come.

City of broken dreams—deep meaningful loss and wasted space, you
are giving it away. You are losing still—to the grasses between curb and
street, to birds and fertility. You are being overgrown, slipping into the
lake which laps against you. On those shores where things must grow, you
are losing to the perch fried memories of my fathers. Fallen city of mud, of
deep green ancient hills, of black soil, of ancient farms below concrete,
your roots are rotting, decomposing in your perpetual breakdown.

NOT IGNOBLE ARE THE DAYS
OF PEACE, NOT WITHOUT
COURAGE AND LAURELED VICTORIES*

At the heart of you is a great drain, an under-consciousness of your
own mortality. This is why you chose to wear your heart on your sleeve—
a big red B pierced by a sabre. You are a city of sacrifice, stupid Christ of
cities, leaving it on the field. Self-conscious righteous city of denial,
abused drunken city of half-baked pizza and charters, you welcome the
world with a defensive steely cold grin, but I know you. You are as soft
and warm as fried dough.

HE WHO FAILS BRAVELY HAS
NOT TRULY FAILED, BUT IS
HIM-SELF ALSO A CONQUEROR*

Great Queen City of lakes, you are the mother city of belief and triumph, a
city of pyrotechnic summers and playgrounds, a pedestrian city of
canopies, a wooden city of aged carnivals and autumnal coffee shops. You

are a city of books, a browsing circular city of street lamps and porches, a city of happy hours and silent prayer. Fun city of bingo, showcase of rhythms, holy city of hospitals and wards, caring city of milk and tears, know your self, proud illusion-less city.

HE WHO SHUNS THE DUST AND SWEAT
OF THE CONTEST ON HIS BROW FEELS
NOT THE COOL SHADE OF THE OLIVE*

Where the Buffalo Creek meets Cayuga, deep waters swirl past the junction of overrun Indian reservations and orphanages, past train yards and ball parks, cemeteries and drive-ins. It's the blood that makes things grow here beneath the shade of elm trees in a tangled forest of wild grapevines just beyond Mineral Spring Road, past the gravel lots of sport trucks and fluorescent tape and shopping carts outback behind your bowling alleys and tool sheds where coal was dumped deep and carbon. In those little muskrat woods rest shards of blue glass engraved with your story, worn smooth and fragile.

> *Note: the three-line verses in upper-case interspersed above are inscriptions, which were engraved on the stadium walls at the Pan American Exhibition in Buffalo in 1901—See Gilder, Richard Watson, *Poems and Inscriptions*, Buffalo: The Century Company, 1901.

In fifty years, Buffalo will either be
a great midsize American city or a
research subject for archaeologists
—Kevin P. Gaughan
*Buffalo News* 12/27/2001

I remember late nights at work at the Lockwood Graduate Library at the University of Buffalo, hearing Peter Bryan, the evening circulation manager tell of digs among your ruins in search of prized glass in lost Babcock switchyards and cinder hills near the Niagara Frontier Food Terminal Market. And having went out there overturning hubcaps and rusted drums, he returned to his wife and daughter, early Buffalo China, and thick tinted bottles. These he collected and displayed in his South Park home, around an altar he made to Lead Belly, on top of his TV.

Autumn at the Albright Knox
We had quiche and coffee,
watched maple leaves cascade
about Giacometti's "Walking Man,"
watched drizzle hit the pane
between vertical venetian blinds,
reading Edward Fry's *Cubism*,
to discover something new
across the street from the Asylum.

Fish Fry

My great grandfather took his rowboat out beneath a metallic sky
beyond the break wall in search of the blue pike you were giving away.
The fish could not resist the squirm of the night crawlers and the boat was
quickly loaded with the silvery swarm. In that shimmering frenzy, he
dreamt of a tavern where he could trade his catch for lager drafts and
stories. The music pulsing so diverted him from the rising storm. The sky
darkened. A crisp breeze gave way to gales raising waves above fifteen
feet. He made for the break wall taking on water, and the pike made their
exit singing with the storm. Nearly inside the wall, the surprise Alberta
Clipper smashed his boat upon the rocks to which he clung. There was no
sign of the nearby city, save a slow pulse from your lighthouse tower.
Wedged inside the boulders, he inhaled gasps of air between the pounding
surf. The rats of your breakwall drowned that night, but he hung on to see
the cool dawn. It was just you and he that night. And that's how I was
born.

If a city can't be London, Alexandria or
Venice, what harm is there in being Buffalo?
—Verlyn Klinkenborg, *The Last Fine Time*,
New York: Alfred A. Knopf, p. 109.

Chrusciki

My mother told me: when returning from dropping my father at work
one snowy morning, she decided to go by the Broadway Market. We had
just moved back to Buffalo after years away. Drawn by the soft glow of
bakeries and butcher shops, she watched the flurries first turn to snow
showers, then squalls. She missed a turn on Fillmore and tried to double-
back on Bailey to Sycamore, but the streets and landmarks were hard to
discern. She became lost in the very neighborhood of her birth.

Snowplows were rushed out to clear the narrow roads and she found herself tailed by them, unable to turn around. She weaved through the passages of close-knit homes, boarded windows and muted slaughter-houses and industrial parks. As she went, the snow spread its mantle and silenced the dense angled streets. She drove for about an hour until she found a clearing. When she looked up, she was directly under the Basilica.

> How gently falls the snow!
>
> The air is calm and still,
> The whispering winds have ceased to blow
>
> O'er wintry plain and hill,
> And now from all the o'ershadowed skies
>
> All noiselessly and slow,
> As sent on tenderest ministries,
>
> So falls the feathery snow.
>
> —Loton, Jabez. "The Falling Snow." *In Poets and Poetry of Buffalo*, edited by James N. Johnston. Buffalo, New York, 1904.

Beouf sur le Weck

On leave from the Navy in the 1950's my father went Downtown with his pals Skip, Buzz, and Zip to the Palace Burlesk in Shelton Square. The plan for this reunion was to see the enchanting Rose La Rose. The four, all in uniform, paid their admission and took their seats in the fifth row. The scene was boisterous for the continuous Vaudevillian matinee of comedians, musical troupes, and skits such as the Keystone Cops and Divorce Court, where the Judge inevitably produced an oversized gavel to bash the promiscuous husband. The crowd was filled with shouts and laughter, but the four sat quietly awaiting the appearance of the sultry Rose La Rose. Then the lights dimmed. The hush was like a velvet blanket and a smoky spotlight sparked and crossed the stage.

Slipping through the crimson curtains came Rose La Rose to the sweet and voluptuous song of the orchestra pit's violins. As she snaked about the stage the curtains revealed a low divan on which Rose La Rose laid her golden and purple robes to reveal her mature breasts and long white-gloved arms. The orchestral serenade quieted as she moved toward the front of the stage. A spotlight waved over the mob, now in hysterics, released momentarily from society's puritanical concerns. Rose La Rose was looking for a partner. As the delirious crowd darted to meet the swaying spotlight, Rose La Rose and the light fixed on the four seated in the fifth row. The crowd drew still as she whispered, "sailor," pointing at my father. This was met with cheers and jeers. And after some halfhearted protestations my Dad made his way up the stage. At this point the memory gets a little foggy.

I asked, "Well...?" And he said, "She sat me down upon the couch, then did some kind of dance around me. I was surprised how old she was up close, but I closed my eyes and didn't move.

"The next thing I know, a number of short awkward little men made their way from back stage and up the aisles, shouting in a clear, lengthy and repetitive call, "Eskeeemoo Pies!!!"

> Down through the windows open wide,
>     To fix the noonday on the floor,
> The fir-tree's gloomy fingers glide—
>     They glide and pause and glide once more.
>         —Peterson, Dr. Frederick. "At the Green Fir
>         Tavern." *In Poets and Poetry of Buffalo*. Edited
>         by James N. Johnston. Buffalo, New York, 1904.

Six years after you arrived …

The strikers demand an eight-hour day, time
and half for overtime, no Sunday work, and
a wage scale with a minimum of forty cents
an hour.
—"5,000 Machinists Strike: Several Buffalo
Plants Close Down Following Walkout."
*New York Times* 3 Mar 1916: 12.

In 1813, all but three structures survived the attack of British forces. No literature from before 1812 in known to have survived. The first bibliographic record was a volume by Jabez Backus Hyde, on a H. A. Salisbury imprint from 1818, entitled, *Indian Hymns*.

Will Poultry

Poor city of fires, your wings are fried. No amount of blaze busters can quench this need to burn. You chop wood behind city hall, and set your dreams aflame. You are the city of Icarus crawling toward the sun, habitually incinerating your idols, boiling steel, liquidating the assets, melting tar-siding and charring roofs, like so much burnt Chiavetta chicken. You coughed an orange sky from a blackened lung. Made it rain pull-tabs. Now the carbon collects everywhere. In schools with coal furnaces, in the soot mounds beneath the skyway, the ashes are shoveled into a circle—a magic ring, which records the conflagrations of your history. Once the throbbing center of Empire, your breached core has been left to smolder.

American Radiator
American Axle
American Standard
An Economics of Extraction & Residues

Burnt during a Long Hot Summer
We Strangers in a Land of Paradise
Suffer Hard Station Post here

Struggle to resist the forces
of an hermetic downward spiral     (ECHC-BPD-ECMC-BPC)
and the violence endemic to this cycle

Rubbed raw by pride of ownership
strengthened by a habitus of ethnic conceit
enclosure laws tore the polis limb from limb
          … leaving no hope but to Gather

A collection of about 400 scrapbooks filled with newspaper articles, compiled between 1930-1975 (many volumes with articles published before 1930).

Grosvenor          F129 B8
Index cards — subject file
WPA     Librarian
Yellowed, Uncombed, Sneezed On

with the word "Dunkirk" approach

... the site of Buffalo from the southwest, scanning it from a vessel's deck on Lake Erie in the days before it was peopled or but sparsely settled, your first observation would be ... a chain of bluffs.

—Welch, Samuel Manning. *Home History: Recollections of Buffalo During the Decade from 1830 to 1840* ... Buffalo: Peter Paul and Bros 1891.

At six she came by boat, and so she missed the war,
to live above a funeral home, two lane bowling hall next door.
Sold lingerie at Sattlers, but we don't go down there anymore.
She had a basement filled with treasures, like rusted bicycles and toys.
Put a quarter in the milk machine by the corner store.

Many of them cannot speak the English language and are a people by themselves, forming a colony on the East Side, where there is a large market and numberless shops which they patronize for the various wares their needs require.

—*Paul's Dictionary of Buffalo.* Buffalo: The Peter Paul Book Company, 1896.

Subsumed in blocks, as an anomalous mass, tribe or race, the first reaction is to strike out in the name of distinction.

At six minutes after 4 am on the sixth of September, President McKinley fell a martyr, a victim of the black structure of anarchy. Buffalo is being built ... nobly, courageously, significantly, fulfilling the dreams of men who have found dreams good, and sometimes true.

—Roy W. Nagle, *Pictorial Buffalo: Niagara Falls and Surroundings*, Buffalo: Otto Retter, 1932.

The second response is to move as one.

1956: Buffalo, May 31 (AP)—
A holiday outing ended in a
voyage of terror for
passengers aboard a Lake
Erie amusement park vessel
last night as teenagers rioted
aboard the ship.

1960: Zanzibar Lounge
Closed Down

       Following the arc of Bethlehem
       The expansion was set outward
       between Seneca and Williams streets
       from Sycamore through Lovejoy
       down Walden Genesee

1988: Zanzibar opened again, one Night,
       Featuring Njabulo, Dr. Bird, Tony Dread ... West West

                            Cream Ale

       Buffalo ... believes that one of the best
       weapons for combating depression is
       cheerfulness.
       —Wilner, M. M. Buffalo Jobless Sing
       'Blues' Away. *New York Times*, Feb 9,
       1933.

It was probably on one of those bright October days, when I realized how spectacular it could be. No place is better than that. Van Miller crackling through someone's old transistor, "The kick is high ..." and a low roar would rise up into the clear autumn air, to hang there for moment, above Orchard Park, with the lake to the west, the Allegheny mountains to the south, and the city skyline glimmering in the north, suspended somewhere between sublimity and solidarity.

       REMO YOU DROPPED A BOMB ON ME
         —a note left below the shuttered TRICO plant c.1985.

Letter to Garcia

During the Blizzard of '77, at 10pm that Friday night, my father and I set out into the storm, climbing two-story drifts and facing seventy mile-an-hour winds to mail a letter on William Street. The following Tuesday, when the skies cleared, I joined a gang of kids to shovel out fire hydrants and mailboxes.

That was the winter I had to feed Uncle Frank's dog behind our duplex apartment. In the late fall after the first snow, Uncle Frank would hang rabbits over the trash cans out back or maybe a deer in the garage. After Christmas he would take my sisters, his boy and girl and I in his Arctic Cat snowmobile. We'd sled down the banks of I90 on cardboard boxes, and beseech truckers to blow their horns by frantically pulling down our outstretched arms as the semi's passed. It worked almost every time.

Sam, the reluctant beagle, when he wasn't out with Uncle Frank shooting pheasants in the rail yards and hobo camps at the base of St. Felix Street, spent the winter perched high in a drift above his aluminum sided dog house. After school, I scooped dog chow from a garbage can and made my way to Sam. Never was a being so happy to see me.

> After the shift the butcher came,
>     dressed in his crimson apron.
> And to his concertina sang,
>     his canine drunk companion.

—ARCHIVE/MANUSCRIPT. Vertical Files, 1905(ca.)-1981, 1952-1981 (bulk) 22.0 cubic ft. Libraries: New York State Historical Documents.

| 1 1 3 | 3 2 3 | 1 2 1 3 |
|-------|-------|---------|
| ʔokwe:nyɔ:h | ʔɛskyɛstɛ? | ʔɔkweʔɔwe:ʔkha:? |
| Can you | teach me | Seneca |

| 1 1 111 1 | 2 32 |
|-----------|------|
| ʔɛkatwɛnɔ:taʔk | ʔakso:t? |
| to speak | grandmother? |

—McElwain, T., *Mythological Tales and the Allegany Seneca: A Study of the Socio-religious Context of Traditional Oral Phenomena in an Iroquois Community*, Stockholm: Acta Universitatis Stockholmiensis, 1978, p. 69.

From Pineridge, Jewish and Polish cemeteries
above the escarpment where the Scajaquada descends

to tunnel below Schiller Park to Cold Spring,
this is the valley of the Seneca in the Cheektowaga borderlands,

home of the Buffalo River reservation,
or a vast subdivision, repetitive and distant,

marked in Summer with bike trails, forts and fire crackers
ripped Lotto tickets and bottle caps.

Mark saw a fox behind JFK high school near Cayuga.
Mark saw a fox, there, across the creek

where cray fish pick between the rocks
fallen cicadas and locomotives eclipse the sun,

where you'd race plumes of black smoke rolling
over kohlrabi patches and throw rocks at orphans,

but they would necessarily win,
having nothing left to lose.

> —Theses, letters, clippings, and other material concerning the Town of Cheektowaga, including census data, churches, cemetery inscrip-tions, industries, and schools; local history topics, including Buffalo, the American Revolution, canals, elections, Indians, medicine, fires, New York State architecture, arts and crafts, and travel.

Where streets once teemed, yards bleed into one another. Narrow houses stand alone in meadows tangled with sumac and rusted springs. Billowing upward a...
                         bank of clouds

In Mastenfields or, Oppenheimer stadium
International league Bisons or pony league
In cotton flannels with iron spikes, saw dust, chalk, clay, rubber
Airing out from the plant or Gerhard Lang's brewery
You laid down a bunt.

Between Hutch Tech and Westinghouse
or Bishop Ryan and "the service."
There was a bank of clouds
rolling high over Humboldt park and fountain pops
a few years before I was born.

At Villa Maria, you had to dance with the nuns
Take chemistry as leaves turned green
You too went to the ballpark
to see your hotshot brother, you the kid sister,
also known as "the kid."

Forget swinging for the fences—you did it with speed.
Getting in the strike zone
Pinched the bat, cushioned the pitch.
Softly. The contact wouldn't make a sound.
The whole park went dead.

Birds stop chirping, ice cone man stopped hawking,
in a moment of invisibility, they were put to sleep.

And when they came to, faces flushed with panic,
you were halfway up the line.

    Down at the edge of the park
    lodged at the edge of the lane
    parked on the edge of the downs
    in a park at the edge of the town

        We gathered berries in the forest when the sky became dark.
        The people shouted because the sun was gone.
        My sisters and I sat down alone.
        There is no need to run at the end of the world
        When the sun came back we gathered more berries.

            —Op. cit. McElwain, T., p. 17.

Such shades and shadows checker the city
building contour by accretion
setting the stage
to begin anew

# CHAPTER FOUR

# SIGNS OF THE CITY: SPACE, PLACE, AND THE URBAN STREET POSTER

## TARA H. MILBRANDT

The public spaces of a city bear traces of the diverse and conflicting hopes, dreams, fears, ambitions, and visions of solidarity that animate and vex its inhabitants in ordinary and extraordinary ways. As a sociological approach to urban culture emphasizes, ways of understanding and ways of inhabiting the city are integrally joined; both emerge out of the socially ordered, yet endlessly inventive, ebbs and flows of collective living. Infinitely more than a location on a map or a mere conduit for human action, the place of the city can be seen as a locus of circulating and colliding desires that derive their significance and force from the elemental fact that human lives are always lived in relation to socially ordered and organized spaces, methods, manners, and times.

This chapter analyzes the dynamic interpretive struggle over the legal status of street posters that took shape in Toronto, Canada during the first decade of the 21st century. On the surface, the passing of a hard-to-enforce city bylaw concerning hand-placed paper signs affixed and displayed in diversely textured ways across the city's public landscape could be considered a minor and essentially bureaucratic event; viewed sociologically, it can be seen to symbolize a transcendent collective spirit whose formalized terms imply a particular vision of an ideal city. I explore the conflicting views of street postering and public space that circulated and collided as different persons and groups struggled to influence City Hall, culminating in the formal sanctification of grassroots forms of "community" speech along city streets.

# The Urban Street Poster within a Landscape
## of Mass Commercialization

*From every thread spinning out of the city, ever new threads grow as if by themselves.* (G. Simmel, *The Metropolis and Mental Life*)

The densely populated streets of early 21$^{st}$ century Toronto, like other contemporary North American cities, are saturated with visual signage and diverse forms of commercially oriented mass communication. From electric billboards glamorizing the styles of the day, to elaborate store window displays, buses, street-cars, and subway trains draped in colorful advertisements, city streets tell and retell the post-modern capitalist story that "the world can be arranged so as to satisfy private desires" (Bonner 1997: 169; Hannigan 1998).

At a more vernacular level, different stories are told in the form of street posters. Speaking through a multiplicity of languages, these signs can be seen wheat-pasted, stapled, and taped to public utility poles, mail-boxes, garbage bins, telephone booths, and other stationary objects along city streets. Creatively soliciting the gazes of pedestrians in Toronto neighborhoods, and *potentially* challenging the hegemonic story told by the commercial billboard that "we transform ourselves" by purchasing commodities (Berger 1972: 131), such visual texts offer "cues and clues" as to who and what forms of social life may proliferate in a given area (Krase 2012: 1). In addition to a plethora of commercial services— including posters advertising cheap postering—diverse scenes, social types, and co-existing modes of life are inscribed onto material objects, from revolutionary political groups and persons who return lost pets, to places where people need cheap roofing jobs done, attend surrealist films, visit anarchist book-fares, hold lawn sales, practice meditation, entertain thoughts of astral travel, want to lose weight, make a quick buck, hear a local band, dream of conversing in Spanish, or need a room-mate. In some instances, highly differentiated forms of consciousness and ways of being in the world are alluded to, as exhibited in the following photocopied sign taped to a light-pole in Toronto's Annex neighborhood:

> Third Roommate Needed ... for July 1$^{st}$... 400/month all inclusive! This is a smoker-gay-david miller-jane Jacobs-cbc radio-Saturday Globe & Mail-creative-friendly-environment.

As a communicative form, the street poster is unique by virtue of the "availability of the means of production" (Timmers 1998: 8); "anyone with a felt tipped pen and a roll of adhesive can do it."[1] The sights and sounds of taping, tearing, stapling, wheat-pasting, and ripping off of posters contribute to the visual and auditory life of the city, particularly in more pedestrian concentrated downtown neighborhoods. Unlike officially sanctioned forms of signage, dominated primarily by the forces of capital, the street poster appears as an exceptionally low-tech form of democratized mass communication. Neither posting nor removal requires the expenditure of money, censorship board approval, or (typically) evasion from authority relations. And unlike the corporate billboards that tower inaccessibly above the passersby, the posters share the streets with their own makers and readers. Indeed, any poster may be torn down, covered over, or written upon by anyone, at any time. The ways in which posters are positioned in relation to each other also reveals the mixing of diverse life-worlds as part of the very texture of urban public culture.

Fig. 4-1. Posters on Public Utility Pole, Spadina Avenue

---

[1] "Be it transitory or transit-worthy, the ad's the thing," *Toronto Star*, 8 Jul 2001.

The ordinariness of the street poster in Toronto was disrupted when a bylaw being proposed by the City's Planning and Transportation Committee was made public in January 2002. If passed, this bylaw would have significantly restricted the permissible placement of posters on public utility poles throughout the city.[2] While previously anyone could poster liberally, repeatedly, and anonymously upon any such pole, prohibitive conditions were hereby proposed and detailed. Exhibiting the spirit of modern bureaucracy in its commitment to rational precision and the leveling of distinctions (Weber 1947), it was stipulated that a poster could not exceed 22 by 28 centimeters, must "consist of lightweight cardboard or paper," be minimally 100 meters from … similar signs and "be dated and displayed for not more than 30 days or 5 days after … the advertised event."[3] Sanctions were outlined, including a $60 removal fee for each violating poster. What inspired this municipal intervention and how was it received?

The harmonized poster bylaw was presented as an intended "solution" to an existing problem: *urban blight*. Following public notice of the City's intent to pass the bylaw, enthusiastic city councilors described postering as a growing problem and anti-social practice, wasteful of public resources. Frequent use of the term "eye-sore" framed poster-filled streets as aesthetically unpleasing, visually *painful* sights to behold. Even some councilors with reservations about the bylaw's viability participated in such representations, emphasizing quantity over content:

> It is a problem, the postering in this city. 99% of (it) is commercial postering. It's not political or social commentary. And much of it is disgusting, not in terms of content but in the sheer volume of paper. People are slapping these things up all over the place. The city recently spent millions revamping Spadina Avenue and (now) everything is covered in posters. (Moscoe 2002)

From the outset, all types of posters, and by extension *posterers*, were treated with a single, indiscriminate stroke. Gestural references were given to "political or social commentary," but commercially oriented content dominated early representations. Unlike the corporation behind the billboard in *its* visual excess, the posterer has not paid for public visibility

---

[2] If passed, the number of public utility poles upon which posters could be placed would have been reduced by up to 98%. Posters placed on mailboxes, telephone booths, garbage cans, were already prohibited, despite evidence to the contrary.

[3] City of Toronto, Planning and Transportation Committee, "Harmonization of the Sign Bylaw Concerning Posters on Utility Poles," Rep. No. 2, Feb. 13-15, 2002, 1.

and so, was depicted as a parasitical "free rider" whose days were now numbered.

City Hall might have imagined that a positive reading of posters was marginal and that the bylaw would pass uneventfully, guided as it was by an instrumentally rationalist conception of social action. For who but a self-interested (commercial) posterer would object to a "crackdown"? There would, however, be no smooth passage. Once the notice of intent was made public, the bylaw evoked vigorous opposition, particularly by those arguing that it threatened to violate citizens' constitutionally protected right to expression.[4] While many people, on all sides, expressed skepticism that it could actually be enforced, its symbolic significance was sufficiently powerful to elicit sustained mobilization and prolific public discussion. Mainstream, popular, and alternative media of all kinds contributed to the emerging understanding that the issue of urban street postering revealed and encapsulated important tensions of the times. The strong response it evoked signaled to the City that the subject would not be resolved quietly, that more was at stake than the clearing of "unattractive street clutter." City Council was all but forced to reconsider the terms of postering in Toronto.[5] The many public meetings, forums, rallies, media focus and general discussion which the bylaw stimulated over the next four years revealed that the issue had powerful resonances that transcended pieces of paper on public utility poles.

## The Specter of Decline and the Offended Resident

The language of "decline" and "disorder"—dramatized by scenes of crime, pollution, and anomie—have guided countless representations of urban life, from dystopic films and everyday judgments, to social science monographs and literary representations of modern times. These representations often equate urbanization with a "loss" of community (Delanty 2010: 18; Hale

---

[4] Spokespersons for *Citizens Concerned About Free Trade* and the *Canadian Civil Liberties Association* joined the discussion with constitutional readings of the bylaw. In Ramsden vs. the City of Peterborough in 1993, a local musician set precedent by successfully fighting for the Charter right to put up posters on public property to announce his upcoming gigs, and so, it was regularly suggested that the restrictive bylaw would "never make it through court" anyway. In publically available documents, the City indicated that it sought to balance protected Charter rights (of expression) with the reduction of "aesthetic blight" in this bylaw.
[5] In accordance with municipal procedure, a public meeting was held in March 2002 to allow public comment to the Committee responsible for writing—and possibly amending—the poster bylaw.

2011; Tonnies 1963). While often dismissed by city lovers as instances of anti-urbanism, the understandings of the city animating such representations are *elements of* the imaginary evoked by a "world of strangers" (Lofland 1973). As revealed in the case under consideration, they are part of the complex story of the city and its particular mix of "mutually oriented social relationships" (Blum 2003: 15).

The newly drafted poster bylaw was embraced by collections of otherwise dispersed residents as a welcome gesture and tangible weapon to fight against impersonal forces of "decline" in Toronto. Interpreted as both sign and symptom of said decline, the profuse and generally unregulated nature of the practice rendered it an object of anxiety for many vocal residents, some of whom took to the stand during public meetings to voice support for more prohibitive restrictions. "This beautiful City of Toronto is being trashed by irresponsible citizens and businesses," deputed one resident,

> ... My neighborhood has been in decline over the past few years, due in no small part to the proliferation of unwanted, unsightly and disgusting posters found on utility poles, Federal mail boxes, Bell Canada telephone booths, and municipal parking boxes ... Let's make Toronto beautiful again ... (Majta 2002)

While proliferating posters were translated as the unambiguous sign of neighborhood decline, the speaker positioned herself as authoritative on the grounds of long-term residency and so, an implied commitment to the well-being of her neighborhood and, by extension, the city. Going on to frame postering as a form of social pollution, the resident positioned herself as a neutral witness to the "degradation" of Toronto's public realm in this way:

> ... Most recently, upon exiting my residence, my eyes were unwillingly assaulted with numerous graphic sexual image posters ... A copy of this visual pollution is attached ... Why then can I not walk down my neighborhood street without having these unwanted filthy sexual images thrown in my face ... (Ibid.)[6]

Although most of the "offensive" examples cited were already prohibited under existing rules, the mobile, fluid, low tech and personal nature of the practice rendered it troublesome.[7] For unlike the sexually explicit billboard, also oriented to being seen and noticed, the poster could

---

[6] On the oriented character of looking vs. "seeing," see Michalko (1998).
[7] Posters on mailboxes, telephone booths, or parking boxes were already prohibited.

evoke danger, discomfort, and disruption since it presumably emerged from the taping, stapling, and wheat-pasting hands of people who inhabit the very streets on which it appears.[8]

Fig. 4-2. Federal Mailboxes, Bloor Street

References to postering as "trashing" the city cast the practice in decisively moral terms. Content considered offensive magnified its visually aggressive ("in your face") character. In a particularly dramatic scene at a public forum held at Metro Hall, a resident approached the podium with handfuls of crumpled paper she announced had been encountered en-route to the meeting. Orienting to the forum as a type of obscenity trial, the "trash" was presented as solid evidence of the aesthetic and social deterioration of Toronto.[9] Referring to a poster felt to be

---

[8] Interestingly, the sexually explicit content is noted here, as the resident is describing the outer fringes of Toronto's "gay village."
[9] See Sewell (1993), esp. 4-42 and T. S. Clark (1970). For an examination of the relation between "purification" and urban space, against the backdrop of the possible "uses of disorder," see Sennett (1970).

*particularly* troublesome—one advertising language lessons with the words "THINK IN SPANISH"—she shouted:

> ... These Spanish, they have destroyed our city with glue! I have lived here
> for 30 years and have watched this city deteriorate ... Everywhere you
> look, Toronto has become dirty! I am retired ... but when I want to take a
> walk, I have to go in battle-mode, ripping posters down ...[10]

Walking in "battle mode" highlights the power in this definition of the situation (Thomas 1923), while suggesting a vigilante-like orientation to the streets. While the offended resident experiences herself as being addressed in ways that call for a response, there is no one present to whom she may direct that response. Aimed at the chorus of citizens describing posters as positive signs of cultural vibrancy, surrogate for the conspicuously absent "Spanish" posterers, she shouted, "It's not fair to the silent majority ... We are entitled to live in a clean city ... All of us reside in the city of Toronto!" Referring to a bothersome "roofing" ad, another person shook his fists, suggesting that if he ever caught those responsible in the act he would "let 'em have it."

The conception of decline presupposes a former (better) state; built into such representations is a eulogy of sorts to a once "beautiful" Toronto. As such volatile scenes, the category of "cleanliness" signifies an image of social order that lies deeper than the literal presence or absence of "disgusting posters" in public places. As the cultural anthropologist Mary Douglas has written, "dirt ... is never a unique, isolated event ... (but) the by-product of a systematic ordering and classification of matter" (1966: 5). Thus to those for whom posters manifest forms of consciousness considered troubling, in both form (in your face) and content (graphic sexuality), a restrictive bylaw would affirm a type of solidarity, delivering a symbolic, condemnatory blow which no individual can achieve on her/his own while moving about the city offended, removing posters from public view.[11]

---

[10] Field notes from "Posters on Public Property Public Consultation Meeting," Metro Hall Council Chambers, 2nd Fl., 55 John Street, 9 Oct., 2002, Metro Hall Council Chambers, 9-11 am; 1-3 PM.

[11] This underscores the sociologically significant difference between being bothered by something as an individual vs. having the symbolic "backing" of the collective in the presence of the bothersome object. Durkheim's classic sociological discussion of crime in the *Division of Labor in Society* is apt here.

## Designer Streets and the Merchants' Alliance

"If Toronto wants to be a world class city, it has to look like one!" The assertion was made during a meeting at City Hall by a representative of postering's most organized opponent: the Business Improvement Area (hereafter BIA) of Bloor-Yorkville.[12] What animates it is the belief that the City has a primary and unquestionable *moral* duty to think of itself as an ongoing (capital) investment (Weber 1958). While rooted in different interests, there is nevertheless a strong kinship between the anxieties articulated along the lines of the "offended resident" and the bourgeois "solution" put forth by this particular aggregate. In public support of street postering restrictions, BIA spokespersons drew upon the boostering discourse of Toronto as an aspiring world class city, a contender oriented to being (seen and recognized as) a 21st century global destination.[13] Once a bohemian hippie destination, this elite enclave and iconic downtown area of conspicuous consumption is (now) a living embodiment of such an orientation.[14]

The merchant's alliance represented the streets as its indisputable turf in each address to City Hall:

... As much as we would like to see the right to postering eliminated altogether, our BIA is strongly in favour of the new bylaw that will provide a limited number of collared poles for postering throughout the city ... (Saunderson 2002)

Rooted in the authority of private stake-holders to "protect" otherwise shared spaces (assets) from harm or abuse, the BIA's relation to city streets is reminiscent of the neo-liberal story of the "tragedy of the commons."[15] Whereas the City must comply with the Canadian constitution in the crafting of bylaws, the BIA reveals itself here as a

---

[12] A BIA (or BID = business improvement district, *US*) is a self-taxing alliance of business and property owners in a defined area recognized by the City, receiving matching (public) funds for "improving" area streetscapes (e.g. planting flowers) and/or hosting community festivals. The model started in Toronto in 1970, and was adopted internationally. Presently, Toronto has 72 such organizations.

[13] Perhaps the BIA was relying on the vulnerability that might accompany Toronto's status as a second tier city striving for recognition, within the context of an international network of urban economies (see Bélanger 2002).

[14] See Henderson 2011.

[15] For a critical sociological formulation of such a position, particularly as it applies to environmental politics, see Pearce and Tombs (1998).

formation that, *if it could*, would "eliminate" all that hinders it from concretizing its particular vision of the city.

The organization's chairperson framed the problem of postering in relation to the defacement of private property and wasteful expenditures flowing from this:

> Our BIA has spent a great deal of money removing posters from private property throughout our neighborhood. The damage caused by leftover glue, tape and adhesive from these posters has made our city an absolute disgrace. The City must take a very firm hand with this matter, as the current situation is out of control and totally unacceptable ... (Ibid.)

While Torontonians were permitted to poster upon *public* utility poles, this organization has installed private, designer streetlights—over 200—throughout the area of Bloor-Yorkville. Each lamp that illuminates (and decorates) these streets has a small plaque with a script engraved upon it indicating it is the "private property of the BIA" and that it is illegal "to damage or deface (such) property." Revealing with exceptional clarity what the Marxist urban writer Mike Davis calls the "architectural privatization of the physical public sphere" (1992: 155), it is technically accurate for the merchant's alliance to describe postering on select light poles in the area it names as vandalism of private property.

The concreteness of this example reveals how decoration and design by business—often described in the language of "community revitalization" —can be used to legitimate a possessive relationship of (private) control over otherwise *public* spaces. The plaques, though, retain visible traces of the BIA's ongoing work of keeping the private lights that adorn and illuminate the streets unmarked. The markings can be interpreted as a silent and mocking riposte to the claim that a light-pole on a public street *could be* considered private property. While the formal arrangement of the BIA may legalize this relationship, posters and other forms of marking suggest that a different kind of truth is at play in city streets. And so, in spite of the material and symbolic resources the BIA may possess, the public street—and all that appears upon it—is open to being temporarily appropriated by the city's mobile and nomadic inhabitants through everyday/night creative tactics (De Certeau 1984: xii-xxiv).

Figure 4-3. Plaque on Designer Light Pole, Yorkville

Coinciding with the postering issue, the Bloor-Yorkville BIA was initiating a multi-million dollar street transformation project; as noted by urban affairs columnist, Christopher Hume, this project could "only go so far without bylaw changes" (2003). "There are million dollar stores on Bloor Street, but not a million dollar streetscape" (de Lange 2003), complained the same spokesperson we heard from previously. While unsuccessful, revealing attempts were also made by the BIA to forbid hot-dog vending and panhandling from Yorkville streets. Mobile and nomadic, such activities legitimate uses of streets as embodied places in which to dwell, pause, eat, and possibly engage with strangers (Sennett 1994). In this way, they disrupt the image of the area as an enclave for "high-end" consumption and place of virtuously productive, i.e. capital generating, activity.

The cultivation of designer streetscapes, exhibited through the BIA's ongoing material and ideological work, legitimates an authoritative relationship to the streets by re-presenting them as the valuable asset of an aspiring world class city, a striving Toronto oriented to becoming a globally competitive site of attraction. Whereas the resident for whom posters signify threat and disorder was animated by her/his lived experience in the city's public realm, above all else, for the BIA the streets are interesting due to their exchange value. Seen through this restricted economic gaze, there is nothing interesting or positive about street posters;

they are simply unwelcome forms. But they are also aggravating reminders to those interested in designing streets down to the last detail that *the street is not a stage-set*, but rather, an open site inhabited by diverse persons and heterogeneous forms of life whose energies exceed any master-plan. It is in relation to this that the BIA implored the City to "take a very firm hand" in the matter.

## Messy Democracy and the Citizen-Activist

"Public space in our city is under attack!" The perspectives advocating regulated, clean, and designer streets form a powerful trinity of speech, the latter supported by significant material resources. In light of the extensive literature detailing the privatization of public space in the North American city, the deliberative process could be viewed as a ruse, orchestrated to produce the mere appearance of public influence. A significant element in Toronto's postering drama, though, was the creative and successful mobilization of persons and groups who coalesced to support postering in the name of vibrant public space and "messy democracy." While it was voiced by a plurality of persons, its most cogent expression came from the *Toronto Public Space Committee* (hereafter TPSC), a small grassroots collective working largely "within the system" (Castells 1983) to defeat the bylaw.[16] This group played a pivotal role organizing a postering rally, launching press releases, encouraging participation at a public forum, organizing a fund-raising benefit concert at the local Bloor Cinema, and offering commentary in mainstream and local news media over the course of the four-year public discussion (and beyond). The defense of postering was transformed into an occasion to celebrate local culture, and collectively engage with the question: *to whom and to what does and/or should the city's public spaces belong?*

The "attack" on postering was rendered urgent against the backdrop of intensified commercialization in/of the public realm. Calling upon people to become involved in the civic struggle, pamphlets circulating at a rally outside of City Hall highlighted this connection:

> Stop the anti-postering bylaw! As more and more corporate billboards and video screen go up, city council is trying to limit community expression by banning postering on 98% of all hydro poles. It's an attack on culture,

---

[16] The TPSC formed in 2001, in response to Toronto's excessive hospitality to the private sector, visible in the increasing commercialization of its public realm. Its slogan over the course of the poster controversy was: *whose space is public space?*

multiculturalism and freedom of expression. We need your help to fight against this new bylaw.[17]

The specter of intensified commercialization that both haunted and stimulated the vigorous defense of postering was problematized in its privileging of *consumer* over *citizen*. In this way, the citizen's defense resonated with other 21st century urban social movements, from more liberal anti-consumerist to more radical anti-capitalist (Klein 2000; McNally 2006). It was also inspired by a neo-Situationist sensibility in its formulation of everyday/night life in a consumer-driven society as homogenizing, routinized, and in need of being actively and imaginatively disrupted (Gardner 2000; Pinder 2005). Speaking from this mix of social criticism and creative celebration during an appearance at a downtown rally, left British folk singer Billy Bragg enthused to a gathered crowd that, "Somehow these people have underestimated the will of the citizens of Toronto not to put up with the privatization of their city. People have to re-take their public space."[18] Such a "will" was made observable that afternoon through a mass postering action of "I LOVE POSTERS" signs. Using the medium as the message, stickers announcing "WARNING! THIS POSTER WILL SOON BE ILLEGAL" were distributed and supporters were asked to attach them to existing posters throughout their neighborhoods, across the city.[19] Revealing the general sociological principle that conflict can engender solidarity, the energies directed at defeating the "anti-postering" bylaw transformed an otherwise negative state-of-affairs into a carnivalesque celebration of grassroots culture and citizen engagement (Simmel 1903a; Schechner 1993; Turner 1983).

## The Aura of Place

A particular reading of "messy democracy" came to crystallize within the collective defense of postering as street posters were translated as signs of local habitation that revealed neighborhood streets as unique *places* replete with history, identity, and vital social energies (Augé 1995: 52). At public meetings, during rallies, on the radio, on blogs, and in local

---

[17] Flyer publicly distributed in Nathan Phillips Square, May 2002. Adding fuel to the citizen-activist's fire, the postering restrictions were proposed during a period in which electronic billboards were appearing in the downtown core and along city highways, due to a variance in the City's signage rules.
[18] Field observations.
[19] For a particularly creative example, see "Lost persons," Toronto Public Space Committee, www.publicspace.ca/poster-lostpersons.htm.

newspaper articles, again and again, diverse Torontonians took to the stand in various ways paying tribute to postering, and describing the ways in which posters infuse the city with character. "It's the lost cat ones that always get me", noted one man, "They're extremely personal. They mean so much more to me than a huge ad for some nightclub. This is how a community talks to itself." (Blackett 2007). It was in this spirit that local public space activist, David Meslin, described posters as "signs that the city has a culture, (that) the city's alive."[20]

Figure 4-4. Community Poster Board, Linux Cafe

Negative connotations surrounding "messiness" were inverted as postering was celebrated and cleanliness became re-defined as a sign of lifelessness, even repression. The sight of poster-adorned streets was thereby re-envisioned as the inspiring sign of a (socially) healthy city, exhibiting a type of urban "authenticity" (Zukin 2010). Variegated and uncensored, posters were represented as the expression of the diverse forms of life, interests, tastes, preferences, proclivities, possibilities, and potentially offensive views that share a home in the city. One of the few

---

[20] Interview on CBC radio, prior to a City Council meeting on postering.

prolific posterers to enter the public conversation explicitly, Reg Hartt, put it this way, "Postering is about freedom of speech, and freedom of speech is about being messy." Hartt's posters, which advertise alternative film showings, from *The Sex and Violence Cartoon Festival* and *The Salvador Dali Surrealist Film Fest*, to *Triumph of the Will* and a documentary about Jane Jacobs at his small private Bathurst Street theatre (*Cineforum*) have adorned poles and hoardings across Toronto streets for decades, and undoubtedly both offended and intrigued many people in their public sojourns.

The messily anarchic urban aesthetic that came to organize the campaign to defend postering became a way to talk about ways of *being in* and *inhabiting* the city more generally. As a writer from Toronto's popular *Now* magazine put it:

... If this new bylaw is passed, a major means of our free speech will occupy only a few narrow corners of our neat and tidy world-class city ... But the process of claiming public space, of allowing people self-expression, will never make the streets Singapore-clean. Instead we should revel in this disorder, for what speaks through our non-commercial posters are our more ragged voices ... (Carter 2002)[21]

To "revel" in this manner would be to treat one's immersion in a heterogeneous environment as a condition of one's capacity to "cultivate a mode of existence ... not imposed ... from the outside" (Simmel 1903b). Within such an orientation, it becomes possible to experience oneself as enhanced and extended by the diverse social energies and possibilities that are visible in the streets one walks, and the neighborhood one inhabits. To develop the more radical implications of such an orientation would lead to the general Marxian principle of "the free development of each is a condition of the free development of all" (Marx and Engels 1978: 491).[22]

---

[21] Representations of postering as "decline," by contrast, were generally dismissed as expressions of a suburban imaginary. Underlying this tension is a deeper issue—the possibly unholy and irreconcilable alliance between "416" (downtown) and "905" (suburb), made official by the amalgamation that produced the bylaw.

[22] Within the activist division of labor in the city, members of more politically radical and/or revolutionary groups (e.g. the Ontario Coalition Against Poverty) did not explicitly partake in the civic debate to defend postering; against the backdrop of the right to a basic income and/or housing, the right of expression can be seen as what David Harvey (2004) calls a "derivative right." To be radical, i.e. *to get to the root of the problem*, denouncing the commodification of the urban public realm would need to be located in a more fundamental analysis of the capitalist mode of production and its implications for everybody's "right to the city," including persons presently without citizenship status. See Lefebvre 2008.

Further, to revel in the city in the manner this suggests is to orient to the city in relation to what it *already is* and to build from this place, from the grass-roots. Seen through this light, even traces of posters alluding to events long past may be viewed as signs of the socially exciting character of the city, and not, for example, outdated information (City Hall), trash (privatized resident) or diminishing exchange value (BIA). Clearly, the battle over the fate of postering in Toronto was about more than street posters *per se*; the outcome was oriented to as significant insofar as it could be read to symbolically affirm (or reject) a particular ethos, vision, and mode of inhabiting the city.

After years of debate and deliberation, Toronto's highly contentious street postering bylaw was at last put to rest when its amended form was passed in 2006 and accepted by City Council in 2010.[23] The most striking difference between the original and its final form was the distinction that appeared in the latter between posters in general and "community" posters in particular:

> COMMUNITY POSTER—A poster promoting citizen participation in religious, civic, charitable or non-profit activities and events, or advertising festivals, community events, political ideas, or missing persons, pets or items."[24]

While posters of all variety could appear on kiosks, only "community" posters could (still) be liberally placed on public utility poles. Postering's most vigorous defenders interpreted the new bylaw as a partial defeat; clearly, though, their vigorous and sustained defense of postering—and all that it brought to public surface—had an impact on this outcome. True, many of the provisions from the original bylaw proposal were retained, including a controversial requirement that contact information be inscribed on the poster text. But by institutionalizing the category "community" poster, forms of expression that could be seen and said to emanate from within the collectivity (the city) were softly sanctified.

---

[23] The bylaw could not actually be enforced until a slate of poster kiosks were installed in key areas throughout the city. Ironically, one of Canada's largest private media corporations, Astral Media, was commissioned for that as part of a long-term contract for a broad array of new street furniture across Toronto. See http://www.toronto.ca/involved/projects/streetfurniture/.

[24] "Article VI: Posters on Public Property," Chapter 693, Signs, of The City of Toronto Municipal Code.

Figure 4-5. G20 Teach-In Poster, College Street

In future struggles over vernacular visual culture, all participants—including new mayors!—will have to orient to the now authoritative category of "community poster" and idea that "promoting citizenship participation" and/or "community events" through the medium of postering has a literal and defensible place in Toronto's streets.[25] While it will invariably become a new source of contestation, engendering unexpected connotations, alliances, divisions, the category of the "community" poster now is an object (now) endowed with the force and prestige of the collectivity, a "thing" in the world to be contended with (Durkheim 1982: 50-59; Berger and Luckmann 1966). This is particularly significant against the backdrop of densely inhabited city streets that might otherwise appear to be little more than "sites of pilgrimage to the commodity fetish" (Benjamin 1978: 151).

If one attends to the look and feel of the city, s/he will find different answers to the question of what makes a good city inscribed in the public spaces that both divide and connect people in everyday/night life. City streets, as the battle over street postering in Toronto has clearly revealed, can be seen as mirrors whose appearance reflects the mixed soul of the collectivity in time. What is at stake is not the mere "look" of the city but rather, the practices and relations to being in the city that its public appearance invites and reveals. After all, the making and remaking of the city is always also the making and remaking of social selves and collective possibilities. The diverse and conflicting responses elicited by the proposal to "harmonize" rules for street postering in Toronto brought this otherwise implicit relationship into the open for a remarkably sustained period of collective debate and deliberation, problematizing the very possibility of a harmonized "solution." Its eventual culmination in the formal sanctification of "communal" over "commercial" speech revealed how sometimes, despite overwhelming odds, grassroots organizing can achieve small victories, leaving marks upon the city which cannot simply or easily be wiped away. While urban culture is not reducible to bylaws, such things matter to people and groups precisely because they symbolize a transcendent and authoritative collective spirit. It is for this reason that they can, and sometimes do, elicit impassioned and committed responses that reveal an ongoing and creative struggle for the very "soul" of the city. Taken together, the multiple shapes and forms this struggle takes, and the mutually oriented responses it elicits, reveals the heterogeneous character of the city and robustness that *is* urban culture.

---

[25] As seen recently, calls to occupy downtown parks, anti-war teach-ins, police accountability demonstrations, G20 protest organizing, anti-austerity marches, student solidarity actions, etc. could constitute "community" postering.

# Bibliography

Augé, M. (1995). *Non-places: Introduction to the Anthropology of Supermodernity.* London: Verso.

Bélanger, A. (2002). "Urban Space and Collective Memory: Analyzing the Various Dimensions of Collective Memory" in *Canadian Review of Urban Research: Space, Place and the Culture of Cities,* 11 (1): 69-92.

Benjamin, W. (1978). "Paris, Capital of the Nineteenth Century" in *Reflections: Walter Benjamin: Essays, Aphorisms, Autobiographical Writings,* ed. by P. Demetz, New York: Schocken Books, 146-162.

Berger, J. (1972). *Ways of Seeing.* London: Penguin.

Berger, P. and T. Luckmann. (1966). *The Social Construction of Reality.* New York: Anchor Books.

Matthew B. (2007), as cited in "Utility Poles and Free Speech," *Toronto Star,* May 13.

Blum, A. (2003). *The Imaginative Structure of the City.* Montreal and Kingston: McGill-Queens University Press.

Bonner, K. (1997). *A Great Place to Raise Kids: Interpretation, Science, and the Urban-Rural Debate.* Montreal & Kingston: McGill-Queen's University Press.

Carter, L. (2002). "Everywhere a Sign: Crackdown on Postering Dicks with Democracy" in *NOW Magazine,* March 28.

Castells, M. (1983). *The City and the Grassroots: A Cross-Cultural Theory of Urban Social Movements.* Berkeley: University of California Press.

Clark, T. S. (1970). *Of Toronto the Good: The Queen City of Canada As It Is.* Montreal: The Toronto Publishing Company.

Davis, M. (1992). "Fortress L.A.: The Militarization of Urban Space" in *Variations on a Theme Park: The New American City and the End of Public Space,* ed. by M. Sorkin. New York: Hill and Wang, 154-180.

De Certeau, M. (1984). *The Practice of Everyday Life.* Los Angeles: University of California Press.

—. (1997). *Culture in the Plural.* Minneapolis: University of Minnesota Press.

Delanty, G. (2010). *Community, 2nd Edition.* New York: Routledge.

Douglas, M. (1978). *Purity and Danger: An Analysis of the Concepts of Pollution and Taboo.* London: Routledge.

Durkheim, E. (1984). *The Division of Labour in Society.* New York: The Free Press.

—. (1982). *The Rules of Sociological Method,* ed. by S. Lukes. New York: The Free Press.

Hannigan, J. (1998). *Fantasy City: Pleasure and Profit in the Postmodern Metropolis.* New York: Routledge.

Hale, S. (2011). "Loss of Community? The Rural-Urban Debate" in *Contested Sociology: Rethinking Canadian Experience.* Toronto: Pearson Canada, 136-166.

Harvey, D. (2004). "The Right to the City" in *The Emancipatory City? Paradoxes and Promises*, ed. by L. Lees. London: Sage, 236-239.

Henderson, S. (2011). *Making the Scene: Yorkville and Hip Toronto in the 1960s.* Toronto: University of Toronto Press.

Hume, C. (2003). "Bloor St's Going Uptown," *Toronto Star*, August 12.

Klein, N. (2000). *No Logo.* New York: Picador.

Krase, J. (2012). *Seeing Cities Change: Local Culture and Class.* Burlington: Ashgate.

Lefebvre, H. (2008). "The Right to the City" in *New Left Review*, 53, September-October, 23-40.

Lofland, L. (1973). *A World of Strangers: Order and Action in Urban Public Space.* New York: Basic Books.

Loukaitou-Sideris, A. and R. Ehrenfeucht. (2009). *Sidewalks: Conflict and Negotiation Over Public Space.* Cambridge: The MIT Press.

Majta, C. (2002). "Forwarding Comments Regarding the Draft By-law to Regulate Postering on Public Highways and Other City Property." *City of Toronto, Planning and Transportation Committee Supplementary Agenda Meeting No. 4. Appendix* (1F). March 8.

Manco, T. (2004). *Street Logos.* London: Thames and Hudson.

Marx, K. and F. Engels (1848). "Manifesto of the Communist Party" in *The Marx-Engels Reader*, 2nd Ed. (1978), edited by R. C. Tucker, New York: W. W. Norton & Company, 473-500.

McNally, D. (2006). *Another World is Possible: Globalization and Anti-Capitalism, 2nd Edition.* Winnipeg: Arbeiter Ring Publishing.

Michalko, R. (1998). *The Mystery of the Eye and the Shadow of Blindness.* Toronto: University of Toronto Press.

Howard M. (2002), as cited in "Killer Fine on Posters: Proposed Bylaw Will Bankrupt Alternative Culture," *Xtra!*, April 4.

Pearce, F. and S. Tombs. (1998). *Toxic Capitalism: Crime and the Chemical Industry.* Toronto: Canadian Scholars Press.

Pinder, D. (2005). "Situationist Adventures" in *Visions of the City: Utopianism, Power and Politics in Twentieth-Century Urbanism.* New York: Routledge, 127-158.

Saunderson, R. (2002). "Forwarding Comments Regarding the Elimination of Postering and the Proposal to Charge a Postering Fee." *City of*

*Toronto, Planning and Transportation Committee Supplementary Agenda Meeting No. 4. Appendix 1* (d). March 8.

Sennett, R. (1994). *Flesh and Stone: The Body and the City in Western Civilization.* New York: W. W. Norton & Company.

—. (1970). *The Uses of Disorder: Personal Identity and City Life.* London: Faber and Faber.

Sewell, J. (1993). *The Shape of the City: Toronto Struggles with Modern Planning.* Toronto: University of Toronto Press.

Schechner, R. (1993). *The Future of Ritual: Writings on Performance and Culture.* New York: Routledge.

Simmel, G. (1903a). "Conflict" in *Georg Simmel: On Individuality and Social Forms,* ed. by D. Levine, Chicago: University of Chicago Press, 70-95.

—. (1903b). "The Metropolis and Mental Life" in *The Sociology of Georg Simmel,* edited by K. Wolff. New York: Free Press, 409-424.

Thomas, W. I. (1923). *The Unadjusted Girl.* Boston: Little, Brown, & Co.

Timmers, M. (1998). *The Power of the Poster.* London: V & A Publications.

Tonnies, F. (1957). *Community and Society.* New York: Harper & Row.

Turner, V. (1982). *Celebration.* New York: PAJ Publications.

Weber, M. (1947). *The Theory of Social and Economic Organization.* New York: The Free Press.

—. (1958). *The Protestant Ethic and the Spirit of Capitalism.* New York: Routledge.

Zukin, S. (1995). *The Cultures of Cities.* Cambridge: Blackwell.

—. (2010). *Naked City: The Death and Life of Authentic Urban Spaces.* New York: Oxford University Press.

# Acknowledgements

I wish to thank Blagovesta Momchedjikova for her tireless work on this stimulating interdisciplinary collection and for helpful comments on earlier drafts of this chapter. I would also like to acknowledge early comments from Kieran Bonner, Sonia Bookman, Roger Milbrandt, and Bill Ramp. A special salute goes to Frank Pearce for his ever-insightful comments about city life and his helpful suggestions for this chapter. This text expands upon parts of my doctoral research. See *Public Space, Collective Desire, and the Contested City* (2006), unpublished dissertation, York University, Toronto, Canada.

# CHAPTER FIVE

## FREIGHT TO "FABULOUS"... LOOKING AT POST-INDUSTRIAL PARKS IN NEW YORK CITY

## MATTHEW A. POSTAL

Viewed with an architectural historian's lens, this essay considers contemporary park design in New York City. Four examples in three boroughs are discussed, paying particular attention to the conditions that led to each park's creation and how specific physical features and artifacts have been preserved and exploited to evoke earlier historic periods, as well as to produce novelty and aesthetic delight.

Whereas earlier phases of urban park design focused on in-land sites and relied on picturesque effects (Central Park) or recreational facilities (Robert Moses-era pools) to provide a refuge from daily experience, these mostly waterfront parks by design recall the city's former role as a leading port, as well as its evolving character in the twenty-first century. Following several decades of neglect and denial, public officials and community leaders have come to accept that the city's economy has changed dramatically and that these changes have presented a singular opportunity to develop new public spaces. Part spectacle and part history lesson, these distinctive post-industrial landscapes provide a unique perspective on the ever-changing urban environment.

Prior to the Second World War, New York City was the world's busiest seaport. From the streets of West Chelsea to the Williamsburg waterfront and Red Hook, these gritty districts were places of work and congestion, where every available parcel was thickly developed with wharves, warehouses, and piers. This changed entirely with the introduction of bulk containers in the mid-1950s. Aging piers and winches could not compete with modern cranes that easily move standard-sized payloads from the holds of ships to storage yards, trucks, and rail cars. This highly efficient system reduced costs, theft and, unfortunately, employment. With limited space available in New York City, the Port Authority of New York & New Jersey looked across the Hudson River to New Jersey. The first, the Sea-Land Container Terminal at Port Newark, opened in 1958, shortly after container ships began to serve North America. This facility was surpassed in 1962 by nearby Port Elizabeth, devoted exclusively to handling container goods. The impact of these projects was swift, drawing freight away from the city's five boroughs.

Fig. 5-1. Brooklyn Bridge Park, Pier 1, 2012

A good place to start investigating the growth of post-industrial parks is on the East River where *Brooklyn Bridge Park* is now under construction.

Extending, north to south, from Jay Street to Atlantic Avenue, at 85 acres it is one of the larger new parks in the city and the earliest (in part) to be conceived (Fig. 5-1). At the heart of the park is Fulton Ferry Landing, a pier where wedding parties frequently gather for photographs. A setting of particularly historic significance, this section of Fulton Street has been a transit hub for centuries—a place where row boats and later steam ferries carried passengers to Manhattan and where various street car routes terminated. The opening of the Brooklyn Bridge in 1883 and the Manhattan Bridge in 1909, however, drew traffic away from the river's edge and by 1924 ferry service ended.

The earliest section to open, previously called Empire Fulton Ferry Park, sits between the two bridges. Conceived in the late 1970s, what originally started as a modest two-acre parcel was actually part of a coordinated effort to revitalize Brooklyn's waterfront (Horsely 1979: B3). While some business groups wanted to maintain the area's commercial character by moving a wholesale meat market here, others wanted to erect low and middle income housing, similar to the Cadman Plaza apartments at the north edge of Brooklyn Heights, a few blocks away. Norval C. White, co-author of the *AIA Guide to New York City*, wrote perceptively in 1968: "I doubt, however, if sirloin steak is either happier or tenderer in sight of the sea. Here, a view of the Manhattan skyline between the two bridges would inspire the most romantic movie director, if not Walt Whitman himself (White 1968: 46). Fortunately, neither proposal won support and a multi-prong strategy was pursued, encouraging the preservation of historic structures and the introduction of cultural activities, as well as the creation of public space.

Empire Fulton Ferry Park is located within the boundaries of Fulton Ferry Historic District, designated by the Landmarks Preservation Commission in 1977—the same year as South Street Seaport in Lower Manhattan. Within the district, the Empire Stores are among the most impressive structures. Built in two phases, in 1869 and 1885, these nine three-and-four-story warehouses face Water Street, as well as the river, adjoining landfill that was once part of the Jay Street Terminal and its connecting railroad. The block-long interconnected brick facades are punctuated by arched openings of varying size and star-ended tie rods. Many arches are enclosed by iron shutters (or vents) that display an admirable rust patina. Con Edison, the site's previous owner, had successfully opposed landmarks designation, arguing that regulation would interfere with plans to erect an electrical plant. To overcome this obstacle, New York State convinced the utility to sell the property in 1977, making historic designation possible and the opening of the park, which originally featured a boardwalk, a few trees, and other "cosmetic" improvements. Though the amenities were modest, the site did offer a strong sense of place, with views of both bridges and the somewhat battered west facade of the Empire Stores. In subsequent years, proposals were made to convert the Empire Stores to new uses but none, even to this day, have moved forward. It is, perhaps, because of the anticipation of future commercial use, with some proposals optimistically modeled on Fisherman's Wharf, a tourist attraction in San Francisco, that the initial landscape was so unassuming—safe and stable but without any real flair. Nevertheless, a modest seed had been planted, showing what a public space on the river could be.

A larger section of *Brooklyn Bridge Park* extends south, ending at Atlantic Avenue. In the early 20th century, this area was controlled by the New York Dock Company, a successor to the Brooklyn Wharf & Warehouse Company, which by 1916 claimed to control three miles of the waterfront, including "the largest warehouse system and pier system on this continent" (New York Dock Company 1916). At the foot of Brooklyn Heights, this company handled freight for the Baltimore & Ohio, Erie, and Lehigh Valley Railroads. They also operated a connecting railroad, as well as railroad car floats, serving Red Hook, parts of New Jersey, and the Bronx. Prior to 1950, this segment of the waterfront was hardly visible from Brooklyn Heights, where only dead-end streets and rear yards faced west. With construction of the multi-level Brooklyn-Queens Expressway, including its top-shelf pedestrian promenade in 1950, the waterfront was revealed and there were soon calls from local residents to limit the height of future construction, as well as to pass laws protecting views of the harbor—an idea that ultimately won approval from the Board of Estimate in 1974 (Fowler 1974: 94). More importantly, in the decades that followed, the promenade offered a panoramic view of the waterfront's steady decline.

By the early 1980s, the six piers and warehouses were handling little freight. Costly maintenance of the aging infrastructure, coupled with current projects in Battery Park City, seemed to provide commercial developers with an edge, but the Friends of Fulton Ferry, eventually known as the Brooklyn Bridge Park Coalition, envisioned a public park. Though some groups found the idea impractical, they suggested it could be funded by leasing 20% of the site to commercial users—almost double what was finally approved. In the 1990s, Larry Silverstein, who currently is rebuilding the World Trade Center, seemed to have the upper hand but this sale failed to go forward and the Port Authority donated the land to the Brooklyn Bridge Park Development Corporation. Landscape architect Michael Van Valkenburgh, who collaborated on a preliminary master plan in 2000, was hired as the designer in 2004 and his firm's plan was approved in 2006.

Van Valkenburgh's team used natural and man-made elements to express the site's evolution, from the arrival of Dutch traders to the present day. Starting at Fulton Ferry Landing, Pier 1 stretches south and west. Built on landfill, a wide promenade runs around the trapezoidal perimeter, as curving paths climb toward the park's uppermost point, where splendid views open towards New York harbor and the Statue of Liberty. Sometimes called the Mohawk, this 38-foot-high ridge slopes down to the promenade, creating a bowl-shaped lawn where films and concerts are presented. To the south and east, a tidal salt marsh that connects to water gardens was planted, evoking the character of the shore prior to commercial activity. Other landscape features reference the ideas of Frederick Law Olmsted, such as the use of berms that will eventually mute the sounds of the nearby highway. Farther down river, the wider-than-average piers that date from the 1950s form a regular perimeter, with deep coves that help protect canoeists and kayakers. The squat multi-bay warehouse sheds have been preserved, but with noteworthy alterations, for future recreational use. Stripped of the metal panel exteriors, steel posts and gables frame vistas within the park and across the harbor. Recycled materials were used to fabricate the handsome pine benches, as well as the stepped granite prospect where people often gather to admire sunsets. Humble choices, likewise, shaped the design of the lighting fixtures, which are attached to giant wood poles scattered along various paths. In this context, such strong vertical elements recall the masts of clipper ships that once crowded the shore and brought wealth to Brooklyn residents.

Gantry Plaza Park opened in 1998—two decades after Empire Fulton Ferry Park. Opposite the United Nations Headquarters, it currently covers ten acres along the East River in Queens. Designed by Thomas Balsley Associates (with Lee Weintraub), the mostly level site provides unmatched waterfront views of midtown. While earlier Manhattan housing developments, such as Waterside Plaza and Battery Park City, bear hardly any trace of past commercial activity, Balsley pioneered the idea of highlighting specific artifacts to bring meaning and pleasure to visitors.

Prior to the consolidation of Greater New York in 1898, Long Island City was an independent municipality, with Hunters Point as its commercial and political center. In the era before suspension bridges and tunnels, people ferried to Queens from Manhattan and transferred to Long Island Railroad trains traveling east. As at Fulton Ferry Landing in Brooklyn, transit improvements would contribute to the waterfront's decline, such as the opening of the Queensboro Bridge in 1909, the

Pennsylvania Railroad tunnels in 1911, and the Queens Midtown Tunnel in 1940. By the 1970s, hardly any commerce remained on this part of the Queens waterfront.

Fig. 5-2. Gantry Plaza Park, Queens, near 48th St., 2012

Hunters Point is the first stop in Queens on the No. 7 subway line. To better appreciate the area's past, walk north from the Vernon Boulevard station to 48th Avenue. Here, the street is wider than most because it once accommodated below-grade train tracks that divided the neighborhood and connected the waterfront to the Pennsylvania (Sunnyside) Railroad Yards. Filled in 1994, this reclaimed area opened as Hunters Point Community Park in 1995. Approaching the East River, float bridges or gantries become visible (Fig. 5-2). Like the figurative bronze sculptures that punctuate the paths of 19th century parks, these large steel structures speak directly of past successes and human deeds. Painted black, orange letters boldly spell out the words "LONG ISLAND," recalling the trains that once served passengers here, as well as the park's geographic location (Gray 2004: RE10; Dunlap 1994: 454).

The four float bridges date to 1925, when they were modernized with overhead suspension systems. A resident of Queens, J. B. French, patented this rail transfer system in 1911 and it was first introduced in the freight yards of the New York Central Railroad at West 69th Street in Manhattan (Flagg). Easier to operate than earlier types of float bridges, gantries allowed standardized barges, also called car floats, to transport and transfer heavy railroad cars with relative ease. At its height, before the Second World War, there were as many as 80 float bridges active throughout New York harbor. Other surviving examples can be found in Riverside Park South, also designed by Balsley, as well as in the Port Morris section of the Bronx, near 134th Street. Described as "marine follies," they function as gateways to four metal piers, offering distinct areas for fishing, sunning and stargazing (Muschamp 1998: AR35). Upriver from the gantries and 48th Avenue, the walkway follows along the shore, bordered by trim lawns, native plants, orange-colored hammocks, and red-colored Adirondack-style chairs.

Lee Weintraub designed Erie Basin Park, which opened in southwestern Brooklyn in 2008 (Ulam 2008). Funded by the international retailer IKEA, this L-shaped mile-long park was created in exchange for zoning variances from the Department of Planning. Here, a rich sense of the site's history and its relationship to Red Hook is felt. The park faces Erie Basin, a man-made semi-enclosed harbor, where four electric loading cranes of varying height rise alongside a promenade, with winding paths, sculpted hills and tall grasses (Fig. 5-3). Now silent, these colossal light blue machines had been part of the Todd Shipyards, earlier known as the Robins Dry Dock Company, which operated one of the largest maritime facilities in the nation until 1983, with two dry docks and multiple piers for ship maintenance and repair.

The ideal way to enter the park is from the south side of Columbia Street, where the path zigzags west, along the edge of the basin. On the left, a 775-foot pier extends into the water. A single steel crane straddles the stained concrete walkway, seemingly ready to resume work at any moment. As in Queens, it functions as a work of environmental sculpture. The boom projects up and out, drawing the eye towards the sky and the water's edge. While the Swedish retailer insisted that an historic graving dock be destroyed to create additional parking, the dock's outline is preserved in cobblestone pavers. Moreover, overlapping signs have been cleverly arranged to cast shadows that suggest ship riggings and various industrial relics are artfully displayed on raised circular pedestals, including thick ropes, chucks and disassembled machinery. Weintraub said he wished to convey "a feeling that something happened here before America was transformed into a place where we actually made something to a place where we now import them" (Ulam 2008: 112).

Fig. 5-3. Erie Basin Park, Brooklyn, west crane, 2012

Unfortunately, Erie Basin Park attracts relatively few visitors. While some observers might explain this by pointing out the absence of athletic fields, or that views into the park are blocked by the store's proximity and huge blue bulk, another reason may be that Weintraub's design is fairly utilitarian. Not only are many of the artifacts rusted and hard-edged but much of the inventively-designed seating appears to be uncomfortable. Lastly, one faces a somewhat active basin that, for some, lacks the glitz and glamour of a Manhattan skyline. Nevertheless, the park's spacious design is a handsome and satisfyingly practical one, balancing the retailer's need to limit maintenance with respect for the site's contribution to Red Hook's history.

In contrast to the panoramic vistas offered at Gantry and Erie Basin parks, the High Line snakes above, alongside, between, into and through structures built for commerce and industry (Fig. 5-4). Because of such unusual characteristics and an exceptional design, this park has captured the city's imagination like none other in recent memory. A block or so east of Hudson River Park, this popular elevated promenade rarely approaches the shore, except near 14$^{th}$ and 30$^{th}$ Streets, but was closely related to businesses that flourished on Manhattan's west side during the first half of the 20th century. Among the parks discussed in this essay, the High Line was the last proposed and the last designed. Covering just 6.7 acres, it is also the smallest—comparable in size to Central Park's Sheep Meadow.

Fig. 5-4. High Line Park, view south from roof of Standard Hotel, 2012

Built in 1929-33 by the New York Central Railroad on properties acquired through eminent domain, it was part of the ambitious West Side Improvement, which attempted to reduce street congestion and improve vehicular circulation. Ultimately, this Depression-era project was poorly timed and in subsequent decades traffic on the viaduct steadily declined— a victim of the Eisenhower interstate highway system. This led to the demolition of two sections at the south end, between the multi-level St. John's Park Freight Terminal at Spring Street, as far as Bank Street in the early 1960s, and between Bank Street and Gansevoort Street in the 1980s. With little fanfare, the remaining tracks, extending north from Gansevoort Street, carried their final deliveries in 1980. This event attracted hardly any attention from the public, and in subsequent years, people who owned property below and adjoining the viaduct sought to have it demolished.

For many decades, the High Line had been known as the New York Central viaduct. In the 1980s, people began use "High Line," a term sometimes used to describe specific trains and rail routes. Some believe Peter Obltez introduced it in the 1980s. A rail enthusiast, he founded the West Side Rail Line Development Foundation and hoped to convert the abandoned tracks to public transit. Though he died in 1996, the name caught on. Journalist David Dunlap used the term in the *New York Times* in 1991 and the Friends of the High Line have certainly benefited from its upbeat, almost romantic, quality (Dunlap 1991: R13).

Nature began to take over the viaduct in the 1980s. Trespassers discovered unusual views and self-planted wildflowers—a rare occurrence in Manhattan. When photographer Joel Sternfeld documented it for the Design Trust for Public Space in 2003, he discovered a surprisingly photogenic urban meadow, with delicate flowers growing alongside rusting metal and the midtown skyline. His striking color images, which have been frequently published and exhibited, not only drew attention to the disused viaduct's poetic character and potential, but provided powerful inspiration for the park's designers.

Robert Hammond and Joshua David founded the Friends of the High Line in 1999. They first met at a community board meeting and were told that the current mayor Rudolph Guiliani supported the owners' longstanding request for demolition. Luckily, the next mayor Michael Bloomberg and the City Council agreed to postpone such action. In Paris, a comparable public space had opened on a derelict mid-19th century railway viaduct near the Bastille Opera in 1993. Though similar in spirit, the almost three-mile-long Promenade Plantee feels less aesthetically ambitious. Not only did the French viaduct's narrow width limit what designers could achieve architecturally but little attempt was made to recall the promenade's previous incarnation as a railway.

From the start, the Friends wanted a unique design and held an open "idea" competition in 2003. An exhibition, including more than 150 of the 720 entries, was presented at Grand Central Terminal. Though many designs were clearly speculative, such as a lap pool, and were probably impossible to build, most shared a common interest in revealing the viaduct's historic layers and its unbroken linear character. In October 2004, the Friends and the City of New York selected the design team, including landscape architect James Corner Field Operations, architects Diller Scofidio + Renfro, and horticulturist Piet Oudolf.

The south entrance rises from Gansevoort Street. Metal stairs emerge from between the grayish-black girders of the viaduct, revealing a leafy green landscape with a northward orientation. The High Line is experienced as a sequence of horticultural and architectural events that bare little relation to parks conceived by past generations. Enclosed by low walls, including some with decorative metal panels where the viaduct passes over streets, the width ranges from 30 to 88 feet. To enhance the linear character, some of the steel tracks have been reinstalled and the elegant cast stone pavers are deliberately narrow and elongated—much like the park itself. Furthermore, rather than interrupt the visual flow with standard issue park benches, the "peel up" wood seating cleverly grows out of the paving. The benches and exterior walls also disguise waist-level horizontal LED fixtures, somewhat diminishing light pollution and the need for conventional vertical fixtures.

Beyond the park's perimeter are uncommon vistas. The High Line passes through commercial areas that were hardly known to city residents before the 1990s, when art galleries started to congregate in West Chelsea following the relocation of two SoHo institutions: the Kitchen, an art and performance venue, which moved to West 19th Street in 1986, and the Dia Art Foundation, which opened at the west end of 22nd Street in 1987. Cultural activities such as these brought new perspectives to the neighborhood. Moreover, the people who passed beneath this once-mysterious steel structure became curious about the area's faded beauty.

Among the viaduct's great innovations was that it runs into and through various commercial structures. While some buildings needed to be modified, others were totally rebuilt to fully benefit from the auto-free freight system. Of the various interior passages, two remain accessible: one built as part of a rental property for the New York Central Railroad and leased to meat packers between 13th and 14th Streets, and the other for large-scale baker Nabisco, originally the New York and later National

Biscuit Company, which demolished part of its factory on Ninth Avenue to create a seamless connection to the viaduct, between 15th and 16th Streets.

One challenge for the designers was how to overcome the viaduct's persistent and somewhat monotonous horizontality. To provide some relief and novelty, two showpieces have been created: an ipe wood paneled amphitheater at 17th Street, in which tiered stadium-style seating faces framed views of vehicles traveling up Tenth Avenue, and the "Woodland Flyover," a metal grate path that gradually rises to a height of eight feet above the former track bed. While most 19th century elevated railways ran above major avenues, at the flyover the High Line squeezes behind former factory buildings, including a 10-story concrete warehouse designed by Cass Gilbert, architect of the Woolworth Building. Here, between 24th and 27th Streets, the path is enlivened by angled seating platforms that permit views of a lush shade garden planted with sumac and magnolia trees.

Nineteenth-century parks presented New Yorkers with a much-needed break from urban life. Olmsted expressed strong reservations about Manhattan's unrelentingly-predictable grid, and certain areas in his parks, such the Ravine in Prospect Park, were fashioned to resemble landscapes found in the Catskills Mountains, an area most city residents hardly knew. The High Line, in contrast, is proudly, almost defiantly, urban, offering visitors an elevated viewing platform that provides unusual views of Manhattan's skyline and the rapidly gentrifying west side, from humble late 19th century brick tenements and early 20th century cold storage warehouses to high-profile contemporary works by such architects as Frank Gehry. Nonetheless, until recent times few could have imagined throngs of park promenaders appreciating this unmitigated man-made spectacle.

This recent wave of park construction is making a significant contribution to the lives of New Yorkers and more examples of this kind are opening in north Brooklyn and the Bronx. Compared to earlier periods of park creation, design and construction, this is still relatively fresh territory and the response from the public and critics has been generally positive. In addition to providing imaginatively-designed landscapes for leisure and recreation, these parks have made sites that were once mostly inaccessible into highly-regarded, what some might call fabulous, destinations. Though New York City may no longer be a major port, the ways in which these once-gritty places have been transformed and interpreted shows an increasingly nuanced understanding of the city's past and present character.

# Bibliography

Berrizbeitia, A. (Ed.) (2009). *Michael Van Valkenburgh Associates: Reconstructing Urban Landscapes.* New Haven & London: Yale University Press.

Flagg, T. and others. "Development of the Car Float Transfer Bridge in New York Harbor," Retrieved (2012) from http://members. trainweb.com/bedt/indloco/developmenttransferbridge.html

Dunlap, D.W. (1991). "Conrail: Looking to a Revival of Its Freight Traffic," *New York Times,* R13. January 20.

—. (1992). "Queens West Begins With a Park," *New York Times,* 454. September 18.

Fowler, G. (1974). "City Acts to Protect View From Heights," *New York Times,* 94. September 29.

Gray, C. (2004). "On Waterfronts of the Present, Rail Bridges of the Past," *New York Times,* RE10. November 7.

Horsley, C.B. (1979). "Developers Map Rebirth For Brooklyn Waterfront," *New York Times,* B3. August 15.

Muschamp, H. (1998). "Where Iron Gives Way to Beauty and Games," *New York Times,* AR35. December 13.

New York Landmarks Preservation Commission (1977). "Fulton Ferry Historic District Designation Report," New York, N.Y.: New York City Landmarks Preservation Commission.

"New York Dock Company," reprint of 1916 advertisement. Retrieved (2012) from http://www.trainweb.org/bedt/indloco/nyd.html

Ulam, A. (2008). "The Park Ikea Built," *Landscape Architecture,* 98, No. 11. March.

White, N.C. (1968). "Waterfront Meat Mart," *New York Times,* 46. December 3.

# CHAPTER SIX

## BACK TO THE FUTURE IN LOS ANGELES:
## A CRITICAL REVIEW OF HISTORY,
## AND NEW INDICATORS OF THE VITALITY
## OF PUBLIC SPACES

## NATHALIE BOUCHER

This text offers an examination of urban history and the contemporary assessment of public spaces through an anthropological perspective. It is based on epistemological and methodological analysis of the literature on lively public spaces and on fieldwork observation of non-verbal interactions in public spaces in Downtown Los Angeles in 2008-2009. By looking at social interactions among city dwellers, urban anthropology brings back to the heart of our understanding the real dimensions that define public spaces, which are to provide access to an open environment, unexpected (and sometimes expected!) encounters, amenities, and atmosphere unavailable elsewhere.

Public spaces host the daily mundane, inspirations for songs and poems, movements of historical contestation, memories of the past, and hopes for the future. They are an essential part of the right to the city; their shape and uses help fix historical and contemporary practices and beliefs onto the urban fabric. To understand today's form and use of public spaces, this text reaches back to Ancient Greece and then to contemporary Los Angeles—the archetype of a metropolis charged with the destruction of its public spaces.

Throughout history and societies, public spaces have played different roles, from market places to meeting points for families (Low and Smith 2006: 4). In contemporary literature, some urban thinkers (from planners to legislators) offer a normative definition of public space: it *should* be inclusive and it *should* host spontaneous encounters between citizens of every class, gender, and ethnic group who practice a wide range of activities at any time of the day (Flusty 1994; Ghorra-Gobin 2002). They are the same who have illuminated us of the demise of public space.

Yet, many of us who live in urban areas may be familiar with the lively "fauna" in public areas—families having a picnic, teenagers frolicking, an old man feeding pigeons. You may have noticed in your urban surroundings the construction of a new neighborhood park, the restoration of a river's banks to its greener glory, or the renovation of an old and forgotten downtown square. Why then have public spaces been considered doomed, if not dead? This fate stems from an ideal—a public space open to all, at all times, for all activities—a universal public space, which is thought to have existed in Ancient Greece (a false premise) and, which has been wrongfully used to criticize the management of public spaces in contemporary Los Angeles.

The public space addressed here is the outdoor, open, physical urban space (as opposed to the virtual or indoor one) (Mitchell 2003; Carr et al. 1992), known also as the plaza, the square, the park, or the garden. These public spaces share various amenities (benches, fountains, paths and planned areas) and visual elements (green patches, art pieces, and paved areas). Some of them are owned and managed by public authorities, others by private interests, and a few constitute a consortium between private and public (Carr et al. 1992: 50).

# The History of the Representation and Production
of Public Spaces

The history of public space begins in Ancient Greece, with the deliberate integration of a local public space, the *agora*, into the urban design (Herzog 2006: 13). For many, the agora represents an ideal of universality, a place where citizenship can be expressed, and where spontaneous encounters can lead to public discussions and the appreciation of otherness (Hartley 1992: 29, cited by Mitchell 2003: 131). Yet, the agora—a place for religious events that turned into a trade site at the end of the 6[th]century—was, for the most part, used by merchants, a particular class to whom the right of citizenship was denied. Citizens talked politics and current events elsewhere, at the gymnasium for example, where noncitizens (6 out of 7 Athenians) were not allowed (Mumford 1964: 170). Although the groups of people visiting the agora for trade were undeniably engaging in encounters and getting familiar with locals and foreigners alike, the agora was nevertheless a place of exclusion, open to all but used only by a group of undesirables (Mumford 1964: 194-198).

The Roman Empire modified not only the role of urban public space, but also its form, which has lasted until today—the contemporary design of many European plazas dates back to that era. The grid plan, which developed at that time, facilitated the creation of the rectangular open space, limited by large archways and lined with wide streets (Mumford 1964: 269, 273). The Roman severity was not reflected solely in the design. Distancing itself from the use of public spaces in Ancient Greece, the *forum* became the site for the expression of military force and the emperor's authority, through parades and architectural elements that recalled the power of the Supreme Chief (Mumford 1964: 255).

As cities declined during the following centuries (because they were under continuous attacks which rendered them unsafe), so did the need for public spaces. Then, in the Middle Ages, protected settlements experienced a demographic boom, while urban planning foresight was neglected. The only places for meetings were the few empty sites and the open spaces in front of churches and cathedrals. This lack of public spaces forced people of all classes to rub shoulders on the church square. This physical co-presence was experienced without fear of social mixing because class status, characterized by specific behavior, was clear to everyone (Low 2000: 81 cited by Carr et al. 1992: 58; Mumford 1964: 370).

During the Renaissance, public spaces evolved greatly, due to new perspectives in urban design and aesthetics (Herzog 2006: 14). However, new inspiration for public space in urban settings came from the New World, where conquistadors discovered gigantic plazas at the center of settlements. Not only did various religious rituals, games, and political activities take place in these open spaces, but the homes of those in power as well as the most important institutions were established around them (Low 2000: 96). This practice influenced not only urban renovation and new designs in Europe itself (84-85), but also urban plans for new colonial establishments designed by European empires (Robinson 1931: 8-9; Ryan 2006: 462). For instance, the plans made for the village of Los Angeles, established in 1781, included such a plaza. After the village was flooded several years later, the plaza was rebuilt in the new settlement a few miles to the West, according to the same principles. It still stands today, under the name of Plaza Olvera (Hutton ca 1849).

New ideas about social contracts and the equality of all souls flourished during the Enlightenment (Rousseau 1992 [1762]) and encouraged more people to take over public spaces and the public sphere, but, at the same time provoked the reinforcement of social distinctions in the city through spatial occupation and appropriation (new neighborhoods and distinctive architecture, for example), behaviors, and discourses (Bernand 1994: 74; Sennett 1976 [1974]: 18). As a result, only individuals carefully selected and similar in terms of social status and respectability (Mitchell 2003: 132-133) were allowed in those public spaces, which were supposedly open to all. This was also the case in the United States, a country with a shorter history in terms of urban planning and plenty of space to develop; public spaces took the form of large grassy commons, places for military parades, or plazas where the Spanish law was enforced. There, just like in Europe, the new bourgeoisie continued to tighten its grip on the city by taking advantage of emerging practices of land speculation and privatization throughout the 18$^{th}$ and 19$^{th}$ centuries (Herzog 2006: 16; Loukaitou-Sideris and Banerjee 1998: 8-18). By then, a greater number of different people (class and gender) were found in public spaces, and visual differences between social classes (clothing, for instance) diminished thanks to mass production and consumption of goods (means of transportation, clothing, etc.).

In response, the bourgeoisie refined its distinguished behavior in public, using public space to spread the new way of being and to bring the lower classes towards more civility, passivity, and self-control in public (Paquot 2008; Rotenberg 2001; Sennett 1976 [1974]: 27). In Los Angeles, for example, children, instead of swimming in the Arroyo Seco, drinking and frolicking on its banks (Lofland 1998: 130; Low, Taplin, and Scheld 2005: 23), were highly encouraged to canoe quietly on the lakes of Westlake Park (now known as Macarthur Park) or Echo Park (Elrick and FoLAR 2007: 19; Low, Taplin, and Scheld 2005: 23) under strict supervision (Hise and Deverell 2000: 4). Land privatization, which fixes social status in the urban fabric, also meant that public activities could be supervised and controlled by private authorities, and separated and isolated in different places (Herzog 2006, 16; Rotenberg 2001, 12-13). In Los Angeles, the Chutes Park, an amusement park reserved exclusively (at the beginning of the 20$^{th}$ century) to African-Americans, is a good example of how private owners can control access (of a specific group) and separate activities (paid entertainment), and thus separate people (the ones who can afford it, and the undesirables—the ones who cannot).

During the 20$^{th}$ century, the urban territory was reorganized: urban space became the object and the means for the organization of social classes and groups (Carter 2010). As public spaces continued to become increasingly open to all—women (Lofland 1998: 132), students (Lanza 2009), war opponents, and suffragettes (Merry et al. 2010)—behaviors continued to be homogenized and normalized, notably through displayed "codes of behavior" in municipal parks and the separation of public spaces according to function or users (Herzog 2006: 16; Low, Taplin, and Scheld 2005: 22). Municipal parks, for example, in the US and elsewhere, were built according to the same model for the "average American" (Loukaitou-Sideris 2012: 199)—white, middle class, nuclear family—without consideration of the specific needs of the local population.

The two Great Wars and economic distress led to a drop in the creation of public spaces in the United States at least, as well as to poorer management of the existing ones (Davis 1992 [1990]: 227). City dwellers left for the suburbs, abandoning public spaces to unionized workers, the unemployed, and strikers (Carr et al. 1992; Lindenberg 1993; Tartakowsky 1997: 2004); and municipal authorities neglected their maintenance. Due to the lack of public money, private interests were invited to take part in the construction of public spaces and to take control of their management (Lofland 1998: 194-195). This was done successfully in many Western cities (Whyte 1980: 14) but contributed towards three practices: the higher securitization (thanks to new technologies and "needs" in light of this new diversity of users and economic riots), greater specialization (spaces for shopping and entertaining) and rapid profitability (through fees for access and activities) of homogenized public spaces (Zukin 1995; Sorkin 1992).

The social movements of the 1960s opened public spaces to women, minorities, and disabled people. This proved that public spaces can be claimed and appropriated by "undesirables," and used for political expression (Doderer 2011), which the authorities considered unsafe (Lefebvre 2000 [1974]: 430; Mitchell 2003: 150). As public space opens itself to all, owners have diversified their control strategies, from displaying signs prohibiting political debates, and gender and ethnic group co-presence (Dennis 2008: 150; Dick Whittington Studio circa 1936-1957, 1939), to installing surveillance cameras, hiring private security agents, or even promoting sterile designs (Lofland 1998: 181-187, Allen 2006). These latter strategies are not badly perceived by city dwellers, if noticed at all, since many believe that public space is unsafe (Minton 2010). In these cases, public space becomes cut off from city life, a process that I figuratively refer to as "strangulation."

# The End of Public Spaces in Los Angeles

Today's public spaces are said to be rare, empty, highly controlled, and visited by similar people (in terms of class and ethnic group) (Sennett 1976 [1974]: 3), especially in Los Angeles, which sets itself apart from other US metropolitan cities by its policies strangulating public spaces. Right from the first settlement, many parts of lands were privatized for real estate development (Davis 1999). The consequences were documented as soon as 1930, when the famous Olmsted Brothers and Bertholomew & Associates counted less public spaces in Los Angeles than the average US city (Davis 1999: 62). Despite this assessment, and the pollution problems in the 1940s, investments continued to be directed towards roads and automobiles, at the expense of parks and public areas (Hise and Gish 2007). Forty years later, in the 1980s, economic restructuring led to a reduction in public expenditures for new public spaces, to the cancellation of many public goods and services, and to a decrease in the maintenance of existing ones (Davis 1996; Loukaitou-Sideris 2012: 193). At the same time, the urban renovation program that spanned from the 1950s to the 1990s, virtually gave promoters and private investors *carte blanche* to rebuild a Downtown neighborhood. They were asked to include public spaces in their developments, in exchange for some benefits in line with construction (such as the permission to build higher buildings). Voids, over-controlled and sanitized spaces appeared at the foot of office and residential towers, more often than not as "quality of life" incentives rather than as real gathering places (Flusty 2000: 151). This gave birth to places with corporate names (a practice criticized today by Rose-Redwood 2012) like the 7 + Fig of the Ernst & Young Plaza (originally named the Citicorp Plaza) and the Bank Of America Plaza (originally the Pacific Securities Plaza). Also, public spaces that were too small, difficult to access, uncomfortable, controlled and hidden, like the Angels Knoll and the Biddy Mason Pocket Park, were built on private land but have been maintained with public money to this day (Flusty 1994: 20-21). The modern architectural trends of the time, which favored the mega bloc structure, the separation of pedestrians and cars, and the corporate plazas, are responsible for the fact that public spaces are shut off from the rest of the city (Loukaitou-Sideris and Banerjee 1998: 222). Furthermore, the combination of private interests, public management, security and urban planning makes it even harder for the "undesirables"—rioters, strikers, the homeless—to access public spaces.

Yet, there has been an ongoing need for the dense atmosphere and the unexpectedness of public life, and the development of festive spaces proved to be a lucrative solution: paid festive spaces with maximum excitement and fun, and with minimum exposure to real-life conditions (Mitchell 2003: 141). Yet, artificial homogeneity and controlled consumption characterize such spaces (Sorkin 1992, xiv)—what Zukinhas termed "Disneylandification" (1998: 836)—which are not exclusive to Los Angeles where they proliferated quickly (Rybczynski 1992; Cruz 2001; Didier 2001; Flusty 1994; Allen 2006). Places like the Plaza Olvera merchandised in the 1930s and the complex L.A. Live built in 2005 (Hawthorne 2008), among others, pretend to be "open" yet they are entirely geared toward the consumption of goods and sensations.

In a recent article (2008), Fleischer creates and inventory of LA's public places, whether privatized, suffocated, or abandoned. As of 2008, only 33% of Angelinos lived within a quarter of a mile of a park; this was the case for 97% of Bostonians and 91% of New Yorkers (Watanabe 2008). The national recommendation is 10 acres of park per 1,000 inhabitants. In Los Angeles, the figure is 6.8 acres (Loukaitou-Sideris 2012: 193). Both of the ways in which the death of public spaces is expressed in Los Angeles—strangulation and Disneylandification—rely on the need for order, surveillance, and control of public behavior (Davis 1992 [1990]: 226, 258; Flusty 1994; Garreau 1991; Low and Smith 2006: 15; Paquot 2008; Sorkin 1992). This is generally understood as the sad ending of a long-dead tradition that was initiated right after the Greek agora. This ideal public space is where, it is believed, no one felt excluded, directed or controlled.

## Quality, Not Quantity; Social Interactions Not Design and Management

Without denying the very low number of public spaces in Los Angeles (Loukaitou-Sideris 2012), I question the quality assessment of the existing places. This assessment, I recall, is based on the heterogeneity of users, and their freedom to practice any activity, at any time. If there is control, limit or direction of the users, their activities or their time of visit, then the public space is considered (by the thinkers who believe the universality of public space to be effective) to be sterile in terms of social mix and interactions.

Mitchell (2003: 131) explains that those who pronounced the death of public space have nostalgic fantasies. The history of public spaces shows that they were in reality never entirely public. From Ancient Greece to today's central parks, when public spaces are open to all, users tend to avoid contact by distinguishing themselves visually (skin color, clothing) or behaviors, or isolate themselves in exclusive environments. The "universal" public space is a confused combination of the "public sphere" as described by Habermas as in the 18$^{th}$ century and the physical public space as thought of by urban planners (Paquot 2008: xvii). When an ideal Greek public space and the public sphere are imagined as being physically integrated in the urban fabric, the definition of public space, overloaded with virtues, becomes normative: since public spaces *have always been democratic*, they *should thus stay* open to all classes, ethnic groups, and gender.

Furthermore, in the specific case of Los Angeles, the public spaces said to be "dead" were never addressed by an in-depth analysis. Neither the controlled and empty plazas of Downtown renovated in the 1990s, nor the other sites, which were being put to death (Pershing Square) or Disneylandification (Plaza Olvera)—but were never explicitly mentioned as doomed—were analyzed using a viable methodology. Finally, no attention has been given to the new public spaces created, like the recent Vista Hermosa Natural Park, the new Grand Park and the future Cornfield, or to the support of investments by California voters, or other proposals and initiatives aiming towards sustainability and greener cities (Hoeffel 2011; Loukaitou-Sideris 2012: 193). If anything, the dark predictions brought attention to a specific type of public space—the uniform private corporate plaza and its dangerous rise in the 1990s—and warned public authorities about the consequences of the lack of public investment in public amenities.

In the United States alone, there are, still today, many public spaces built before the 1980s that are thriving and appreciated—such as Washington Square Park in New York (Project for Public Spaces 2005; Flusty 1994: 53; Whyte 1980: 98). Thanks to favorable public policies and citizens' interventions, many public spaces are being created or revitalized, which confirms their dynamism and resilience (Project for Public Spaces 2005; Broverman 2010; Dakota 2009; Drake Reitan 2012a, 2012b, 2012c; Hawthorne 2010). Revitalization strategies go from full reconstruction to mere additions like benches, or new events, such as a weekly farmers' market. Of course, the recent revitalization of downtowns, with new population and money coming back to urban centers, has a lot to do with the reanimation of central parks and squares (Herzog 2006: x). At first glance, these lively spaces are different in many ways, but there is no doubt that, even in the globalized era of virtual relations and individualism, they fulfill a unique role in cities. They host spontaneous interactions and informal contacts; they serve as familiar landmarks, which can be a source of comfort, security, community identity, and democratic aspirations (Forrest and Kearns 2001: 2129; Low, Taplin, and Scheld 2005). Contrary to what predictors of the death of public spaces have claimed, there are today public spaces that are lively, desired, and used, even among the ones that were once pronounced doomed.

Yet, we need to discover the users of today's public spaces in Los Angeles. Who are they? What is their background? Do they interact? Unfortunately, too little researchers looking at lively public spaces shed light specifically on the qualitative dimensions of public spaces (Navez-Bouchanine 2002: 43). That was noted by Whyte back in the 1980s:more and more Americans used public spaces, but their public behaviors were not well known and thus, more empirical research was need (Whyte 1988: 1-2). Loukaitou-Sideris (2003) has conducted such research in Los Angeles, but she focuses on children's presence in parks and playgrounds. Matei and his colleagues (2001) focused on xenophobia behind the general perception of public spaces. These researches do concentrate on public spaces as a setting, but they do not consider that an influential variable. Other research does, but it more specifically pertains to beaches, a very unique environment in the vast array of shapes that public spaces can take (Davidson and Entrikin 2005).

## Reframing the Evaluation of Public Spaces' Vitality

Before examining the vitality of public spaces in Downtown Los Angeles in 2008-2009, I reviewed the literature on social activities in lively public spaces. I identified four elements linking citizens in and around these sites. These elements are observable through positive or negative, verbal or non-verbal interactions. As the Chicago School has explained, any interaction, pleasant or not, allows for a "communicational exchange" that links actors who are otherwise separated (Park 1938, 1990 [1926]).

The first indicator is *sociability* between different users, in terms of social identity, age, ethnic group, and gender. This encompasses the vast range of interactions, from brief and fortuitous non-verbal to regular verbal exchanges. Far from indicating the loss of community sense (Wellman and Leighton 1981; Wirth 1990 [1938]), these short interactions among strangers contribute to the individual's well-being and to the general quality of urban life (Pennec 2006), notably by further linking the strong relationships lived out elsewhere (Henning and Lieberg 1996). While it is important to admit that social interactions between different people are limited, sociability is crucial in establishing the staging of *interactions* among users as the main function of public space (not simply the co-presence of different users).

These interactions are also essential to the formation of public trust, or what I like to refer to as *informal security*. Following Jacobs, I believe that the sum of brief contacts between users of public spaces develops a feeling of belonging, a network of trust and respect, and recourse for personal or collective needs (Jacobs 1993 [1961]: 66). Informal security, which implicitly governs behaviors and actions, co-exists with formal security devices and resources, and often the two work together to promote the same consensual (and dynamic) definition of comfort and safety (Boucher 2012: 249-250).

Another indicator of the vitality of public space lies in its *representational role*. When appropriated by neighbors or city dwellers (Project for Public Spaces 2005), public spaces become landmarks where the image of the neighborhood, the city, or even the nation is projected (Dansereau, Éveillard, and Germain 1994: 6; Hayden 1996: 9).

This process of appropriation and place-making is not without social conflicts. Because space is never without content or value (Dikeç and Garnier 2008), individuals are invited to organize themselves in it, to contest it, to transform it, to become emancipated from it (Lefebvre 2000 [1974]: 70). This idea, developed by Lefebvre, has meant for researchers like Mitchell (2003: 129), Harvey (2006), and Low (2000: 130-131) that public space is a site where political forces are expressed. In other words, a place is public if it is appropriated and if that appropriation is contested, ideologically or physically. I call this indicator the *contestation in public space*.

The criteria presented here as indicators of the vitality of public spaces have successfully been put to the test (through detailed observation of interactions and semi-structured short interviews) in five public spaces in Downtown Los Angeles (Boucher 2012):

- Plaza Olvera has a Mexican atmosphere that calls for small talk and sociability, which is barely contested, thanks to the regular users—retired Latinos who happen to fit in the décor and have great informal control over the behaviors of other users;
- Pershing Square is mainly used by the homeless who manage the site in an impressive yet informal way. Interactions with other users are rare. For this reason, references to Pershing Square as a "dump" is common, and thus highly contested by new Downtown residents;

- Because it is a corporate plaza whose function as a white collars' cafeteria al fresco is never contested, the Watercourt has a very low level of diversity (in terms of ethnic group and class, although other heterogeneity criteria are considered by the white collars themselves);
- Grand Hope Park is a neighborhood park where students and residents rarely rub shoulders because they use different areas. This implicit use of space is imposed through security rules and reinforced by non-verbal behaviors, all of which are highly respected;
- Quite the same happens in Vista Hermosa Natural Park, but between local teenagers and families, who use the park at different hours, making sure they rarely meet and that no conflicts emerge for control over activities and users.

All of these places show different results in terms of sociability, informal security, representation, and contestation, but none is considered "dead," not even temporarily. Furthermore, the sociability, informal security, representation, and contestation in and of those public spaces are not frozen in time and space; the assessment I performed may change, for example, with new amenities introduced in the parks or a shift in the main users. The recent movement of contestation surrounding the access to the LA River and its imminent expanded public access is another example (Glick Kudler 2012; Senate Bill No. 1201 2012). A main advantage of those criteria is that they take into consideration the evolution, the dynamics and the resilience of public spaces and their social dimensions, by placing the users (individually or in groups) and their interactions back at the heart of the creation and reproduction of places, despite the globalized forces reflected in their design and management.

Thus, my project focuses not on the quantity of public spaces at large, but rather on the quality of existing places. It calls for a reframing of the question of their vitality at the dawn of the 21$^{st}$ century. In public spaces, differences co-exist. They nourish the process of learning about otherness, and, as a result, generate unity in the city (Navez-Bouchanine 2002; Simon 1997: 44). They are resources for collective living (Le Gall and Meintel 1997: 212; Rémy 2001). When reviewing the history of public spaces, as focused on the unattainable ideal of universality, one can see the source of erosion of contemporary public spaces: an increase in homogenization, control, surveillance, and merchandizing.

No wonder then that those who were focused on that ideal claimed the death of public space in the 1990s. They were rightfully alarmed by a design and management practices that prevailed at the time and that threatened the ideal public space. This ideal, based on the universality of users and uses, was seen (wrongly) in the historic context. The history and contemporary evaluation of public spaces should be aligned with their main purpose in cities: to encourage encounters, to create networks of trust, to play roles of representation, to host movements of contestation over the use of these spaces, and debates about other issues. These dimensions, less tangible than institutional management and physical design (Low and Smith 2006: 6), focus on the social experience of public spaces and relate to the set of perceptions and actions that makes them a place for urban sociability.

# Bibliography

Allen, J. (2006). "Ambient Power: Berlin's Potsdamer Platz and the Seductive Logic of Public Spaces" in *Urban Studies, 43*(2), 441-455.

Bernand, C. (1994). Ségrégation et anthropologie, anthropologie de la ségrégation. Quelques éléments de réflexion. In J. Brun & C. Rhein (Eds.), *La ségrégation dans la ville*. Paris: L'Harmattan, 73-83.

Boucher, N. (2012). *Vies et morts des espaces publics à Los Angeles : fragmentation et interactions urbaines*. Ph.D., Institut national de la recherche scientifique—Centre Urbanisation Culture Société, Montréal. http://www.ucs.inrs.ca/sites/default/files/centre_ucs/pdf/Boucher_Nathalie_PhD_2012.pdf

Broverman, N. (2010). Brightly colored chairs, food carts coming to the new Civic Park. *Curbed LA*. November 07. http://la.curbed.com/archives/2010/07/hawthorne_placated_maybe_excited_by_new_civic_park.php.

Carr, S., Francis, M., Rivlin, L. G., & Stone, A. M. (1992). *Public Space*. Cambridge: Cambridge University Press.

Carter, H. W. (2010). "Scab Ministers, Striking Saints: Christianity and Class Conflict in 1894 Chicago" in *American Nineteenth Century History, 11*(3), 321-349.

Cruz, M. (2001). L'espace public entre commodité et identité: l'exemple de deux rues à Los Angeles. In C. Ghorra-Gobin (Ed.), *Réinventer le sens de la ville. Les espaces publics à l'heure globale*. Paris: L'Harmattan, 103-112.

Dakota. (2009). "Latest Civic Park Designs: Everyone Weighs in" in *Curbed LA*: December 3. http://la.curbed.com/archives/2009/03/latest_civic_park_designs.php

Dansereau, F., Éveillard, C., & Germain, A. (1994). *Le rôle des espaces extérieurs résidentiels dans la dynamique du lien social.* Paper presented at the Conférence internationale de recherche sur l'habitat, Beijing.

Davidson, R. A., & Entrikin, J. N. (2005). "The Los Angeles Coast as a Public Place" in *Geographical Review, 95*(4), 578-593.

Davis, M. (1992 [1990]). *City of Quartz: Excavating the Future in Los Angeles.* New York: Vintage Books.

—. (1999). *Ecology of Fear: Los Angeles and the Imagination of Disaster.* New York: Vintage Books.

Dennis, R. (2008). "Public Spaces—Practised Places" in R. Dennis (Ed.), *Cities in Modernity: Representations and Productions of Metropolitain Space, 1840-1930.* Cambridge: Cambridge University Press, 144-179.

Dick Whittington Studio. (1939). A fountain in Pershing Square in downtown Los Angeles with a sign prohibiting public speaking, debating, and blocking walks [Photography]. Los Angeles: University of Southern California. Libraries.

—. (circa 1936-1957). The Biltmore Hotel as seen from Pershing Square, with men sitting on the park benches, some of which are "reserved for women and children only" [Photography]. Los Angeles: University of Southern California. Libraries.

Didier, S. (2001). Parcs de loisirs et nouveaux espaces publics: le "Disneyland Resort" D'Anaheim. In C. Ghorra-Gobin (Ed.), *Réinventer le sens de la ville. Les espaces publics à l'heure globale.* Paris: L'Harmattan, 149-158.

Dikeç, M., & Garnier, J.-P. (2008). Éditorial. *Espaces et Sociétés, 134.*

Doderer, Y. P. (2011). "LGBTQs in the City: Queering Urban Space" in *International Journal of Urban and Regional Research, 35* (2), 431-436.

Drake Reitan, M. (2012a). "An Orchard Spirals Out" in D. C. Sloane (Ed.), *Planning Los Angeles.* Chicago: American Planning Association. 212-213.

—. (2012b). "Planning a Great Civic Park" in D. C. Sloane (Ed.), *Planning Los Angeles.* Chicago: American Planning Association, 240-241.

—. (2012c). "Regreening the LA River" in D. C. Sloane (Ed.), *Planning Los Angeles.* Chicago: American Planning Association. 137-138.

Elrick, T., & FoLAR. (2007). *Los Angeles River.* Charleston, S.C.: Arcadia Publishing.

Fleischer, M. (2008). "Parks and Wreck: In Search of the Emerald City" in *L.A. Weekly.* July 16. Retrieved 10/09/2011, from http://www.laweekly.com/2008-07-17/news/parks-and-wreck/

Flusty, S. (1994). *Building Paranoia: The Proliferation of Interdictory Space and the Erosion of Spatial Justice.* West Hollywood: Los Angeles Forum for Architeture and Urban Design.

—. (2000). "Thrashing Downtown: Play as Resistance to the Spatial and Representational Regulation of Los Angeles" in *Cities, 17*( 2), 149-158.

Forrest, R., & Kearns, A. (2001). "Social Cohesion, Social Capital and the Neighbourhood. *Urban Studies, 38* (12), 2125-2143.

Garreau, J. (1991). *Edge City.* New York: Doubleday.

Ghorra-Gobin, C. (2002). Dévalorisation de l'espace public et spatialisation du fait ethnique. In C. Ghorra-Gobin (Ed.), *Los Angeles: le mythe américain inachevé.* Paris: CNRS, 145-181.

Hartley, J. (1992). *The Politics of Pictures: The Creation of the Public in the Age of Popular Media.* London: Routledge.

Harvey, D. (2006). "Space as a Keyword" in N. Castree & D. Gregory (Eds.), *David Harvey: A Critical Reader.* Malden: Blackwell, 270-293.

Hawthorne, C. (2008). "It Has No Place" in *Los Angeles Times.* Dec. 3. http://articles.latimes.com/2008/dec/03/entertainment/et-lalive3

—. (2010). "Civic Pride Shaping Civic Park" in *Los Angeles Times,* October 14.    http://www.latimes.com/entertainment/ news/la-et-civic-park-20100714,0,5715540.story

Hayden, D. (1996). *The Power of Place: Urban Landscapes as Public History.* Cambridge, Massachusetts: MIT Press.

Henning, C., & Lieberg, M. (1996). "Strong Ties or Weak Ties? Neighbourhood Networks in a New Perspective" in*Scandinavian Housing and Planning Research, 13*, 3-26.

Herzog, L. A. (2006). *Return to the Center: Culture, Public Space and City Building in a Global Era.* Austin: University of Texas Press.

Hise, G., & Deverell, W. (2000). *Eden by Design: The 1930 Olmsted-Bartholomew Plan for the Los Angeles Region.* Berkeley: University of California.

Hise, G., & Gish, T. (2007). City Planning. In H. L. Rudd, T. Sitton, L. B. de Graaf, M. E. Engh, S. P. Erie, J. A. Grenier, G. R. Lothrop & D. B. J. Nunis (Eds.), *The Development of Los Angeles City Governement; An Institutional History 1850-2000.* Los Angeles: Los Angeles City Historical Society. Vol. 1, 329-369.

Hoeffel, J. (2011). Villaraigosa wants a more livable L.A., with 50 pocket parks, *Los Angeles Times.* November 16. http://latimesblogs.latimes.com/lanow/2011/11/villaraigosa-wants-a-more-livable-la-with-50-pocket-parks.html

Hutton, W. (ca 1849). *Drawing by William Hutton of the Los Angeles Plaza as it appeared in 1849*. Los Angeles: University of Southern California, Libraries.

Jacobs, J. (1993 [1961]). *The Death and Life of Great American Cities*. New York: The Modern Library.

Lanza, F. (2009). Politics and the City: Student activism and Urban Space, Beijing 1919. *Contemporanea, 12* (1), 5-28.

Le Gall, J., & Meintel, D. (1997). Espaces observés: ethnicité et appropriation territoriale. In D. Meintel, V. Piché, D. Juteau & S. Fortin (Eds.), *Le quartier Côte-des-Neiges à Montréal; Les interfaces de la pluriethnicité*. Paris: L'Harmattan, 211-229.

Lefebvre, H. (2000 [1974]). *La production de l'espace* (4th ed.). Paris: Anthropos.

Lindenberg, T. (1993). Politique de rue et action de classe à Berlin avant la Première Guerre mondiale.*Genèses, 12*(12), 47-68.

Lofland, L. H. (1998). *The Public Realm. Exploring the City's Quintessential Social Territory*. New York: Aldine de Gruyter.

Loukaitou-Sideris, A. (2003). "Children's Common Grounds—A study of Intergroup Relations Among Children in Public Settings" in *Journal of the American Planning Association, 69* (2), 130-143.

—. (2012). "Green Spaces in the Auto Metropolis" in D. C. Sloane (Ed.), *Planning Los Angeles*. Chicago: American Planning Association, 191-203.

Loukaitou-Sideris, A., & Banerjee, T. (1998). *Urban Design Downtown: Poetics and Politics of Form*. Berkeley: University of California Press.

Low, S. M. (2000). *On the Plaza: The Politics of Public Space and Culture*. Austin: University of Texas Press.

Low, S. M., & Smith, N. (Eds.). (2006). *The Politics of Public Space*. New York: Routledge.

Low, S. M., Taplin, D., & Scheld, S. (2005). *Rethinking Urban Parks: Public Space and Cultural Diversity*. Austin: The University of Texas Press.

Matei, S., Ball-Rokeach, S. J., & Qiu, J. L. (2001). "Fear and Misperception of Los Angeles Urban Space—A Spatial-Statistical Study of Communication-Shaped Mental Maps" in *Communication Research, 28* (4), 429-463.

Merry, S. E., Levitt, P., Rosen, M. S., & Yoon, D. H. (2010). "Law from Below: Women's Human Rights and Social Movements in New York City" in *Law & Society Review, 44* (1), 101-128.

Minton, A. (2010). Ville privée, vie contrôlée. *Courrier international*, February 22. http://www.guardian.co.uk/commentisfree/2010/feb/22/ doesnt-work-didnt-ask-why-cameras.

Mitchell, D. (2003). *The Right to the City; Social justice and the fight for public space*. New York: The Guilford Press.

Mumford, L. (1964). *La cité à travers l'histoire*. Paris: Les Éditions du Seuil.

Navez-Bouchanine, F. (2002). *La fragmentation en question; des villes entre fragmentation spatiale et fragmentation sociale?* Paris: L'Harmattan.

Paquot, T. (2008). Préface—De "l'espace public" aux "espaces publics". Considérations étymologiques et généalogiques. In Y. Jébrak & B. Julien (Eds.), *Les temps de l'espace public urbain: construction, transformation et utilisation*. Québec: Éditions Multimondes, ix—xxii.

Park, R. E. (1938). "Reflections on Communication and Culture" in *The American Journal of Sociology, 44* (2), 187-205.

—. (1990 [1926]). La communauté urbaine: un modèle spatial et un ordre moral. In Y. Grafmeyer & I. Joseph (Eds.), *L'école de Chicago; naissance de l'écologie urbaine*. 2nd ed. Paris: Champs Flammarion. 197-212.

Pennec, S. (2006). Les pratiques de la ville entre anonymat et proximité; garder une relation urbaine au monde. *Les annales de la recherche urbaine, 100*, 51-58.

Project for Public Spaces. (2005). Top 12 Public Squares in the U.S. and Canada. November 20. Project for Public Spaces. http://www.pps.org/reference/uscanadasquares/

Rémy, J. (2001). Public-privé: entre pratiques et représentations. *Villes en parallèle, 32-33-34*, 23-29.

Robinson, W. W. (1931). *The Story of Pershing Square*. Los Angeles: Title Guarantee and Trust Company.

Rose-Redwood, R. (2012). "Against the Selling of Naming Rights to Public Places" in *AAG Newsletter, 47* (7), 13.

Rotenberg, T. (2001). "Metropolitanism and the Transformation of Urban Space in Nineteenth-century Colonial Metropoles" in *American Anthropologist, 103* (1), 7-15.

Rousseau, J.-J. (1992 [1762]). *Du contrat social*. Paris: Flammarion.

Ryan, M. L. (2006). "A Durable Centre of Urban Space: the Los Angeles Plaza" in *Urban History, 33* (3), 457-483.

Rybczynski, W. (1992). "Why Cities?; How to Rebuild Los Angeles" in *The New York Times*. June 6.

Sennett, R. (1976 [1974]). *The Fall of Public Man*. London: Faber and Faber.

Simon, P. (1997). Les usages sociaux de la rue dans un quartier cosmopolite. *Espaces et Sociétés, 90-91*, 43-68.

Sorkin, M. (1992). *Variations on a Theme Park: the New American City and the End of Public Space*. New York: Hill and Wang.

Tartakowsky, D. (1997). *Les manifestations de rue en France 1918-1968*. Paris: Publications de la Sorbone.

Tartakowsky, D. (2004). La construction sociale de l'espace politique: Les usages politiques de la place de la Concorde des années 1880 à nos jours. *French Historical Studies, 27* (1), 145-173.

Watanabe, T. (2008, July 20). "Vista Hermosa Park Opens: It's Downtown L.A.'s First New Public Park since 1895" in *Los Angeles Times* http://articles.latimes.com/2008/jul/20/local/me-park20

Wellman, B., & Leighton, B. (1981). Réseau, quartier et communauté. *Espaces et Sociétés, 38-39*, 111-133.

Whyte, W. H. (1980). *The Social Life of Small Urban Spaces*. Washington D.C.: Conservation Foundation.

—. (1988). *City: Rediscovering the Center*. Garden City: Doubleday.

Wirth, L. (1990 [1938]). Le phénomène urbain comme mode de vie in. In Y. Grafmeyer & I. Joseph (Eds.), *L'école de Chicago; naissance de l'écologie urbaine* (2nd ed.). Paris: Champs Flammarion. 255-281.

Zukin, S. (1995). "Whose culture? Whose city?" in J. Lin, C. Mele, F. Stout & R. T. LeGates (Eds.), *The Urban Sociology Reader*. New York: Routledge, 282-289.

—. (1998). "Urban Lifestyles: Diversity and Standardization in Spaces of Consumption," in *Urban Studies, 35* (5-6), 825-839.

## Acknowledgments

Sincere thanks to Blagovesta Momchedjikova for a very inspirational visit to the Big Apple in 2012, and for putting this book together. A longer version of this paper was part of my thesis, commented by Julie-Anne Boudreau, Annick Germain, Hélène Bélanger and Yves Pedrazzini, whom I thank sincerely. The fieldwork behind this work was made possible by the financial support of the Social Sciences and Humanities Research Council of Canada, the Fondation Desjardins, the Canada Research Chair in the City and Issues of Insecurity, and the Institut National de la Recherché Scientifique, Centre Urbanisation Culture Société.

# PART II

# CITY IDENTITIES:
# IN TRANSIT AND SITU

# CHAPTER SEVEN

# DANCING BRIGHT: IDENTITY POLITICS AND THE PERFORMANCE OF EX-SOVIET ÉMIGRÉ ALLIANCES IN THE TWIN CITIES

## MARGARITA KOMPELMAKHER

My project is best located within the disciplines of performance and dance studies. It draws on the technique of choreographic ethnography to provide a close reading of bodies as they move and interact with their urban surroundings. A choreographic reading destabilizes the notion of the "urban" as a stable text and analyzes the dynamic relationality between objects and bodies as they construct the space of the urban. It is able to lend valuable information missed by ethnographic approaches that privilege the "voices of the city" when it foregrounds kinesthetic and embodied modes of producing and transmitting cultural knowledge.

This essay analyzes the way that ex-Soviet immigrants negotiate the politics of identity within the civic sphere of the Twin Cities. It complicates the way that performances of marginal identity get framed in the field of performance studies as scripts of resistance and attempts to undo a one-to-one relationship between identification and culture. I call attention to the dance floor as the pivotal site that regulates the construction of a pan-Soviet imaginary "cityspace" even as it reveals dance moves that register differences in nationality, class and gender within this space.

# A City Without An Identity

I worry about missing my stop every time. The view from the bus window is pitch black as it passes a stretch of empty parking lots and office buildings. I remember that my destination comes up right after this stretch and start to pay better attention to the road. A bright "Teahouse" sign with a logo of chop sticks breaks through the darkness and a few other lights begin to outline the façade of a strip mall in the suburbs of Minneapolis. I ask the bus driver to let me off.

I walk past the lights of the Teahouse toward an unassuming restaurant with a basic white sign on which beige letters spell out *Baku*—the name of the capital of Azerbaijan, a former Soviet republic now an independent nation. The color contrast on the sign is so slight that *Baku* only identifies itself to a guest at parking lot distance. To the right of the sign is a row of heavily draped windows obscuring any visuals of the inside. The restaurant seems ill suited for a US advertising environment even though it is technically open to the general public. Whereas other businesses typically strive for visibility, *Baku* does not seem to need to flaunt itself to the public to bring in customers. Every time that I have come to the restaurant on a Saturday night, it has been full of clients who are eating, drinking, toasting and dancing behind the heavy drapes.

I imagine that the patronage of the restaurant has to do with the word-of-mouth transmission of information between members of the ex-Soviet émigré community: a term that I use to describe an alliance between multiple immigrants organized around a nebulous spatial mark of the former Soviet Union. My reading of this space is informed by my own experience growing up within such a community in California, where I spent my teenage years being dragged around to restaurants that practiced a similar mode of visibility. *Baku* follows the specifications of a quintessential *banquet* restaurant for the ex-Soviet émigré community in the US. Calling it a restaurant is somewhat misleading as it also plays the roles of communal dance hall (after about 9pm on Fridays and Saturdays) and makeshift community center on Mondays through Wednesdays when the restaurant is closed (a flyer at the bar says that next week there is an event with a Russian hypnotherapist). *Baku* specializes in special occasion events for large parties—50th birthday parties, wedding celebrations, Russian-style bar/bat mitzvah dinners etc.

Inside *Baku*, Russian pop music is blasting and a female MC with microphone is power singing with back-up vocals from the one-man keyboard band next to her. I am seated at a table wedged between the main hallway and the kitchen door—not the most desirable spot for privacy but one that offers great sightlines of the rest of the dining room and the dance floor/stage area. My dinner guest, a woman in her late forties, is my mother's friend who has agreed to dine with me this evening and provide a cover for my research at *Baku*. We are seated at one of only two four-person tables in the restaurant. The rest of the dining room is lined with three long rectangular tables covered with white tablecloths and bottles of liquor and wine spread evenly across their length.

The sight of the adorned tables conjures up memories of "banqueting" at similar places like *Baku*. My family had immigrated to the US in the late 1980's from the former Soviet republic of Belarus and an immigrant from Azerbaijan also owned a banquet restaurant in the town where I grew up. In relocation to the United States, the distance between Baku and Minsk does not seem so far for ex-Soviet immigrants. This remapping of places is part of the work conducted at *Baku* to facilitate the creation of an imaginary city within the actual city of Minneapolis—an ex-Soviet immigrant paradise in the US.

Looking around carefully, I realize that the vaguely Caucasian décor at *Baku*—with its arched doorways and reddish-brown wallpaper that resembles tapestries—comes off as more of a cosmetic touch rather than the desire to reproduce a far away city. *Baku* does not sustain itself either economically or culturally through an "authentic" connection to the real Baku. Russian, not Azerbaijani or English, is the dominant language spoken in the restaurant between guests and wait staff. The cover of the dinner menu features a photo of an old landmark in Baku, pre-Soviet days, but the dishes offered on the inside loosely outline the contours of the former USSR, with delicacies that stretch from Siberia to the Ukraine. The slippages in the menu is more evidence of the way that place is remapped in order to create the fictional cityspace of *Baku* in the Twin Cities, a city whose demographic breakdown of ex-Soviet immigrants heavily slants toward those from the loosely "European" republics.

I find Italio Calvino's book *Invisible Cities* a helpful departure for my analysis of the fictional city space created at *Baku*. Calvino writes that a city exists in the "relationships between the measurements of its space and the events of its past" (Calvino 1974: 10). For Calvino, the city is a dynamic relationship between the visible measurements of its material spaces and the invisible dimensions of history and memory that circulate within these spaces. I attempt to understand the relationship between the physical space of *Baku* and the experience of relocation for the ex-Soviet immigrant within the Twin Cities. This relationship speaks to the way that ex-Soviet immigrants, coming out of a particular social and political history, attempt to perform an invisible cultural community while negotiating a US system of identification.

Performance scholar May Joseph, in *Nomadic Identities*, writes that "publically proclaiming one's identity is a distinctly U.S. expression of democratic political performance" (Joseph 2000: 11). This notion of participatory democracy in the US context links the power of visibility with the ability to perform identity in the public sphere. The equation of power with proclaiming public identity is the basis for the policy of multiculturalism in the US, whereby citizenship is peppered with the idea of multiple communities and identities.

In the case of ex-Soviet immigrants, identity in the public sphere is a fragile notion conditioned by a history of power relations in the Soviet Union. Proclaiming an identity in public increased visibility to the state and made one more vulnerable to its apparatus. The safest resistance to these power relations was to remain incognito in the public sphere. Although people in the USSR participated in a vast number of cultural practices that reflected a diverse territory, markers of difference were best relegated to the private sphere and performed invisibly in relationship to civic space. As such, ex-Soviet immigrants negotiate a historically informed skepticism toward a principle component of US public life—the public performance of identity.

*Baku*'s low-contrast sign and heavy drapes demonstrate this skepticism. The restaurant (and the community it attracts) resists public representation of itself as an identifiable Other in Minneapolis. Instead, it prefers to remain a dis-identifiable "city" in the sense that it does not choose to make itself visible in the public sphere. To dis-identify is not a tactic of invisibility whereby *Baku* is trying to hide its location in someway—to resist a negative identification—as might be the case with illegal immigrants who deal most pressingly with the issue of visible identity in its less empowering sense. Such a tactic pre-supposes a stable notion of identity that can be, or has been, marked and has needed to go underground to avoid representation. Instead, *Baku's* mode of operation intervenes in the political use of identity that divides culture into mainstream or marginal, resistive or collaborative, varieties. It attempts to practice culture by process of dis-identification in the following way:

It functions as a surrogate for the private home space in which a communal, familial experience is the aim rather than asserting an identity. *Baku* as a home space is about the experiential register of performance without the intent of representation. It dis-identifies from the end of public identity performance to the outside, the civic sphere. But this ideal space of performance as experience and pure means is complicated by the fact that *Baku* is not a home space, but exists in a public strip mall, and that the people sharing the dance floor from various regions of the former Soviet Union are *not* necessarily those that would gather at your home otherwise. To sustain its position as a surrogate for the home space, *Baku* manages the relationship between the public and the private spheres so as to provide the experience of the private and build the illusion of the familial sphere between multiple parties of people.

## Bright Moves That Make a Difference
## On The Dance Floor

A small mass of bodies is lightly bouncing on the small parquet dance floor. I look across the dining room and notice empty chairs at one of the long tables and make the association that this must be a family group on the dance floor. Later I would find out that the table is celebrating Polina's birthday. Polina is seated at the head of the table and participating in a casual toast with one of the men. She is the matron of the group with no male counterpart next to her. To her side is an empty seat occupied by one of her grandchildren, a young man with a rosy face and a shadow of a mustache. He is on the dance floor with another of Polina's grandchildren, a younger sister or cousin, perhaps about ten years old and wearing a sparkly neon-green blouse and short ruffled skirt.

A man in a trendy decorated jeans and a muscle T-shirt joins the two grandchildren on the dance floor and begins to dance with the girl in the neon-green blouse. *Her father?*

Dancing is integral to the banqueting culture at *Baku*. Its most rudimentary function is to break-up the sedentary food and drink courses and get the body moving so as to both dance off the food and drink and stimulate it for more of the same. The core step on the dance floor is a basic two-step: For women, the quality of the two-step technique is light, flowing, and includes a sway of the hips, as where men typically bounce up and down with their knees to achieve a more virile and playful aesthetic.

The "father" of the neon-green blouse moves differently from what I am used to seeing among men on the dance floor. He moves his hips and pelvis. His arms are extended up and out to the sides in a motion that claims the space and demands attention. My dinner guest also notices the hip motion and I mention to her that I am not used to this much hip rotation from the male dancers from Minsk unless it is in jest. It looks vaguely "middle eastern" and I speculate that perhaps this family is from somewhere in the Caucus region.

This marker of difference intervenes in *Baku's* practice of dis-
identification by highlighting the way that dance moves in this space
register national, class and gender difference. The man from Polina's table
with the hip rotation does not perform the choreography I associate with
men from "northern" Soviet countries. His hips and widespread arms
articulate an "oriental" physicality that does not fit into the norm at *Baku*.
The males from the north perform a brand of masculinity that engages in
the athletic and joyful dimensions of dance and distances itself from the
feminine aspects of dancing. In contrast, the hip rotation and pelvic moves
feminize the dancing of men from the Caucus regions in *Baku* and the
moves serve to mark regional difference between the ex-Soviet men from
the "south" and their northern counterparts. These two notions of
masculinity can be further understood by referencing a conversation that I
had with a Belarusian man at *Baku* about the reasons why Georgian and
Azerbaijani men owned so many Russian restaurants in my hometown and
in the Twin Cities. He said that they are: *better in the kitchen. They know
how to do that. We are engineers and would be embarrassed to work like
that.*

The conversation with the man from Belarus outlines the loose
distinction of "south" and "north" when he refers to the "they" that are
better in the kitchen than "us." The dancing at *Baku* participates in the
circulation of regional difference within the ex-Soviet community and
serves to reinforce a power relationship between men who are considered
masculine and men who are considered feminine in this space. According
to the quote, northern men are associated with labor on and off the dance
floor that is deemed intelligent, technical and systematic—i.e., the
engineers—while their counterparts from the southern countries are
associated with work related to the feminine, intuitive, and
creative/entrepreneurial spheres of hospitality, i.e., work in the kitchen.
The ways that the male dance moves code regional difference risk being
translated into a class difference as well. They are bright moves that count
at *Baku*.

Next, the shadow-of-a-mustache lets go of the girl in the neon-green
blouse and she takes center stage. She begins to articulate her fingers in
sharp, pointed gestures that coincide with what looks like salsa footwork.
*She takes studio dance classes for sure*, I think. Her small, sexualized and
disciplined body looks poised in ways not mirrored in the bodies of the
older women who have formed a circle around her to cheer on her show.
At times the young girl is almost embarrassed by the attention she is
receiving and moves toward one of the women in the circle, undoubtedly

her mother, to receive some affirmation before she continues to work the floor.

For women in *Baku,* social dancing is mediated by age. The visibility of dance classes in the neon-green blouse's dancing, and the encouragement offered to her by the older women in her circle, speak to the way that choreography is a site for the transmission of lessons in womanhood from one generation to another. Younger girls are validated for dance moves that outside of *Baku,* in the Twin Cities, would probably be considered too adult or sexy for family celebrations. Gendered choreography is part of the cultural training where sexuality carries a double currency. On the one hand, sexuality is linked with training for the marriage market and the demand to look and act sexy in order to entice a member of the opposite sex. On the other hand, sexuality has nothing to do with sex per se but with technical prowess and skill as showcased by the technique of the young girl in the neon-green blouse. In this second valuation, sexuality is not simply a situation of being—a look or an essence—but a doing, a skill that develops over time and involves training. The dance technique transmits training in the culturally appropriate shapes and cadences of womanhood.

After Polina's table has their turn on the dance floor, the women from the long table near the draped windows enter onto the dance floor. Most of the women in the group have on some version of a pants suit or pencil skirt/blouse combo with high heels. One young woman enters the center circle formed by the women and as she dances her short black skirt rides up her legs. As this is happening, the women in the circle take turns running into the center and pulling it down for her. Everyone in the circle giggles at each pull even though the woman with the miniskirt looks mildly embarrassed.

The miniskirt choreography highlights how sexuality has its own system of evaluation and markers of success. Even though sexy dance moves are part of an important skill set in this space, there exist thresholds of appropriate/inappropriate dance moves and dance attire. The movement of the skirt riding up the leg and its subsequent policing points to the border of sexuality. The dance of the skirt length reveals the fragile border, of just a few inches, between a successful performance of female sexuality and its easy slippage into something negative—trashy, indecent, "you're trying too hard," etc.

## Dancing Pan-Soviet Alliance

By 10pm the dance floor includes dancers from all the tables in the dining room. The MC dims the dining room fluorescent lights and this further highlights the disco lights running across the bodies on the dance floor. The rules of voyeurism change with the moment of dimming. I turn around and see gazes focused toward the dance floor. Yes, it has becomes harder to see your food, but somehow much easier to look at the bodies in the space. An hour ago the dining room and dance floor was being marked out and negotiated by individual parties and stealing glances across these tables was a surreptitious act. No longer. Look on.

As the dancing continues so does the intermingling between the family tables. A woman in a grey pants suit from the same table as the miniskirt enters the dance floor and sets her sights on dancing with the neon-green blouse. The grey pants suit holds the neon-green blouse by her hands and they dance in a playful manner. Later the grey pants suit will daringly pull the shadow-of-a-moustache from his seat and begin to dance with him as well, although he will seem far less comfortable with this than his sister/cousin.

The dance floor is not only a space of family reunion, but also the stage for the performance of a pan-Soviet alliance in the Twin Cities. A typical Saturday night at *Baku* starts with a dance floor that is used privately as an extension of the familial table. As the evening progresses, the dance floor becomes the critical site that facilitates the encounter between the familial table and the other familial tables—the dancing of pan-Soviet community. The woman in the grey suit is an example of how difference is negotiated and bridged in the move from one familial table to another through dancing. The grey suit moves in step with a social choreography of accessing community: first she dances with the girl in the neon-green blouse, then uses this connection to secure an invitation to the young girl's table, and finally participates in a toast with the matron of the table, Polina.

In migration from the former Soviet Union to the United States, the cultural trajectories of immigrants at *Baku* diverged from their country of origin. The movement trajectory of the grey suit to Polina's table shows how ex-Soviets in the US might perform a pan-Soviet imaginary in a new location even while the former territories of the Soviet Union are busy carving out separate national notions of belonging. Alliances at *Baku* are in response to a different set of conditions in another country. The dance floor provides a space for the strategic construction of these alliances when it straddles public/private relationships to produce the imagined "home" community.

## Dancing Brighter Than White

Out of the corner of my eye, I take notice of a couple coming off the dance floor where a few others continue to dance. The female dance partner is wearing white sneakers, black leggings and a beige T-shirt that spells out something about "West Africa." Her male partner has a full head of white hair and is wearing jeans. They sit down at the other four-person table in the room. I know without a shadow of a doubt that this is not a "Russian" couple. Actually, this is *the* American couple stereotype of my "banqueting" memories. Not one that I actually ever *saw* on the dance floor, but the ghost my mother evoked to highlight our cultural distance and discipline me: *go put on some earrings and high heels. Why is it that you don't dress up? You look like a disheveled American.* There was an underlying horror amongst many ex-Soviet women that their daughters would turn into those white sneaker monstrosities. After a while of living in the United States, I remember that jeans started to infiltrate the émigré circles, mostly among young women or women wanting to look younger. Even then, your jeans needed to look "bright"—maybe with a rhinestone or two—and they sure as hell could not be worn with white sneakers.

Unfortunately white sneakers and her partner did not get the dress memo. If they had, they would have found out that there is no such thing as being overdressed for a "banqueting" event, but there is such a thing as looking too casual. A casual-ness associated with American-ness. This couple...they were *too* American.

Although the proclamation of public identity is parcel to the democratic process as highlighted by Joseph, the ability to access invisibility and an unmarked identity is a currency of power in the US context. Rick Knowles, in his book *Theater & Interculturalism*, notes how Whiteness Studies over the past twenty years has been tracing the extent to which "White" has become less of a distinct race than a universal gold standard for the human race. Invisibility takes on the meaning of the white dominant. White is "the strength to remain undistinguished—the struggle to be ordinary, to be as passive as omnipresent, to be an essential feature of everyday life and yet unaccountable" (Knowles 2010: 52). The invisible "White," is therefore power manifested in remaining unidentified within structures of power and to assume the position of power while remaining unaccountable within the structure.

The racial system of the United States affords a distinct privilege of invisibility to many ex-Soviet émigrés that might not be offered to other immigrant groups. The desire to dis-identify is complimented by the fact that this is a social possibility. But the process of migration has also created new categories of difference for ex-Soviet émigrés. In migration to the United States, the gold standard of White invisibility looks different. The cultural gap between the white sneakers on the dance floor and the high heels at the banquet tables highlights how ex-Soviet immigrants differ from the White (American) standard. In the Soviet context, the bright body had been the golden standard of beauty and therefore a neutral and invisible norm. But in the United States, the ex-Soviet woman appears to be too "bright"—inappropriately bright, either too young, like the dancing of the girl in the neon-green blouse, or too trashy, like the skirt sliding up the leg of the woman in the miniskirt. At *Baku,* a woman from Uzbekistan shared with me a story about her putting on her favorite pink lipstick and being stared at the whole time she rode the bus to work. *Why do American women always dress in muted colors? Black. Brown. We like to be bright,* she said.

In many ways the example of the white sneakers shows how identity does infiltrate *Baku's* inside and reflects the way this immigrant group experiences their relationship to the public sphere. Although the woman in the white sneakers is the obvious foreign body in this space, her presence jeopardizes the delicate process of dis-identification that works to sustain the loosely "Russian" community in this space. The outside has come inside and this encounter cuts into the circle dancing of community in a significant way: they experience the mainstream cultural standard of the "White" dancing body in relationship to their own, newly becoming visible, "brighter" one. The dancing circle reveals itself as the illusion it has been all along.

Leaving, my dinner guest and I stall on the paved sidewalk area directly in front of the restaurant. We are about to say goodbye to one another. Next to us a handful of Baku-dians have come out to smoke.

*So what are you writing about for school at the moment,* she asks. I think of how to answer this question. Do I tell her the "secret" reason for our trip to *Baku?*

*Well I have been studying the Russian avant-garde of the 20's and have recently been interested in contemporary political theater in Belarus, but actually, what I am writing about now—is you.* I pause for a moment to determine if I should keep going. She looks confused.

I continue: *Ok, well of course not you as an individual. I am writing about immigrants from the former Soviet Union and how performance practices intervene in issues of cultural belonging or un-belonging.*
Silence.
She responds: *Aha. I think I understand. And I think you should stick with the other projects. There is nothing interesting about me or us, Rita.*
*Why?* I ask.
*Trust me. Don't embarrass yourself or us. Write about something else. I have a book about the Russian Futurists and Constructivists for you to borrow,* she says.

On the bus back I am stuck with the problem of representing *Baku* in a written publication when the people in this space desire dis-identification. To not "embarrass yourself or us" is code language to warn me that official culture is something that happens somewhere out there, way beyond the personal sphere (and best in the past). I have heard this before. Similar to the young woman in the miniskirt, I am being trained in a culturally specific navigation of issues of public disclosure. Writing culture, like dancing, is also about watching out that your skirt does not ride up too high.

## Bibliography

Calvino, I. (1974). *Invisible Cities*. Orlando: Harcourt, Inc.
Joseph, M. (2000). "Nomadic Identities" in *Performance of Citizenship*. Minneapolis: University of Minnesota Press.
Knowles, R. (2010). *Theater & Interculturalism*. London, New York: Palgrave McMillan.

# CHAPTER EIGHT

## OCCUPATION OF THE CROSSROADS: NEGOTIATION OF IDENTITY IN CONTESTED SPACES OF URBAN DEVELOPMENT

## TOLONDA M. TOLBERT

Employing the interdisciplinary fields of Comparative Literature, Performance Studies, and Anthropology, this study engages urban public sites of cross-cultural contact as text. Through *reading* the performance of cultural engagement, one gains insight to what is at stake in the close-to-the-bone urban co-occupation of areas in contestation; revealing losses and gains engendered at the crossroads of urban development. As an ethnographic study, this project documents a population in the moment of destabilization, looking at the relationships amongst community members through the lens of black vernacular expressions, and interrogating the rituals of communal identity construction in an urban environment.

This essay grew out of research and experiences coordinating a community documentary, capturing the history and change in an urban neighborhood through the eyes of youth and elders. Written from the unique perspective of a researcher, resident and community leader, this small-plot ethnography utilizes participant observation to capture the intimacy surrounding the rough edges of a community in flux—an ongoing gentrification narrative in urban locales. As a point of departure, this project spotlights the contested urban space of the public sidewalk, as the stage of cultural negotiations for a community in transition, revealing the "tipping point" of change and thereby exposing both emergent identities and tensions between competing cultures and claims of belonging in urban contexts.

This interpretive ethnography examines a historic brownstone neighborhood in Brooklyn, New York—Prospect Lefferts Gardens (hereafter PLG)—currently experiencing the shifting demographics of economic development. Using small-plot ethnography, I focus on a single block, which both marks the frontier of social change and is the literal border of the historical neighborhood.

*Occupation of the Crossroads* focuses on how a group of men in this community, threatened with impending displacement, assert themselves within a shifting value system. What coping mechanisms do they use to navigate social change? How do they claim ownership of space? Through the lens of their social construction of *home,* I examine their public encounters as defining moments of exchange and change across lines of race/ethnicity and gender. I interrogate how this male community of African descendants uses black vernacular oral traditions to both strategically define self-value and to negotiate intersecting experiences of oppression. The oral traditions are employed as the theoretical tools to *read* social encounters; mapping the exchange of kinship bonds, the assertion of gender roles and demarcating territory. My focus on the oral tradition is limited to storytelling and nation language—the preferred public modes of cultural engagement.

The stage for these observations is the contested urban space of the public sidewalk. For these men, the sidewalk functions as a literal *rite of passage*—a transitory space to make and remake identity. I view these sites of public co-occupation, detailing the performativity and rituals of face-to-face cultural contact. These encounters act as threshold moments that map dynamic power struggles over values and space in the city.[1]

# Inception: Feeling the Heat or Seeing the Light

In the fall of 2008, as the last throws of the summer heat radiated through the concrete, I emerged from the subway. Plumes of black smoke poured out of an apartment building on my street. The lights and sirens of fire trucks abruptly assaulted me. Ambulances hovered near the entrance of the apartment, catching the new refugees, escaping near doom.

Mesmerized by the awesomeness of the fire, I stood in communion with neighbors, contemplating the inception of such a blaze. Observers began the narrative of the how and the why of the inferno. Some found

---

[1] All assertions and interpretations are preliminary observations based on semi-structured interviews and participant observation with the community in flux, between 2008-2012.

comfort in the deep groves of bias, blaming *Jewish lightning*, claiming that landlords set the fire to collect the insurance. Others blamed homegrown crack-heads who accessed the building's corridors to self-medicate; still others saw disrepair as the culprit. Huddled together we found comfort in each other's company as we watched the drama.

The majority of the on-lookers were members of the African Diaspora, a potent mix of Afro-Caribbean, African American, and a few Continental Africans. Others congregated around the borders of the blaze—new migrants into this neighborhood—White youth. Trailblazers exploring new frontiers, "discovering" this neighborhood they could afford on their own. They were gentrification casualties, who left formerly affordable areas of Manhattan and Williamsburg, Brooklyn, seeking more affordable housing. Although I share the same story of migration, from the East Village to Brooklyn, what drew my eye to them was not this shared history of dislocation, nor was it the starkness of white skin against black smoke and Black people, but rather, their sheer emotional response to the fire. Before I ever saw them, I heard them—wailing. They were on their knees in the street staring at the burning building, and weeping. This real-life drama unfolding, their primordial pain struck me, and I wept for them inside. All attention went from the destruction of the building to these living, breathing embodiments of loss.

When I could no longer bear witness to their pain, I sought relief in conversation with a young mother I recognized from the playground. I quickly discovered that she too lived in the building, as did several others around me. I shared my sympathies with those now watching their lives being dismantled. My interactions with the Black residents were notable because they weren't distinguished from conversations I had with other onlookers. Each Black resident had certain calmness and distance: "All be God Damn!" and "Lord have mercy!" were their most dramatic responses. The juxtaposing of this scene was uncanny—White residents on their knees wailing and Black residents just shaking their heads. Then I realized that these two groups, who shared spaces but not history, were undergoing two completely different experiences of loss: one so adjusted to loss/tragedy, responded with muted emotion, the other so new to loss/tragedy was transformed. That night, the six-alarm fire injured seventeen firefighters and two civilians, displacing more than forty families. And I realized that I was living at a crossroads—a transitional space between transitioning peoples, and through the flames I began to see the light.

# PLG Then

PLG was originally the property of John Lefferts, a Dutch farmer during the turn of the nineteenth century. This time marked a turning point in Brooklyn land-use. Developers turned farmlands into suburban residences and Lefferts followed suit, carving his land into 516 lots for sale (Brooklyn Historical Society 2011).[2] To ensure a strictly middle class development, his son James attached a restrictive covenant to each deed, restricting development, in perpetuity, to single-family residences—no commercial use, no rooming houses or multiple family dwellings. Under this covenant, the new middle class could feel relatively secure knowing that what they viewed as disruptive effects of tenements and boarding houses would be kept at bay (Lefferts Manor Association 2010).

Lincoln Road is also where two ideas of urban development collide: majestic Victorians[3] on one side of the street, on the other—tenement buildings. Erected between 1925 and 1938, the apartments are the neighborhood anomaly, originally attracting white-collar professionals of Dutch, Irish and Italian roots. As the buildings fell into disrepair, tenancy became more working class (Krase 1982: 54).

The late sixties saw Black population growth. Local urban mythology recounts their introduction into the neighborhood. A dispute amongst neighbors resulted in one neighbor moving and selling to an Afro-Caribbean family to spite the (White) neighbor who stayed on. There are many stories of difficulties for those first Black *pioneers* in the area, including people building backyard "hate fences" (Hevesi 1993) to shield them from sharing social space with the new neighbors of color.[4] The onset of Black settlement in the area began a slow trickle of white flight, opening more opportunities for upper middle to working-class Blacks.

The Caribbean influence on this area substantially altered the definition of a single-family home. The cultural assumption behind the single-family covenant was the normative idea of the nuclear household, in which individuality and independence from both your immediate and

---

[2] In the end the heirs to the Lefferts estate had sold 600 lots, for private single-family home development (Lefferts Manor Association 2010).
[3] Victorian houses that are part of the national registry of historic buildings. All of the private homes were built between 1896-1935. (Ibid.)
[4] This is an interesting point in the social history of the community because neighbors talking over back-fences is a reoccurring trope within current real estate advertising. Moreover, several neighbors on my block even removed their backyard fences as a symbolic commitment to community, allowing the children a bigger shared play space.

extended family were privileged values. North-American cultural norms were in direct conflict with Caribbean familial norms. As multigenerational families moved in, Caribbean definitions of *family* expanded the notion of the single-family covenant. As the American adolescents of the neighborhood were socialized to move away from home, Caribbean youth were encouraged to stay closer to home, often having an active role in the care of children or family elders. This new definition of family continued to stretch when Caribbean immigrants would often take in children of friends from their native countries. The title *Auntie* or *Uncle* has a nuanced meaning of *like* family on the Caribbean tongue,[5] while maintaining its blood relation meaning in the States. These different cultural framings of family were unspoken amongst neighbors in PLG, but the lack of articulation did not mean the diminishment of the cultural influence.

## PLG Now

Currently, people of African descent populate seventy-eight percent of PLG.[6] To date, the area maintains a Caribbean flavor, with grocery stores, retailers and restaurants catering to this population. The Caribbean distinction is dramatized in public spaces through the enactment of nationalism: it is normative to have a national flag on clothing, cars, or on homes. Where African-Americans often identify racially in public, for those with Caribbean roots national identification holds more currency. The Black/White dichotomy of the States lacks the space for intra-racial diversity. The Caribbean experience of a more nuanced racial identification, manifests in a national marker of difference amongst Caribbean communities of Brooklyn, and more prominently, from African-Americans.

In the last ten years this area has become hyper-visible to upper-middle class Black professionals, seeking an affordable area to raise a family. There is also a significant enclave of multiracial families in the neighborhood, both LGBT and heterosexual. Most of those families are some variation of Black joined with other races. The social distance of the past has transformed itself in the twenty-first century, manifesting in multiracial families of all hues and structures.

In the last five years there has been a significant urban buzz around the neighborhood. *Time Out New York* (2008) named PLG as one of the "up-and-coming neighborhoods," and their bottom line in the article was "A

---

[5] Martin P. Felix, Creole translator and cultural resource on Lesser Antilles cultural practices. Personal communication, June 23, 2012.
[6] Prewitt, May 2011.

neighborhood in transition." *In transition* has become the real estate code word for a community shifting its racial composition. The pendulum is swinging back as young White families (re-)discover the affordability and amenities of this formerly devalued historic brownstone area. The 2010 Census of PLG attest to that re-discovery with a 127% increase in its White population.[7] New York city's (in)famous ability to recycle neighborhoods, puts PLG next in line to be repackaged for a different population.

## Case Study: The Gatekeepers

Entering this block that embodies the crossroads, one immediately encounters a group of Black males standing in front of apartment buildings. The subway spills out onto this street, a gateway into the neighborhood. The gentlemen flank the sidewalk creating a corridor of humanity, through which one must pass to get home. Some people avoid the corridor altogether and cross to the other side of the street, to join the Victorian homes looking on from a distance. Others brave the gauntlet, encountering, engaging and enmeshing themselves amongst these Gatekeepers.[8] This group of males is a consistent presence on the street, viewing themselves as guardians of the community, self-empowered to monitor those who enter the neighborhood. Most of these men have grown up in the neighborhood. The reasons for their omnipresence are varied: some are retired, others are under-employed, and several are long-term unemployed. Most of them live in the apartments, and others live in houses around the community with their extended families.

The Gatekeepers' definition of home is connected to occupying the land. Many have deep roots in the neighborhood having gone from playing on these sidewalks as children to standing watch over them as adults. Others have lived all over Brooklyn and consider the whole borough their home territory. Those, whose families achieved the American Dream of home ownership, maintain a sense of entitlement about their home space that extends to the public space of the sidewalk.

The Gatekeepers' intimate ties to the street and street culture keep them in the know about happenings in and around the community. Recent neighborhood gossip, incidents involving police, happenings with local businesses and trade/barter networks are all fodder for their oral forums.

---

[7] The 2010 Census of PLG also revealed a 17% loss in its Black population, 28% loss in its Asian population, 10% loss in its Latino population. (Prewitt 2012, Spring).
[8] I will be identifying this group as the Gatekeepers throughout this essay because this group of males identify themselves as the guardians of the neighborhood.

They function as urban griots sharing the inside track on communal information—one of the valued commodities that they traffic in trade (Williams 2009: 257).[9] These practices exist on the sidewalk where orality imbibes their stories with transformative qualities. Each gentleman infuses his own ethnicity, ego, bias, priorities and values in how those stories are told and re-told. These oral practices are dependent on face-to-face interaction, each responding to his audience. For instance, in the aftermath of the fire, the various stories of its inception lingered on their tongues for months, as did the information of where displaced residents went and whether they would return. In this sidewalk realm, those with the greatest story-telling skill have the highest social collateral and are seen as authority figures. The internal peer validation and lack of traditional employment reinforces their commitment and pride to these communal roles and services they provide.

## The Specter of Displacement

The sidewalk is a privileged vantage point for witnessing the current community transformation and the Gatekeepers have a particular sensitivity to those tectonic shifts. In the morning a few of them gather as the hustle to work begins. The retired men are on morning duty, forced by former work habit to rise and start the day. The men discuss having once known the majority of the residents that came through this corridor (#101, personal communication, March 21, 2009). Morning small talk in Creole[10] with those not in a rush is part of their daily routine. The weather, reports about the prior evening's goings on, compliments towards the women dressed for success—all these are the fodder of morning conversation and engagement. As the community grows to include more Caucasians, the portion of those that they know dwindles, and the visual cues of a changing community are unambiguous.

This shift was accompanied by the fall of middle class Black families, unevenly impacted by the 2006 economic downturn. The 2010 PLG Census demonstrated a pronounced income gap.[11] The economic crisis

---

[9] In his article, Williams goes into great detail of how men negotiate the street as part of family and communal economies, the exchange of information being a large part of those economies.

[10] Throughout this essay I use the term "nation language" and "Creole" interchangeably.

[11] Out of 2566 PLG households, there were 159 households making over $200,000; almost 1,541 households making below $50,000; and 864 households making below $25,000. (Prewitt 2012)

disproportionately affected minorities; the Pew Research Center found that:

> [T]he bursting of the housing market bubble in 2006 and the recession that followed from late 2007 to mid-2009 took a far greater toll on the wealth of minorities than whites. From 2005 to 2009, inflation-adjusted median wealth fell by 66% among Hispanic households and 53% among black households, compared with just 16% among white households. (Kochhar, Fry & Taylor 2011)

This resulted in a significant portion of Blacks from this area, returning to the Caribbean on early retirement deals, or for a younger population, *reverse* migration[12] (Coates 2011) to southern states. Those families lacking mobility options are threatened with potential home loss by default mortgages or overdue taxes.

The specter of potential displacement amplified the need to mark one's territory into a performance of ownership. Feelings of a home space under siege permeated my conversations with the Gatekeepers (#102, personal communication, May 8, 2010). Some have palpable hostility toward any changes in the community, because they signify a threat to their residential status and therefore the elements that define the core of their identity. The necessity to assert one's *belonging* empowers those who reside at the crossroads. The performance of ownership begins with a physical presence at the entrance to the residential area, at times blocking entrance. Residents must either walk in the street or engage with them to gain passage. When passage is blocked, newer residents, often read it as a transgressive activity—contesting the city's norms of mobility. In the context of New York—a place identified by the daily movement of millions of people, all with someplace to go—the Gatekeepers' lack of an alternative destination and omnipresence on the sidewalk, places them in a transitional space. The sidewalk is often understood as a means to an end, not an end in and of itself.

The sidewalk also serves as a *safe space* for several Gatekeepers, who often discussed the pressure they felt from their landlords to leave. Most of the Gatekeepers have been long-term renters with rents much lower than the current market value. Anxious landlords threaten eviction if rent is late, some even offering buyouts. There is a general feeling that the formal

---

[12] Coates elaborates on the current migration movement of Blacks nationally, a reverse trend from the Great migration of Blacks which took them from the south to the cities up North to find working opportunity after slavery had ended. Currently more Blacks are migrating back down south with Atlanta as one of the more popular locations to move to because of economic opportunities.

authorities of the community are becoming hostile toward the Gatekeepers' presence.

The evidence of this hostility takes place at community meetings focusing on crime. The conversation starts by discussing burglaries and muggings, and then turns to quality of life crimes like dumping, graffiti, and loitering. Any time the latter is discussed the issue of the Gatekeepers' omnipresence surfaces. Interestingly, many new neighbors don't know that these men are residents. It is often assumed that they are drug dealers since several smoke marijuana on the sidewalk. I have had several conversations with new neighbors concerned about men loitering both at the apartments and around particular stoops. Many times it isn't men at all but rather local teenagers being read as adults. Often, the young men keeping vigil on the stoops have conservative families prohibiting them from leaving the block. This new heterogeneity of the community becomes more challenged with misunderstandings, mis-readings, and miscues.

Change in PLG begins to reveal conflicting realities. Newer residents offer a different understanding of the use of public space. Community building is still the goal, but a community that is generated in public yet nurtured in private spaces. The increased heterogeneity of the residents is mirrored in the local businesses, as new start-ups seek to meet the changing needs of a community. For example, when a new wine store opened, both the types and prices of wine had to speak to the broad economic spectrum. The challenge of the crossroads is that one must straddle both worlds appealing to multiple audiences to succeed. A difficult balance to negotiate, as grocers add organic produce to their inventory, it often goes bad because the demand is present but limited; and therefore, a new transient quality emerges in some business sites.[13]

## Nation Language

Most of the communication amongst the Gatekeepers is done via nation language. In the Caribbean, the discourse on cultural identity has overwhelmingly focused on an authentic language of cultural self-expression (Wynter 1973; Glissant 1989). Kamau Brathwaite (1984) defines nation language as:

> [T]he language which is influenced very strongly by the African model, the African aspect of our New World/Caribbean heritage. English it may

---

[13] This was evidenced in multiple cafés and restaurants cropping up in the neighborhood (#103, personal communication, June 23, 2012) and shutting down within one to three years.

be in terms of some of its lexical features. But in its contours, its rhythm
and timber, its sound explosions, it is not English, even though the words,
as you hear them, might be English to a greater or lesser degree. (13)

Professor Sara Herbert (2004) expounds on this definition, stating that:

Ultimately, nation language is one method that people from the Caribbean
use to reclaim (or to form) their individual identity as a people. Their
identity has been influenced by colonial, European powers, by native
Amerindian culture, by the imported culture of the African slaves.
But their own culture and identity is separate from all of these influences;
it is something unique to the Caribbean.

Therefore, the use of nation language serves to both indicate kinship bonds
and to exclude, creating simultaneously an intimacy and a distance
depending on your level of cultural literacy.[14]

Within the African Diaspora, linguistic nodes of cultural affiliation
extend across national boundaries to reconnect the descendants of the
African slave trade. The Gatekeepers use nation language to distinguish
intra-racial kinship bonds. They employ nation language to both publically
identify themselves and to identify those sharing the same ethnic
background. The reciprocal nature of this kinship affiliation stresses a
performativity on both ends. The Gatekeepers extend an invitation out to
African descendants in the form of a greeting or comment in their nation
language: "Whey you dey? or "Whagoin on, boi?"[15] The recipient either
recognizes this node of affiliation, or not and decides weather to
acknowledge it or not, through whatever means is at his or her disposal.
Regardless of one's cultural background, the decision to respond or not
becomes an issue of the will to publically connect.

---

[14] I've adopted V. Clark's notion of "diaspora literacy." This aspect of the
Gatekeepers' oral tradition is most difficult to discuss because of my own
insider/outsider status as an African American with no Caribbean Roots. Initially,
this was a barrier to gaining access to the Gatekeepers for informal interviews:
they would immediately begin speaking to me in their nation language, assuming
my Caribbean background, and then code switch into Black English to discuss
these elements with me. Their immediate recognition of my outsider status
ethnically, put a certain distance between us, the impact of which I'll never know.
[15] "Where ya at?" (Black English)/"How are you?" (Standard English, a generic
greeting); and "How are you?" (Standard English; a male-to male greeting). All
nation language translations are by Martin P. Felix.

# Crossing the Invisible Line

For the most part, the moments of conflict that I witness are rare. A clear pattern takes shape for those moments when the Gatekeepers either lead with or respond with aggression to some residents. Regardless of the race or gender of the resident, the tipping point for the Gatekeepers seems to be the same in each situation—a general lack of acknowledgement. When any member of the community refuses to *see* the Gatekeepers, this challenges their very existence. A resident walking by without looking their way, or whose body language is in avoidance mode, immediately becomes a moving target. They read these non-engagement actions as blatant disrespect—in a society that often renders them invisible—they refuse to go unacknowledged.

In the context of a neighborhood in flux with many new residents, ignoring the Gatekeepers and what they deem as their intrinsic role in the community is understood as a direct challenge. When this occurs, it incites an in-your-face response that involves closing in on personal space, speaking in nation language, raising voices, and becoming a direct focus of the whole group. I have never witnessed this becoming a physical confrontation but the threat of physicality is present. Efforts to render them invisible result in them responding in hyper-visible ways.

# Gender Bender

The Gatekeepers' engagements with women[16] are dramatic performances, seemingly in efforts to solicit responses from women and their peers.[17] As women head to work, the assertion of black male heterosexuality is on display via compliments, invitations and expressions of potential sexual exploitations. One would assume that the specter of traditional gender roles looms heavily over these interactions. In this context, however, the commentary of the Gatekeepers is often outside traditional Western gender norms. Asking to be a woman's personal assistant, to wait at home for her or to take care of her children, is within the Gatekeeper's norm. So while exhibiting a certain element of bravado and competition, oral performances

---

[16] My observations of exchanges between women and the Gatekeepers varied depending on the race and age of the women, how many men were present, and if it was day or night.

[17] As a woman, I found their answers to my questions around their engagement with women to be burdened with bravado, as they also viewed me as a potential sexual encounter. But in my observations of the Gatekeepers, I noted that almost all women of child birthing age are actively spoken to.

also go beyond assertions of traditional gender roles, stretching the possibilities for Black male identities.

The women who appear harassed by the Gatekeepers are those attempting to avoid the Gatekeepers. Exchanges often begin with some compliment: "Hail up me Empress!" and "Whas up sugadumplin?"[18] If such comments do not elicit a smile or eye contact, the comments grow more vulgar. But those women who give direct eye contact with the Gatekeepers or greet them first, get minimal return comments, which are usually formal greetings rather than commentary or critique. This seems to be an obligatory *verbal dance* that males attempt to engage females in and that appears to be driven by sexual conquest. Yet this *exaggerated masculinity* (Harris 1995: 280)[19] has the underlying focus on peer approval.

## Dis is Where We Do Us!

These denizens of the sidewalk—the Gatekeepers—stand witness to the transitions of a community. But they are not bystanders; they are active players in the creation of this urban community, simultaneously representing both the center and the margin of this area in flux. They are self-empowered in their constructive role through the orality of the sidewalk culture. Within that culture, their creation of a literal *rite of passage* places them in position to grant admission into the community, functionally reversing the current power trends. Their employment of the co-occupied space of the sidewalk opens up opportunities to redefine *self* and *other*, outside the realm of the material. The oral traditions act as the vehicles, creating the occasion for change and exchange. For the Gatekeepers, these oral traditions play the same instructive role that they have for generations—identifying community and documenting the impact of the larger social structure.

The Gatekeepers organize their community around relationships on the sidewalks of Brooklyn. The oral nature of their relationships serves as the scaffolding from which they build the borders of their community. When asked why they choose to congregate on the sidewalk, the simple response was, "Dis is where *we do us!*" (#104, & #102, Personal communication, August 12, 2010). In this statement, the "we" implies kinship and community while the "do" has connotations of the performative aspect of

---

[18] "Hail to the Queen!" "What is happening, sugar dumpling?"
[19] This article discusses hyper-masculinity as a response to a culture that de-masculinizes black men.

creating community. There is also the implicit expectation that one must actively participate in the creation of the self within community. In the context of a changing neighborhood, with tensions between competing claims on space, the need to *do* one's identity and community in public space speaks to the threat of displacement.

The performance of community and the theme of kinship expands, not only to the Gatekeepers themselves, but also to those residents who engaged with them. Patterns of engagement take many forms, falling into three categories: critique, challenge, and affirmation. Regardless of the tactic of engagement, recognition is demanded in some way, shape or form. To be *seen* by those you consider your own and by those you consider "other," validates your lived experience.

The use of the oral traditions to critique social systems has a long history of both resistance and empowerment within Black communities (Christian 1980; Gates 1988). The signs, symbols and language of black vernacular traditions create a site where only those who have literacy within this cultural milieu are able to gain full access.[20] These street traditions serve as tools of social negotiation, often functioning to resist external authority and to redeem the social value of identity for the Gatekeepers. Their comments often signal their system of values as applied to those who pass through, and have a reciprocal relationship of validation to their peers. Their lived experience of invisibility and oppression creates a distrust of external institutions and people of authority, generating a climate where peer approval becomes the only authority that matters.

Resistance to external authority is best exhibited in their engagements with women. In the context of the "Pressures to meet European American standards of manhood as protector, disciplinarian, and provider" (Harris 1995: 279), the Gatekeepers negotiate these external expectations through their verbal dance with women. This dance simultaneously asserts Black male masculinity while also expanding notions of manhood outside of Western male patriarchy. This social response can be read as a conscious refusal to internalize these external standards within a system of inequities. The crossroads provides a site to question traditional assumptions and assert alternative versions of manhood.

The crossroads is often associated with angst—two options, going in different directions and a decision to make. Perhaps we view the

---

[20] Part of this essay uses my dissertation *To Walk or Fly?: The Folk Narration of Community and Identity in Twentieth Century Black Women's Literature of the Americas.* In that dissertation, I elaborate on the role of the black vernacular tradition in the various cultures of the African Diaspora.

crossroads through the wrong lens; perhaps it is a site of creation as much as a site of elimination. Perhaps it is the dynamic moment when a community is both and neither, margin and center—like the Gatekeepers themselves. The crossroads creates the potential for a third space to emerge, where both community and identity run fluid, just waiting to be *seen* and the story to be *told*.

As of fall 2012, much of the residential population of the apartments has transformed to young, White families with cherub babies flocking out onto the sidewalk, strollers occupying the public space where domino tables once stood. Seasonal landscaping has filled in a previously barren scene with a skeleton crew of the Gatekeepers remaining: more elders than youth, no longer omnipresent but rather a twilight presence, hanging in the shadows not center stage, diminished voices echoing the sounds of change.

# Bibliography

Brathwaite, E. K. (1984). *History of the Voice: The Development of Nation Language*. London, England: New Beacon Books.

Brooklyn Historical Society. *An American Family Grows in Brooklyn: The Lefferts Family Papers at Brooklyn Historical Society*. Retrieved from http://www.brooklynhistory.org/exhibitions/lefferts/

Christian, B. (1980). *Black Women Novelists*. Westport, Connecticut: Greenwood Press.

The City of New York Landmarks Preservation Commission. (1979, Oct. 9). *Prospect Lefferts Gardens Historic District Designation Report* (Landmarks Preservation Commission Report No. 128 LP-1024).

Clark, V. (1990)."Developing Diaspora Literacy" in *Out of the Kumbla: Caribbean Women and Literature*, ed. by C.B. Davies & E.S. Fido, Trenton, New Jersey: Africa World Press.

Coates, T. (2011). "The Reverse Migration, Cont" in *The Atlantic*, Mar. 5 http://www.theatlantic.com/national/archive/2011/03/the-reverse-migration-cont/73015/

Condè, M. (1995). *Pensar la Crèolitè*. Paris, France: Éditions Karthala.

Gates, H. L. Jr. (1993). *The Signifying Monkey: A Theory of African-American Literary Criticism*. New York, NY: Oxford University Press.

Glissant, È. (1989). *Caribbean Discourse*. Charlottesville, Virginia: University of Virginia Press.

Harris, S. (1995). "Psychosocial Development and Black Male Masculinity: Implications for Counseling Economically Disadvantaged

African American Male Adolescents" in *Journal of Counseling & Development,* 73(3), 279-287.

Herbert, S. (2004). *Caribbean Poetry: Barbados.* August 20. http://www.courses.vcu.edu/ENG-snh/Caribbean/Barbados/ Caribbean/lanuage.htm

Hevesi, D. (1993). "Enclave Outgrows its Racial Tensions" in *New York Times.* October 15.

Kochhar, R., Fry, R., & Taylor, P. (2011). "The Wealth Gaps Rise to Record Highs between Whites, Blacks, and Hispanics: 20 to 1" in *The Pew Research Center.* July 26. http://www.pewsocialtrends.org/011/07/26/wealth-gaps-rise-to-record-highs-between-whites-blacks-hispanics/

Krase, J. (1982). "Apartment Houses: The Big Change" in *Self and Community in the City.* Washington, DC: University Press of America.

Lefferts Manor Association. (2010, July 4). "The Changing Face of Lefferts Manor 1983-1993—Lefferts Farm Divided." July 4. http://www.leffertsmanor.org/changing-face-lefferts-manor-1983-1993-lefferts-farm-divided-lefferts-manor

Prewitt, M. (2011). "Latest Census finds PLG's Black Population Fell 25% in the Past 20 years" in *Lefferts Manor Echo.* May.

—. (2012). "With Rising Affluence and Retail Growth, Income Inequality Widens in PLG" in *Lefferts Manor Echo.* Spring.

*Time Out New York: Kids.* (2008). "Neighborhoods: Prospect Lefferts Gardens". April 15.

Tolbert, T. (2010). *To Walk or Fly?: The Folk Narration of Community and Identity in Twentieth Century Black Women's Literature of the Americas.* (Doctoral dissertation). ProQuest/UMI. (3397521).

Williams, B. (1985). "Owning Places and Buying Time: Class, Culture, and Stalled Gentrification" in *Journal of Contemporary Ethnography, 14,* 251-57.

Wynter, S. (1973). "Creole Criticism: A Critique" in *New World Quarterly, 5,* 12-36.

# Acknowledgements

I would like to thank my husband, Donald Jurkoic, for unceasingly supporting all of my intellectual endeavors with both words and actions.

# CHAPTER NINE

# RECOVERING THE BODY'S LIMIT:
## *SAN FRANCISCO* (1936),
## NEW ORLEANS (2011)

## J. EMMANUEL RAYMUNDO

Using different domestic and transnational scales, Postcolonial Studies, American Studies, and African American Studies grapple with iterations of identity and mobility in the wake of actual internecine conflicts and wars and corresponding theoretical debates about territory, peoplehood and nation. A tangible and digestible site through which these various academic disciplines intersect is the city, which I take as a prime site of difference and cohabitation. Even more specifically, each discipline is drawn together through the body—that simultaneously constant yet ever changing biological and social vessel of communication, experiences, and meanings—that is perched between the biological and social worlds.

Investigating the sensory dimensions of earthquakes, this essay traces the visual and sonic absence of Orientals in the movie *San Francisco* (1936) despite the documented historical fact of Asian immigration to California at the turn of the 20th century. Juxtaposing the performance of the iconic song "San Francisco" with the lesser known and barely audible song in the movie referred to as "The Philippine Dance," this text wonders about what these performances portend for the apocalypse they portray and its victims, especially its mute Orientals who are seen sporadically throughout the film. Here, we question the entangled cultural practices, institutional regimes, and environmental phenomena that reconfigure the body's limit and the body itself, which is simultaneously visible and concealed by the natural and social worlds, and a testament to the challenges posed by urban heterogeneity.

*San Francisco* (1936) provides a lens into the historical resonance of urban disasters on screen and in real life. This is especially the case when viewing the historic 1906 San Francisco earthquake depicted in the movie in New Orleans in 2011, while the city is rebuilding itself after its own disaster—Hurricane Katrina from 2005. The persistence of disaster and its bearing on contemporary life, which inspired the initial drafting of this essay, also haunted its revisions, as I left New Orleans for Philadelphia in the face of Hurricane Isaac, in August 2012. The juxtaposition of these cinematic and actual climatic events is neither meant to obfuscate nor obliterate their historic and circumstantial specificities. The 1906 earthquake came without warning; Katrina's impact was exacerbated by the failure of the levees and was a case of the natural laying bare the inadequacies of the infrastructural. As of this writing, Isaac's strength is constantly changing (from a Category 1 to a Category 2 Hurricane) and is shadowed by Katrina's specter especially since, coincidentally, Isaac is scheduled to make landfall seven years to the day Katrina hit the city. What is evident in each circumstance is the normality of environmental precariousness. As Brian Massumi has argued, such continuous environmental threats in the form of "disasters" become "indistinguishable from the general environment, now one with a restless climate of agitation" (Massumi 2011: 20). "Between irruptions," he claims, "the threat of a large scale disruption" transforms or "blends in with the chaotic background, subsiding into its pre-amplified incipience, already active, still imperceptible. The figure of the environment shifts: from the harmony of a natural balance to a churning seed-bed of crisis in the perpetual making" (Ibid.). Thus within the already volatile natural world lives the unstable urban world and all the means and measures to stabilize it, in order to preserve life itself.

I discovered *San Francisco* at the Prytania Theater, the only single-screen movie theater in Louisiana, in operation since 1915. On Wednesday afternoons (and Sunday mornings) the theater ran a series of "Classic Movies." Partaking in this long-running tradition seemed like one of the local habits I should try to acquire. In the Prytania's air-conditioned anonymity, I could silently commune with my neighbors over a movie depicting a natural disaster that had happened elsewhere, a century prior, thus joining the collective yet symbolic exorcism of the disaster that had befallen our city, for which some of us were present while others had only known second-hand. Watching the cinematic depiction of the disaster was like seeing the uncanny overlap of two New Orleans traditions—the celebratory "second line" (the revelers following the "main line" of the brass band parade) and the mournful "jazz funeral" (a funeral procession with music). Indeed, daily life in New Orleans since Katrina was simultaneously an attempt to mourn and transcend the disaster. In this city, celebration, routine, and mourning had fused together forming a particular kind of metaphoric "second line," described by writer Dan Baum as "a jazz funeral without a body" (2009: 120). In fact, the absence of bodies was quite real in the city: as of December 2005, when the city ran out of money and suspended its search, 1,400 bodies remained unaccounted for (Bowser 2006).

Among the missing bodies on screen in *San Francisco* is the body of the Oriental. The rarity of Orientals depicted on screen runs counter to the factual presence of peoples of Asian descent in California and San Francisco in particular during the period as seen on celluloid. In 1900,[1] San Francisco was the 9th largest city in the US with a population of 342,782[2] that accounted for nearly a quarter of California's total population of 1,485,053.[3] Of this total population, 55,724[4] were Chinese and Japanese, and what could otherwise be classified as "Orientals." In line with Edward Said's classic idea of Orientalism as a mode of mute and objectified representation, the Orientals in *San Francisco* remain rarely seen or persistently silent. Whereas traditional Orientalism was hidden, Rey Chow claims that contemporary Orientalism (especially in films) is graphic, even forcibly so, insofar as the viewer's gaze is exclusively locked on what is in the frame (2011: 559). Reiterating Martin Jay's warning that "Western culture has been thought to be highly ocular-centric" (Cheng 2011: 167), Anne Cheng argues that the issue at stake is the crisis of visuality rather than the allocation of visibility (Ibid.). The focus of my examination is the collusion between this invisibility and audibility of Orientals in disasters and through the movie *San Francisco*. Within the interwoven layers of the film—the environmental (the earthquake) and the performative (the musicality)—the body becomes the main register of natural phenomena and vehicle of artistic expression. To what degree is then the Oriental paradoxically both seen and heard?

---

[1] The U.S. census is decennial and is conducted at the start of the decade. Since the San Francisco earthquake depicted in the movie happened in 1906 and in between a census period, the figures used are for the last completed census in 1900.
[2] United States of America 2003: 13.
[3] United States of America 1902: xx.
[4] Ibid.

## *San Francisco* (1936)

*San Francisco*[5] opens on New Year's Eve 1905 and the city is awash in bacchanalian celebration to the cheers of "Happy New Year," renditions of "Auld Lang Syne," and "Hail, Hail, The Gang's All Here." The New Year's Eve celebration is interrupted by a fire truck's clanging of bells as it weaves its way through the choked city streets: a nearby apartment building is in flames. The intimate relationship between celebration and despair as essential to the life of this city is set up in the opening scenes of the movie. The juxtaposition of merry-making and distress, gaiety and gravity, is crucial as contradictions are brought into stark closeness, which will be mirrored by the characters themselves. The fire that has engulfed the apartment amidst the revelry has displaced the wide-eyed Mid-western transplant Mary Blake (Jeanette McDonald). Homeless and jobless, she lands at the Paradise Café, a nightclub owned by the Barbarry Coast's most popular and most notorious businessman and womanizer, Blackie Norton (Clark Gable).

*San Francisco* is as much a political as it is a romantic drama. The personal antagonism between the scrappy Blackie and the aristocratic Jack Burley for Mary's affection plays out against their professional rivalry. Blackie is conscripted by a group of Barbarry Coast businessmen into the race for the Board of Supervisors on a single-issue platform of strengthening the Coast's fire codes to prevent the eruption of fires like the one on New Year's Eve. Such regulations are against Burley's vision for the Coast as a "picturesque" section of the city that should not be further developed and levied with the resulting taxes. Natural erosion aside, which is not at all discussed in the movie, *San Francisco* is ultimately about the differing visions of the city as a permanent settlement and how to ensure its longevity: from implementing stricter fire codes to fostering relationships, both romantic and civic, amongst its inhabitants.

## The Limit

The concept of the limit in relation to the natural and political (or constructed) worlds is at play for both men. For Jack Burley, the Coast has

---

[5] Made by Metro Goldwyn Mayer, *San Francisco* was directed by Woody van Dyke and sound designed by Douglas Shearer. It featured Clark Gable, Jeanette McDonald, and Spencer Tracey, and garnered five Academy Award nominations including Best Picture. Made for about $1.3 million, the movie was a critical and commercial hit that grossed $5.3 million at the box office (Turk 1998: 184). The movie's title song has become equally well known.

reached its limit, its capacity for development and should return to its original, natural state as a promontory overlooking the ocean—a place for sightseeing and leisure. Furthermore, he has reached his fiscal limit of paying for costly upgrades and taxes on the property he owns. The businessmen drafting Blackie into the race, however, have yet to reach theirs and promise to support him "up to the limit." The limitless promises pledged to Blackie aren't just monetary. At a boisterous political rally for his candidacy, the "Ladies Blackie Norton Club" is extremely enthusiastic in their support: they endorse Blackie "right to the limit." The unbounded and unlimited political rhetoric accomplishes its goal of stirring the crowd. Determining the exact point of a limit, much like predicting the next earthquake, is not easy. While seismologists are able to identify faults and discontinuities of planar surfaces, it is harder to establish when these different geologic plates will shift and the intensity of the resulting earthquakes. While seismologists can identify a plate's shape, its start and its reach, they cannot as easily predict when it will break or the shape and extent of the break. Thus the limit—in terms of our knowledge of the quake and its strength, is unknown—as is what will happen from campaign to election day.

Be it financial or rhetorical, the types of limit evoked by Blackie's supporters underscore the natural limits of the city Blackie is campaigning to represent. With its cliffs cascading into the Pacific and the fog blanketing the city as if it were one with the clouds, San Francisco and the peninsula it is on occupy the terrestrial limit. In Blackie's case, the limit is tied intimately to the Barbarry Coast: this is where the Paradise Café is located and where Blackie has been conscripted to run in the political race because of his popularity and likelihood of victory. Blackie is so beloved and associated with the Barbarry Coast that the rally's Master of Ceremonies introduces him as "our candidate, born on the Coast, raised on the Coast, lives on the Coast, of, by and for the Coast." Hence, Blackie, the Barbarry Coast's central character, embodies, albeit in contradictory ways, the geographical periphery, edge, limit of the Coast. Collapsing identity into geography is an honorific that strategically serves Blackie's political goals but glosses over the changing nature of that very Coast. Along with propositions for stricter fire codes as part of larger, district rezoning plans, the Coast, bordering on the water, is susceptible to erosion, just like the whole city is, in the wake of an earthquake of unknown magnitude. If the Coast changes or disappears, what happens to its representative character and native son whose identity has become so entangled with it? Under what conditions, through what register, and in what form does the limit take shape and transform itself?

## Performing "San Francisco" at the Limit

As earthquakes dislodge tectonic plates and everything that rests on their surfaces, first seeing and then feeling the earthquake challenge each other, displacing traditional sensory hierarchies. Similarly, *San Francisco* practices the musical tradition of dislodging and displacing conventional modes of understanding, as synthesized in "San Francisco," the eponymously titled song. It is the key example of the limit pushed unto itself to the point of transformation, echoing how Paul Gilroy looks to music as a means of de-stabilizing the authority of texts as the "preeminent expressions of human consciousness" (1993: 74). "San Francisco" is first played in the opening credits and repeated in various iterations throughout the movie. The song undergoes various stylistic renderings depending on when and where it is performed. Mary first sings "San Francisco"—in an operatic pitch and in adagio, for Blackie when she is hired at the Paradise Café. Blackie interrupts her rendition, plays the piano in double and triple time, and instructs her to "heat it up!" "San Francisco" receives more uptempo renditions at Mary's first performance at the Paradise Café and then at Blackie's campaign rally.

However, it is at the Chicken's Ball, a variety competition amongst all the Coast's nightclubs, that the signature song is given its most eclectic and engaging rendition, bringing together the different styles of performances presented thus far. The Chicken's Ball has taken on an added importance for Blackie whose liquor license has been suddenly suspended resulting in the Paradise Café's closing. Blackie has also lost Mary who has returned to Jack, to sing opera at the Tivoli. With his performers in jail, Blackie is out of the running for the Ball's $10,000 prize that he hoped to win to use to buy back his liquor license and re-open the Paradise Café. Though no longer Blackie's performer, Mary, now Jack's fiancée, volunteers to sing on behalf of the shuttered club. "Play 'San Francisco,'" she directs the orchestra to the audience's approving roar.

The orchestra strikes up a quick note only to slow down as Mary heads from the front of the stage. Dramatically turning her back to the audience, Mary places her clinched right fist to her chest as if to summon courage before turning around and walking back to center stage, hand clasped and poised in front of her waist. After a deliberate start, the orchestra almost falls silent except for the strumming of the violins. Mary's hand unclasps and reaches out, as she sings:

My home upon the hill, I find I love you still …

She enacts the opening of a window through which she sees and grasps the city, or at least that "tiny corner of this great big world to make the place we love." The song takes on several interwoven meanings when Mary sings, especially since the preceding lyrics don't actually reveal her message right away but demand of San Francisco to "open" its "golden gate":

> I've been away but now I'm back to tell you ...

Mary has been itinerant, shuttling back and forth between the Paradise and the Tivoli, the saloon and the opera house, and the different worlds they represent. If she is singing that despite her absence "I love you still," to whom is she professing her love? We know that she loves the city of San Francisco--but as epitomized in the Barbarry Coast's nightlife? Or Nob Hill's Victorian domestic tranquility? Is it Blackie or Jack?

Mary reserves her answer and holds the audience in suspense through her stylistic delivery, drawing out the "San" in "San Francisco" into an elongated, multisyllabic pronunciation. She sings the city's name and the title in an undulating stretch, not exactly a melismatic flourish, which adds to the song's dramatic impact nonetheless. Inching from center stage to left then right, Mary literalizes the lyrics by knocking on an imaginary door as she sings and declares:

> You let no stranger wait outside your door ...
> I'll wander no more.

Pledging her declaration of loyalty to San Francisco, Mary returns to center stage to sing the song's closing lines about the paradoxical nature of travel. Clutching her chest, increasing the tempo of her delivery, she sings:

> Other places only make me love you best.

By the time she raises her sinewy arms in pugilistic triumph and in correspondence with her increasingly higher pitched voice about the city as the "heart of the golden west,"[6] she is no longer asking the crowd to "welcome" her "home again"; she is declaring:

---

[6] At the turn of the 20th century, San Francisco was the heart of the booming West where fortunes, financial and personal, could be made. Affluent American settlers along the California coast sent letters, which appeared in newspapers, and editors urged their "readers to 'go West.' The *New York Herald* cited the added attraction of California heiresses who were beautiful and virtuous." (Merck 1963: 48)

I'm coming home to go roaming no more.

Mary's improvisational, unplanned performance on behalf of the Paradise Café (and Blackie) illustrates her true allegiance.

Already on their feet, the crowd joins Mary in the encore, taking over most of the singing. The camera pans the audience to reveal dancing men and women, twirling arm-in-arm in celebration. Mary moves around the stage but her singing has now become an accompaniment, humming the tune in an operatic pitch. Through a declaration of love for the city sung in the standard fare familiar to the audience who are entranced in this Dionysian-like celebration, Mary reintroduces the operatic to the masses: she uses her voice as a high pitched instrument, as if she were one of the brass or woodwinds in the orchestra blaring the tune and providing the soundtrack to this scene of excessive joy. That the winner of the Ball will be judged on "artistic achievement" determined by the audience places the onus on Mary to fuse the artistic and the popular into her performance. She needs to meet a particular aesthetic criterion that is legible for a wide audience. The artistic must be the popular. Enacting a form of civic and "cabaret citizenship" (Vogel 2009), audience and performer are, in this hall, at this moment, engaged in an improvisational embodiment of their social contract as citizens—joined together by an event that will be matched in intimacy only by the earthquake that will soon strike the city and that will require these bonds of affection and conviviality displayed here, in order to overcome it. To no surprise, Mary wins the prize by a wide margin. She hands the prize to Blackie who throws it away. Dejected, Jack escorts the crestfallen Mary out of the Ball as the Great Earthquake of 1906 strikes.

## The Philippine Dance

Mary's rousing performance of "San Francisco" and the ensuing earthquake are two famous (and obvious) high points of the movie. But if we take a cue from Chow, Cheng, Gilroy and a host of African American diasporic theorists, who are asking us to pay attention to "what the music said" (Neal 1998) and look at the confrontation between in/visibility and in/audibility, then we should focus on what happened right after Mary's performance, or outside the conventional climax of the movie, or beyond the edges of the camera's frame. And so, following Mary's performance at the Chicken's Ball is a competing act named "The Golden Gate Trio," with "The Philippine Dance" song. As noted earlier, *San Francisco* is notable for the near absence of Asian Americans or "Orientals." In the "Philippine Dance" song, for instance, only the opening lines are audible:

There's a big sensation going around town called the Philippine Dance...
There's a big sensation going around town you oughta see it back in France...

"The Philippine Dance" contradictorily articulates the absence of Orientals in *San Francisco* through a partial visual and sonic acknowledgment of the Philippines and the United States' newest colonial territory at the turn of the 20th century. After the first two lines, the camera cuts to Blackie entering the bar and the lyrics about the apparent sensation that is "The Philippine Dance" recedes and fades into the background. We never find out what the sensation is all about. That the Oriental, through the Philippines, is an unknown sensation is in stark contrast to the sensation of the earthquake, which is central to the movie.

The collusion between invisibility and inaudibility of the Oriental body has its roots in the tandem of earthquake and fire that destroyed San Francisco. The city is heterogeneous, composed of different parts, and so too is the rumbling apocalypse that shattered it. An earthquake is composed of three different types of elastic waves. The least damaging kind is known as the "surface wave" and is near to the ground. The P or "primary wave," moves through rocks and liquids at the fastest speed. The S or "secondary wave," travels at a right angle and can only move through solids. While S waves are the most damaging to infrastructure because of their side-to-side and up-and-down motion, P waves are usually felt first; they are similar to sound waves (Milsom and Eriksen 2011; Prodehl and Mooney 2011). An earthquake, then, is heard before it is felt, and that is how the hierarchy of senses that the body registers gets shuffled.

But the body has not escaped the question of "What comes after?" In the discourse of the aftermath of regimes and ideologies ("post-colonial" (McClintock 1992), "post-socialist,"[7] or even "post-racial,"[8]) the "human" (Hayles 1999) has also come into scrutiny: registering sensory experiences and emotions outside the human body is no longer impossible, take the robot or cyborg (Haraway 1990), or the super-sensitive advanced technology for detecting and measuring natural environmental phenomena

---

[7] Political theorist Nancy Fraser (1996) frames the "post-socialist" condition as a conflict between the "politics of recognition" and the "politics of redistribution." Political struggles center around claims to recognition not material redistribution.

[8] Barack Obama's election to the presidency suggests a "post-racial" climate, as well as a genre, in the United States. On a recent Amazon search, nearly 700 books that included the term "post-racial" turned up. The race to use the term to sell the idea is perhaps more profound and telling than the concept itself.

(such as the seismograph, for earthquakes). Yet taking into account the role of P waves in the damage caused by earthquakes, we cannot wholly replace the human body as a sensory barometer; we can, in fact, place it along a scale or register as a truthful, necessary measure of how we sense and process natural phenomena, including earthquakes. If P waves are similar to sound waves that rattle windows, then the body is reacting just as much to the sound of glass shaking and tables rocking as it is to the accelerated and exaggerated motion that it senses. Especially in a modern city like San Francisco—with large and tall buildings such as the Lyric Hall where the Chicken's Ball was held—the body is reacting to both visual and sonic cues of natural phenomena that induce panic and terror. In an urban milieu, the body is joined with others and encased in constructed surroundings through which environmental events like earthquakes are filtered. The body's reactions are not spontaneously epiphenomic or biologically idiopathic but rather mediated—through the undoing of the surroundings.

The "Philippine Dance" is a sensation, for us at least, because of its imposed visuality coupled with its partial audibility, which produces fragmentary knowledge about the subject it introduces. Through the medium of film, our gaze follows the camera, as instructed by the director. We are squarely focused on "The Golden Gate Trio" as they are wheeled on stage and prepare for their performance. As Blackie enters the hall, the camera (and our visual attention) cuts to him but the trio's crooning of "The Philippine Dance" is still audible. Though it is trailing off, getting harder to decipher, bits about a "Sally Wong" and an "Eagle Rock" are still audible and serve as background to the news served to Blackie: that he could not bail out his performers or pawn his jewels to buy back the club's license. With the visual attention focused on one subject but the sonic interest dispersed to multiple possibilities, the viewer's gaze experiences a kind of "jouissance," as Rey Chow would say, a "sense of a violent prying open of the possibilities of visualization" (Chow 2011: 559). With the viewer's attention straining in opposite directions, towards the visual and the sonic, neither gets fully satisfied.

The Philippines in the trio's act is, as a place, at once present and hidden, audible and indecipherable, while the Filipino is, in Dylan Rodriguez's terms, "suspended." For Rodriguez, the term "suspended" is about the denial of Filipino agency in its initial encounter with and eventual engulfment by the United States' white supremacy (209: 160). This process of simultaneous denial and engulfment happens "out of direct view," "above and behind," but nevertheless "continually shadowing, and altering…" Filipino agency (209: 160-161), which ultimately results in, according to

Rodriguez, a "suspended apocalypse" (209: 160-161). The Filipino is, both cinematically and politically, "suspended" and "out of direct view": in/visible and in/audible but nonetheless altered.

Indeed, we are uncertain as to the exact *type* of Oriental that we encounter in the movie *San Francisco* since the possibilities are never exhausted and the limits never reached. On the one hand, there were real statistical limits and impositions barring Oriental immigration and settlement to the United States. Most prominently, the Chinese Exclusion Act of 1882 barred Chinese immigration to the U.S. for 10 years and outlawed Chinese from becoming naturalized American citizens. The Geary Act of 1892 extended the provisions of the Chinese Exclusion Act for another 10 years and required persons of Chinese descent to carry identification papers. In 1904, Congress extended the Chinese Exclusion Act indefinitely (Lee 2007 and Soennichsen 2011). Yet despite the legal barriers preventing Chinese immigration and intermittent raids, the Chinese lived in the United States. In 1880, just before the initial law, there were 103,465 Chinese.[9] In 1890, just before the Geary Act's extension, there were 94,987.[10] And in 1900, just before Congress' indefinite Chinese Exclusion Act of Chinese, there were 111,054.[11] Filipinos in particular occupied an ambiguous and otherwise suspended position within this schema. Manifest Destiny and American exceptionalism intersect through San Francisco. The "city upon a hill" is situated at the geographic limit of where a city could be built in the contiguous continental United States. And Filipinos stood on this intersection as an exception—they could travel across legal barriers and national boundaries as American nationals since the Philippines was an American territory.[12] But the "exceptionality" of Filipinos, when it came to their right of entry to the US (or their facility with the English language) was part of their colonial miseducation, political prototyping, and "little brown" brothering.[13]

---

[9] Statistics of the Population of the United States at the Tenth Census 3.

[10] Report on the Population of the United States at the Eleventh Census lxxv.

[11] Twelfth Census of the United States xxiv.

[12] Milestones: 1921-1936.

[13] Rodriguez traces the colonization and miseducation of Filipinos as simultaneously "exceptional" and in line with oppression of other subjugated peoples of the American empire, namely African Americans, through R. Constantino's reading of C. G. Woodson's *The Miseducation of the Negro* (164).

# Return

I returned to New Orleans in mid-August 2012. I left again a week and a half later as Hurricane Isaac headed for the city. As beer, daiquiris, and the infamous Hurricanes are poured into plastic and styrofoam to-go cups for consumption in the city streets, emergency protocols dictate evacuees to bring a "To-Go Bag" that includes "copies of all important documents, in waterproof, transportable containers."[14] As a foreigner, I automatically grabbed my passport and employment authorization papers. In an emergency like an approaching hurricane, the primary task is to preserve life as it is contained in the body. Once the body is out of harm's way, the body needs a signatory and epistolary witness to account for its existence, which is what a piece of paper can provide. To that end, I grabbed my *Penn Card*, which could open metal doors monitored by electronic eyes that would allow me, as contained in my body, to pass through a maze of buildings in West Philly and the campus of the University of Pennsylvania where I had spent the previous year and where I was now fleeing towards, for temporary shelter.

From Philadelphia, I watched the news like a pre-emptive wake. This would be no Katrina, the news assured; the levees would hold, the Corp declared. What remained to be seen was the storm surge and how much water Isaac would bring in terms of rainfall and flood, especially since it looked like a slow moving front that would squat and linger over the region. Water, along with fire, is the antithesis of paper, which, together with our very bodies, was the essential stuff to take out of the storm's path. At a faculty orientation when I first moved to New Orleans, a Tulane librarian lamented how Katrina flooded the library's basement (Corrigan 2012), ruined hundreds of thousands of holdings but also brought with it FEMA "Recovery Funds" to replace lost items and then some.[15] Katrina's

---

[14] A driver's license, Social Security Card, proof of residence (a deed or lease), birth certificate, insurance policies, stocks, bonds, wills, deeds, copies of recent tax returns. See: http://new.nola.gov/ready/gather-supplies.

[15] The Federal Emergency Management Agency (FEMA) and the Louisiana Recovery Authority (LRA) provided Tulane University with $16 mln to build two additional floors on its current library in place of the basement that was flooded during Katrina. http://www.mmrs.fema.gov/news/newsrelease.fema?id=49444. Tulane also processed insurance claims totaling $241 mln and received a FEMA supplement of $95 mln, http://mmrs.fema.gov/news/newsrelease.fema?id=49131. These funds allowed the university to replace lost items and purchase new ones. For example, before Katrina, the Tulane Library had less than 1,200 DVDs. As of September 2012, the library has 14,000.

floodwaters had ruined paper, such as books, yet had created new opportunities, like the fire from the 1906 earthquake in San Francisco did. With records, including birth certificates, destroyed by quake and flames, "paper sons" to would-be immigrants could claim to be sons of American-born Chinese whose birth certificates were lost in apocalypse (Kuhn 2008: 220). Disaster, from fire or flood, became an opportunity to lay claim to what paper constituted before—a citizenship status or library, respectively. Rodriguez' "suspended" apocalypse gives us a frame through which we can view *San Francisco* (1936) for the disaster it depicts just as rescue workers scour another disaster for survivors. In an environment that cannot distinguish among its own various states, as Massumi cautioned, rescue workers must be committed to expanding their field of vision and scope of hearing, in order to be able to identify the bodies amidst the rubble and the precarious, indistinguishable limit between these bodies and their own.

# Bibliography

Baum, D. (2009). Nine Lives: Death and Life in New Orleans. New York: Spiegel and Grau.

Bowser, B. A. (2006). Search Effort Continues for Katrina's Missing. PBS News Hour. Mar 21. Podcast. http://www.pbs.org/ newshour/bb/business/jan-june06/missing_3-21.html.

Cheng, A. (2011). Second Skin: Josephine Baker and the Modern Surface. New York: Oxford University Press.

Chow, R. (2002). "Framing the Original: Toward a New Visibility of the Oriental" in PMLA, 226.3, 555-563.

Corrigan, A. (n.d). "Tulane University- Howard-Tilton Memorial Library. Hurricane Katrina and the Library's Collections" http://library.tulane.edu/collections/katrina_recovery.

Emerson, J. & Hyman B.H., Van Dyke, W.S. (1936). San Francisco. USA. MGM.

Fraser, N. (1996). Justice Interruptus: Critical Reflections on the Postsocialist Conditions. New York: Routledge.

Gilroy, P. (1993). The Black Atlantic: Modernity and Double Consciousness. Cambridge: Harvard University Press.

Haraway, D. J. (1990). Simians, Cyborgs, and Women: The Reinvention of Nature. New York: Routledge.

Hayles, N. K. (1990). How We Became Posthuman: Virtual Bodies in Cybernetics, Literature, and Informatics. Chicago: University of Chicago Press.

Kuhn, P. A. (2008). Chinese Among Others: Emigration in Modern Times. Lanham: Rowman & Littlefield Publishers, Inc.

Lee, E. (2007). At America's Gates: Chinese Immigration during the Exclusion Era, 1882-1943. Chapel Hill: University of North Carolina Press.

McClintock, A. (1992). "The Angel of Progress: Pitfalls of the Term 'Post-Colonialism'" in Social Text, 31/32, 84-98.

Merck, F. (1963). Manifest Destiny and Mission in American History. Cambridge: Harvard University Press.

Massumi, B. (2011). "National Enterprise Emergency: Steps Towards an Ecology of Powers" in P. T. Clough and C. Willse (Eds.), Beyond Biopolitics: Essays on the Life of Governance and Death (19-45). Durham: Duke University Press.

Milsom, J. J., &, Eriksen, A. (Eds.). (2011). Field Geophysics. 4th ed. New York, NY: Wiley.

N.A. (2012). "Are you ready? Hurricane season is here. Gather supplies." 26 June. http://owl.english.purdue.edu/owl/resource/560/10/

—. (2009). "Tulane's Library to Benefit from Additional FEMA Funding," 2 September. http://www.mmrs.fema.gov/news/newsrelease.fema?id=49444

—. (2009). "FEMA Funds Help Tulane University Roll Again After Katrina." 21 July. http://mmrs.fema.gov/news/newsrelease.fema?id=49131.

Neal, M. A. (1998). What the Musica Said: Black Popular Music and Black Popular Culture. New York: Routledge, 1998.

Prodehl, C. & Mooney, W.D. (Eds.). (2011). Exploring the Earth's Crust: History and Result of Controlled-Source Seismology. Boulder: Geological Society of America.

Rodriguez, D. (2009). Suspended Apocalypse: White Supremacy, Genocide and the Filipino Condition. Minneapolis: University of Minnesota Press.

Soennichsen, J. (2011) The 1882 Chinese Exclusion Act. Boulder: Greenwood Press.

Turk, E. B. (1998). Hollywood Diva: A Biography of Jeanette McDonald. Berkeley: University of California Press, 1998.

United States of America. U.S. Census Bureau. (2003). No. HS-7. Population of the Largest 75 Cities: 1900 to 2000. Washington D.C.: U.S. Census Bureau.

—. (1902). Twelfth Census of the United States—1900 Census Reports Volume II—Population Part II . Washington D.C.: U.S. Census Bureau, xx.

United States of America. U.S. Geological Survey. (n.d.) The Great 1906 San Francisco Earthquake. Retrieved from http://earthquake. usgs.gov/regional/nca/1906/18april/index.php.

United States of America. (1900). Census Office. Twelfth Census of the United States. Washington D.C.: Government Printing Office.

—. (1897). Census Office. Report on Population of the United States at the Eleventh Census. Washington D.C.: Government Printing Office.

—. (1880). Census Office. Statistics of the Population of the United States at the Tenth Census. Washington D.C.: Government Printing Office.

United States of America. Office of the Historian. (n.d.) Milestones: 1921-1936. Immigration Act. http://history.state.gov/milestones/1921-1936/ImmigrationAct

Vogel, S. (2009). The Scene of Harlem Cabaret: Race, Sexuality, Performance. Chicago: University of Chicago Press.

## Acknowledgements

Thank you to Blagovesta Momchedjikova for her editorial guidance. I am grateful to Lisa K. Hooper, Music and Media Librarian at Tulane University, for talking to me about the FEMA "Recovery Fund." I would not have known about the "http://new.nola.gov/ready/gather-supplies" website without my friend Sara Hudson who was the visionary and the labouring force behind the new resource for the city. Margeurite Nguyen was essential for an initial discussion of the "second-line." This essay is dedicated to her and our time together in New Orleans.

# Chapter Ten

# Seed the Clouds: Lessons from Arabia

## Michelle Lee Dent

Informed by the practices associated with feminist ethnography, which seek imaginative and subtle ways to discuss gender politics, the intimacies of women's work, and women's subjectivity, this project centers around the journey of the participant observer, a pedagogue, in a foreign city. This more intimate methodology becomes a vehicle for exploring the uncomfortable fact of being so disconnected from life back home while living and working in a new environment. In this exotic landscape everybody—students, faculty, and staff—grapple with the learning that comes with culture shock and the productive misery associated with learning "to see" culture with the kind of second sight that often only comes when confronted by senses of displacement and estrangement.

This essay takes place from somewhere within the ethnographic present where I am in the midst of a year-long assignment that has me living and working in the Arabian Peninsula. I have been contracted as an Affiliated Faculty to help create a writing program during the launch of the new campus that my university is building in partnership with the Crown Prince of the United Arab Emirates. The globalization of higher education is indeed a noble enterprise, but not without risky challenges to academic freedom, and not independent of volatile financial markets, which will become more evident as the Arab Spring catches fire and the Occupy Wall Street movement smolders.

# In Flight

Etihad Airways flight 6005 will soon begin its descent into the Abu
Dhabi airport. We are nearing the end of the 14-hour journey from New
York's JFK airport; the cabin is hushed with the quiet of sleeping
passengers and the hum of the luxury aircraft and crew. A few of us are
still awake, the glow of our in-flight movies keeping us company. It's that
still point in the night, again—traveling with what amounts to a small
village and yet solitude blankets at least one person. Somewhere on the
ground it is still New Year's Day, at least I tell myself it is so, even though
it's clear that I am stretching the clock to suit my own purpose. Thanks to
the warp of time zones and circumnavigation, it is now nearly January
3$^{rd}$in the Gulf region.
     My thoughts drift. I dwell on the odd pleasure of having been almost-
stranded in Brooklyn during last week's blizzard, catching a subway just
before the whiteout, making my way home, marching backwards in a
strange dance up Ditmars Boulevard in Queens, attempting to gain footage
against the pounding force of wind and snow. A car skids along in slow
motion, and another is stuck spinning its wheels. I drift again imagining
that I am one of the women from early 1900s Alaska about whom I have
been writing. I begin to fancy that I am trekking through the Yukon and
Klondike, mushing behind a dogsled, wearing a long cumbersome black
wool dress, dreaming of a warm berth on a steamer that is bound for the
gold fields of the Far North.

     Down the rabbit hole I go.

     The snow storm lingers in my mind as I am jolted back to the luminous
details of the in-flight map in front of me: *Mosul, Kirkuk,* and *Tigris.*
*Mesopotamia.* Perhaps I am more disoriented than I thought–Mesopotamia?
Not only am I traveling across this great geographic expanse to the other
side of the world, this trip also involves strange temporal leaps as a page
from an ancient history lesson now flutters against my memory; the golden
city of *Ur,* the Code of Hammurabi intermingling with the clatter of high
school students grappling with blue books and thesis statements. None of
it ever made much sense to me as a bored sophomore struggling with AP
history. Mesopotamia is a distraction, of course. Luxury travel cannot
tolerate the harsh truths of war, and tyranny, and military intervention.
     Such foolishness, I have been living in the region since August, and on
clear mornings I wake to see the cobalt blue of the Persian Gulf outside
my high-rise window, so of course I am crystal clear about the geography,

but somehow returning now, after the winter holiday, I still am not prepared for the fact that we are currently flying over Syria and Iraq—ancient lands, which the airline industry most certainly prefers to highlight, but also ground zero to decades-long ideological battles, from the 1979 Islamic Revolution and Iran hostage crisis, to the 1990s and the "Desert Storm" war, and then, to the 9/11 attacks, Osama Bin Laden, George W's revenge in Afghanistan, the 2003 invasion of Iraq, and the tyranny of men like Saddam Hussein and Donald Rumsfeld and Dick Cheney.

There it all is, 30,000 feet below—Bagdad, Mosul, Kirkuk—making concrete that which often remains an abstraction; a sudden reminder of the ways in which expatriates, tourists, and sometimes even students and their teachers are tacitly given permission not to see, as the boundaries between tourism, education, and political allegiance blur. In this brave new world, there is the hypnotic effect of traveling within the kind of security zone that my students refer to as the NYU bubble—combined also with tunnel vision, blind ambition, and the distractions of consumer binging that come with living in an oil rich country, a desert landscape littered with deluxe mega-malls.

I scribble in the front pages of my tattered copy of *Pattern Recognition,* the William Gibson novel I was reading earlier, returning to the phenomenon he calls "soul delay," the process whereby trans-continental flights deliver the body ahead of the soul, which "can't travel more than 100 miles an hour" and therefore drifts in limbo before finally catching up—"reeled in on its silver thread" (Gibson interview). Perhaps this is the malady through which I find myself wondering about the details of no-fly zones and the Gulf Wars, sobering up to the proximity of mountainous Northern Iraq and the Kurdish territory directly below the aircraft. I shift my attention to the window. I am paying attention now, expecting Kuwait, and the primal fires of its oil fields, scattered like stars across the black void of night, all of which the map tells me, is coming up.

## Lone Wolves

When I teach first-year college students to become more sophisticated writers, there is always a short-lived honeymoon, that tiny window before they realize there is something about reading, thinking, and writing that not one single person, up to this point, has ever asked them to do. Ultimately students usually come to see this process as liberating. In the beginning, however, the set of cognitive shifts that must occur can, and should, fall upon students with a productively seismic effect. When this moment arrives, on cue, in my classes in Abu Dhabi, it hits with a gale force. A small mutiny begins to take shape. I hunker down, we keep working, I wade through a plagiarism outbreak; we practice peer review, critical reading, working with citations, and properly representing other writer's ideas whether you agree with them or not. When the right moment comes, I ask the students about their upset. *What's going on guys? Why are you running around like a bunch of angry bees and stressed out squirrels?* They identify with these images, and as they laugh at my characterizations and also at themselves, they unwind a few degrees, and they see they have the freedom to talk with me about their concern and stress, but that that doesn't mean they are free to not do the work. Our contract becomes clearer; they gain a little more focus, but they are still mired in their own tentativeness, and I see that I also have been tentative. We talk about risk, we look at it in other people's writing, I have them practice it in their own writing, but still they hold back.

And that is when, in the middle of a particular lackluster lesson, I begin teaching them to howl. I lead—*aoooo! aooo! aooooooo!*—and they stare at me with bafflement, and a certain embarrassment. I keep howling, and pausing, waiting for the antiphonal response until finally it comes and one by one they let go, nearly everyone taking a moment in the spotlight, each howl surprisingly unique. Afterward, there is a new energy in the class, and when I ask them to go "meta," and to consider *why* I just asked them to do this, they are surprised that there's more to it than a simple stress buster exercise. Slowly a couple of hands go up and they begin piecing together that to be a writer, there is a critical moment when you must step away from the beehive or the wolf pack, to make sense of your own mind's eye, rather than running around frantically looking for the right answer. Much later I realize that I've unwittingly adopted the language that the State Department uses to describe terrorists acting alone. Not exactly part of my plan, but good writing can, and should, expose, disrupt, that which is meant to linger beneath the surface. Writing is a critical act; a love letter pushing for more—we build new worlds, and subvert others.

## Dreaming Alaska

Nearly three months into the Abu Dhabi assignment, I wake one morning thinking about Alaska and the Chilkoot Trail, remembering the young hikers I met at a hostel in Skagway, Alaska the summer before shipping out to Abu Dhabi. I am more tender kneed now than even a year ago, but I want to hike the Chilkoot someday, the arduous 33-mile trail that stampeders took in the late 19<sup>th</sup> century, and from which many never returned on their way to the Yukon and Klondike Gold Rush. It was a trail of hope that more often than not ended in despair and disappointment. I am also thinking about Charlie Chaplin's film *The Gold Rush*, something to do with the tilted interior space of his little arctic cabin as it slides precariously to the edge of a snow packed mountain: disaster looms, but Chaplin's pratfalls make viewers giddy. *Man proposes, but nature disposes.* And then it happens again, I am dislocated, between worlds, Alaska rising like the tip of an iceberg into this desert landscape, showing up like an unexpected, but not unwelcome, weather front.

I am on my arid morning walk to work standing on the corner of Airport Road and Hamden Street—pondering the cosmic shift that has me suspended between New York, Alaska, and Arabia—waiting for the light to change as the tide of Indian and Pakistani workers washes by me: hungry men also on their way to work, on their way to climb a steep and unsafe scaffold and the next glittering skyscraper, a modern gold rush of need and desperation, a new stampede of laborers building a city of gold. It is November and the temperature still hovers around 100 degrees Fahrenheit. Indoors central air conditioning blasts against bodies wrapped in fleece, cashmere, and silk. We live in a strange vacuum of prosperity where in another month's time the Arab Spring will begin unfolding on the horizon; the Pyramids will be crossed off the list of expat tourist destinations; the awesome revolution in Tahrir Square will have begun. But now the traffic light changes, the stampeders pass me, the pungent smell of their sweat already strong at 8am in the morning. I am a Western female—a straightforward New Yorker, middle-aged, professional—grappling with a sense of my own erasure in a Muslim country, an invisible guest (a ghost) from another place, another time-zone. There they go with lunch pails in hand, and here I am, on my way, dreaming of the Klondike and the Chilkoot Trail.

# Wormhole Wedding

The November Eid holiday approaches, and the city of Abu Dhabi grows quiet as friends and colleagues jet away for quick vacations and many Muslims depart for Mecca. Emiratis retreat to family compounds, turning inward to a closed domestic sphere that will remain a mystery to me throughout my assignment. I am ever reminded of being a stranger in a strange land. American Thanksgiving is approaching, and this year the season is reminding me of my first arid Thanksgiving after leaving home for California and college. In Abu Dhabi I wander around local department stores and dollar stores, where mechanical toys bleat pathetic renditions of "We Wish You a Merry Christmas," and at a certain point I am so lonely that I email a former lover from back home. He writes back, and I proceed to charm him with mundane details of my new life. Loverman takes this as a welcome escape from another failing romance back in Brooklyn. "Sounds like you're living in a wormhole," he says. Something to do with time/space displacement, the science of which is lost on me, but I like the premise of all the same. We will carry on like this for months. Later, I will boldly invite him to meet me in Istanbul for a dirty weekend, a wormhole wedding. We will rendezvous under the liberating anonymity of the gloomy northern megalopolis—seduced by the city's own melancholic relationship to its Ottoman ruins and the rising mist of the Bosporous, by the Blue Mosque and the Hagia Sophia. Istanbul will put another name to this feeling of soul delay—*hüzün*—a Turkish word, which, writer Orhan Pamuk, describes as a "cultural concept conveying worldly failure, listlessness, and spiritual suffering." It is a malady Pamuk claims that "Islamic culture has come to hold...in high esteem" (91). With this, another piece of the puzzle surrounding of my own "year of melancholy" (90), will fall into place.

## Turning 50 in Abu Dhabi

Today I am 50. It is also the end of the fall semester and the lone wolves have turned our last class into a celebration, with ice cream cake, and a funny little crown for me and party hats for them. As we go around the class, each student reads selections from their portfolios, commenting on how far they've come, and applauding each other's new skills. Toward the end of class they nudge me for the howl cue, and all but Elias, a taciturn and brooding writer, partake. Elias still refuses to howl in public, but even he is pleased and amused. Later I will go to a lecture at the Al Mamoura Institute, to hear a talk about Gulf Politics and diplomacy given by the former ambassador of Abu Dhabi. After the lecture I'll slip out, apologizing to friends, and dodging acquaintances, preferring to spend some time alone.

Sitting at a table for one in a sleek Japanese restaurant at the Emirates Palace, I study the Alaskan king crab the waiter has just served me. Prepared with a spicy pepper sauce, and delivered with all the necessary tools and picks for breaking through the shell, it is messy beyond belief. After a few helpless moments, I leave manners aside, giving myself over to the spectacle of cracking the shell and picking out the meat with my fingers, sucking it out of the crustaceous nooks and crannies. I am hunching over to contain the mess, looking out over the top of my glasses—blind, but daring. Of what? The Emirati and Saudi guys across from me could care less about how I tear at this crab. Instead there is something of that odd sense of erasure again, a theatricality even, that tingling sense that I am seen and unseen, lost in a parallel universe, conjuring Eurydice, in exile, from her life, from her love, her city, her Orpheus.

*What will I remember of this?*

The waiter brings another glass of Louis Roederer champagne, clears the empty plates and I turn to my notebook, still pondering, while he goes to prepare the check. What *do* I want to remember?

*I was here, fully, passionately, taking in all that this radically new culture would give, absorbing, struggling, and watching, carving out my own space, leaving traces, evidence—fingerprints.*

When the waiter brings the check, because I am 50, I am pleased by its roundness, a sign that I have sufficiently wined and dined myself on my birthday. As I stand to leave, the kind waiters nod and smile—*goodnight madame, thank you madame.* And then the worried maître d' approaches—*what are you writing about madame? Is madame writing a book?* "No, no," I say. "It's just that it's my birthday, so I want to remember it." He smiles. I howl.

## Seed the Clouds

It is the beginning of January and I am combing through the extravagant Marina Mall, a 15 minute taxi ride from "home," a skyscraper dormitory where my university's faculty, staff, and students scuttle around in a vertical city. This mall is another of the haunts where I often drift on Friday mornings, arriving before all the stores are open—a reconnaissance of peacoats, sweaters, lingerie, and shoes—as I wait patiently for the Friday prayers to end so the Diesel blue jean shop will open up its denim mysteries to me and the shop boy will flirt and cajole and admonish me to "please put back those jeans," insisting that "they're for guys,"—and that the beautiful indigo skinny jeans with fancy girl stitching and silver sequins are The Ones.

Outside, the day is marked by unusual drizzle—here, they "seed the clouds"—a sinister sounding idea involving crop-duster planes and chemicals, the only way to artificially insure at least 5 days of rain a year in a hot arid climate. I emerge from my shopping spree collapsing in a taxi with all my spoils and a piece of dark chocolate with hazelnut filling ("only one Madame?"). Glad for the other shop boy at Zara Home, who smiled so knowingly and fetchingly while I lingered over a set of mother of pearl coasters and while the woman he was waiting on badgered him about the nomenclature of bed linen ("It's the Spanish way Madame." "Oh, you don't do it the way the *rest* of the world does it?"). And we make eyes at each other in the middle of it. The glance, the consenting spark, only here in this palace of consumer dreams.

All the while I am contemplating this thing about the worm hole. I suppose that *is* where I now find myself, in some new terrain, exiled, estranged from both my new life in Abu Dhabi and my former life in New York, wistful over other cities that have shaped me: Cleveland, Santa Barbara, Seattle, and Juneau—calculating the details of the trip to Istanbul. It is an experience to remind you that you are indeed as mortal as you first understood yourself to be so many years ago, a lost undergraduate in California zooming down that hill on your Schwinn bicycle, the smell of eucalyptus trees and the briny ocean, the pulse of a ballet class rising in your thighs. We get only this! Only all of this! Race cars, artichokes, elderflowers, the Q train. And still we seed the clouds. And wait for more. Always more.

## Soon the Birds Will Disappear

Soon the birds will disappear, escaping to less suffocating climes. Today, however, they are making a joyful noise, and my little writing class is cocooned in the corner of the garden patio of our makeshift campus; the three boys winning me over in their petitions to *please* let's have class outside. It is April now, and the weather is "nice"—somewhere around 90 degrees Fahrenheit, with a relatively cool breeze: cloudless. The garden is lush and the sodded yard a rich verdant green. Soon the scorching heat will come again, scattering humans and birds alike to cooler quarters.

In two more days the birds will already be farther away, a soundscape disappearing into a vacuum. There goes one of those comedic yellow-beaked crows now—packing up his birdsong, and trucking along. In the distance, the sound of construction machinery: cranes, bulldozers. And what of the memory of Istanbul that is pushing against the proprietary boundaries of my little class? I scrutinize each boy: is he awake? Did he do his homework? Does he have *another* excuse? I prompt the three of them, cajoling and insisting as I guide them toward their own inner eye, each of us in our own way searching for the thing that is just beyond our reach as writers. There on the periphery is my own wild heart. Cold and rainy Istanbul and the cacophony of its prayer call, sounding more like the tumultuous cry of lovers and seagulls just before daybreak than the austere piety of its Abu Dhabi counterpart.

This reverberation of time zones will soon be punctured by the lone aching voice of the Abu Dhabi muezzin. Still my students are at their task, their lunch trays pushed aside, the sleepiness that comes quickly upon the heels of mental labor is still a few minutes away. I have their attention, but not for much longer. The afternoon prayer call begins; its minor chords break our concentration, adding a full stop to the day's work, encouraging retreat and solitude. Where do I, the lone female traveler, find myself in that call that translates, literally, "Brothers come to Allah"? Here in Abu Dhabi I respectfully participate in the conservative dress codes of the Gulf Coast Countries, but it would be inappropriate to wear the elegant black gown and head covering—the *abaya* and *shayla*—of an Emirati woman. I am, however, bound by a more ephemeral version of the veil, the *hijab*, and I come to realize this may have something to do with the peculiar double consciousness, the sense of erasure and solitude that frequently clouds this journey.

I am not Muslim, but I am moved by the prayer call as an expression of melancholic grief, and I am curious about the rock solid calm—the certainty, the faith—that accompanies it. The Sufi mystics characterize this feeling of *hüzün* as a journey of trying to reconnect with the Beloved, and Western readers, especially those of us enchanted by the love poems of Rumi, confuse this with earthly love, rather than with the transcendence associated with coming home to Allah, connecting with God, the ultimate lover. I begin to surrender and trust that, *Insh'Allah,* I will find my way home soon enough. For now, though, *this* is home. And I wonder, is it possible that this feeling of exile, this estrangement is home itself?

My students and I read an essay called "Souls on Ice," where author Mark Doty locates his grief of having lost his lover to AIDS at the same moment he becomes transfixed by a display of mackerel outside a local market. Later, when I took the students on a field trip to the Abu Dhabi fish market—the souk—we bonded over our own unique encounter with mackerel, their beautiful silver shimmer. As we stood there, taking it all in, there was Jackson, pensively watching hard-working Iranian and Afghani men cleaning the blood and guts of fish netted in the Arabian Gulf; Jack and the other boys silently assessing the mix of grime and blood, a lack of sanitary conditions that they realize they have taken for granted back in their home countries. The boys report to me that they see several men have missing finger tips. But it's Jackson who surprises me as he quietly announces to no one in particular, "So basically we're standing in a graveyard."

# An End to Journeying

In his 1955 memoir *Tristes Tropiques,* anthropologist Claude Levi-Strauss bemoans the "vogue" for trendy mid-century travelogues, dismissing them as the facile mutterings of a new generation of travelers set in motion by tourism and the increased affordability of booking passage to faraway lands. And yet, translated literally as *sad tropics,* Levi-Strauss asks "… what else can the so-called escapism of travelling do than confront us with the more unfortunate aspects of our history?" For Levi-Strauss this isn't anti-modernism so much as it is a political project: "The first thing we see as we travel round the world," he tells us, "is our own filth, thrown into the face of mankind" (38). *Tristes Tropiques* is in part an experiment in the poetics of writing culture, a vehicle through which he is asking readers to distinguish between the leisure and the comforts of bourgeois travel and the *dis-ease* of travel driven by the necessity of being pushed beyond one's own cultural assumptions and myths. Levi-Strauss clarifies:

> Exploration is not so much a covering of surface distance as a study in depth: a fleeting episode, a fragment of landscape or a remark overheard may provide the only means of understanding and interpreting areas which would otherwise remain barren of meaning. (Levi-Strauss 1955: 47-48)

Levi-Strauss's account of his early 1930s fieldwork in Brazil becomes part of my own compass for making sense of Abu Dhabi. His experience of helping to build the University of São Paulo from the ground up also echoes with the United Arab Emirates' current modernization project.

Last week I finally capitulated and bought an iPhone after months of relying on Etisalat calling cards and a crappy little LG mobile phone. I now have weather and time zones for New York, Abu Dhabi, Istanbul, Kathmandu, and Southeast Alaska at my fingertips, and I flip through them late at night and early in the morning, reminding myself where I am, and where I've been. I am also looking through the random hieroglyphics of my flight itineraries and impressionistic fragments scribbled in the margins of notebooks, cautiously expecting they might add up to something more meaningful than *the weather was strange.* Having finished my Abu Dhabi assignment I have since returned to New York, where only now I am beginning to discover that I am suffering a peculiar sort of reverse culture shock. I am "home" in my neighborhood and city, but I have not yet fully arrived. I am a little lost, not quite in-sync with my former life, my former self. As I write, I look for ways to talk about cities as real material places, as places that matter, literally, but also as spaces of imagination, and estrangement. This has me thinking about clouds—places for airplanes, dreams, obfuscation, and now, apparently, data. Also: climate, and weather systems, and the ways we are borne from one place to another through atmospheric pressure. Enter jetlag, turbulence, air streams—soul delay.

## Bibliography

Doty, M. (2008). "Souls on Ice" in *Occasions for Writing: Evidence, Idea, Essay,* eds. R. DiYanni and P. C. Hoy II, Boston: Wadsworth. 92-95.

Gibson, W. Interviewed by Wes Unruh, *Green Man Review.* http://www.greenmanreview.com/book/interview_william _gibson.html.

—. (2003). *Pattern Recognition.* New York: Berkley Books

Levi-Strauss, C. (1955). *Tristes Tropiques.* Trans. by J. and D. Weightman. New York: Penquin Books.

Pamuk, O. (2004). *Istanbul: Memories and the City.* Trans. by A. A. Knopf. New York: Vintage International.

Ross, A. (1991). *Strange Weather: Culture, Science, and Technology in the Age of Limits.* London/New York: Verso.

# CHAPTER ELEVEN

## TALES FROM THE HEIGHTS: MOHAWK IRONWORKERS IN NEW YORK CITY

## SAMUEL NEURAL

The primary purpose of this anthropological work is to describe and interpret some of the ways in which people encounter, form attachment to, and remember places. In the 20th century, Mohawk ironworkers helped erect some of the highest skyscrapers in North America. They established a community in Brooklyn, New York, known as "Little Caughnawaga," while keeping strong ties with their hometown, Kahnawake, in Québec, Canada. Mohawk ironworking in the United States has been well researched until the 1970s but little is known about the phenomenon in the years that lead up to the 21st century.

Focusing on a young Mohawk's experience as an ironworker in Brooklyn, New York, in 2001, this ethnography examines the temporary residence of someone living and working away from his home and family in Canada. The recorded stories here, based on extensive conversations between the ethnographer and the former ironworker, are about urban places that are experienced both through a different set of work-related practices and through memory, thus forming a particular kind of cultural legacy.

During the 20<sup>th</sup> century, Mohawk ironworkers from the Caughnawaga community (named later "Kahnawake") located in the south shore of Montreal, Canada, became involved in the structural steel industry in cities across North America. Living originally through agriculture, hunting and gathering, in multi-clan villages and a matrilineal social system, the Mohawks were the keepers of the Eastern Door of the Six Nations Iroquois Confederacy, which included also the Oneida, Onondaga, Cayuga, Senaca, and Tuscaroras nations. Mohawks first established the Caughnawaga settlement in 1676 (Katzer 1972).

The reservation community evolved from the French mission of St. Francis Xavier—a refuge for Iroquois converts to Catholicism in 1669. In 1716, after several relocations, some Mohawk families ended up at the present site of Kahnawake on the south shore of the St. Laurence River, near the Lachine rapids, at Montreal's "doorstep." The Kahnawake Mohawks were successful as fur traders and warriors in the 18<sup>th</sup> and 19<sup>th</sup> centuries. In the late 19<sup>th</sup> century, agricultural and trading practices were gradually replaced by farming and local industries (logging and brick building; mills, dams, and railroad construction). But as the city of Montreal grew rapidly around the Mohawk community (which was officially regarded as a reserve after the Indian Act of 1876), Kahnawake began to suffer the pressures of urbanization and assimilation.[1] By the 20<sup>th</sup> century, the village was criss-crossed with railways and highways, built on expropriated Mohawk land hemmed in by the skyscrapers of Montreal to the north and the fast-growing suburb of Chateauguay to the south. This increased the participation of men in the iron industry and local employment in the nearby city, and soon after 1912–in larger cities of eastern and central Canada as well as the United States. Brooklyn, Detroit, and Buffalo, in that order, received Mohawks migrants and retain, to this day, some Mohawk families.

In his study of ironwork in New York, Blanchard (1983) shows how ironworkers experience the city as a cultural continuity primarily through their trade. This is due to the multitude of tasks that their work requires, which allows them to convey and share with each other both cultural values and technical skills, by which they re-appropriate specific places in the city. For Michel De Certeau (1984), the individual produces his or her own place in the city through the "practices" of walking, naming, narrating and remembering, while for Steve, a Mohawk ironworker, this happens

---

[1] Despite their conversion to Catholicism and the many changes surrounding their reserve, Mohawks never abandoned the three-clan structure (Turtle, Wolf, Bear) and continued to respect their longhouse faith keepers and war chiefs (Blanchard 1982).

through particular work operations such as shooting studs, patching, flashing, tack welding, as well as through "after work" occupations. Steve's anecdotes give significant density to social locations glimpsed at specific moments of his own New York experiment, as well as exposure to the selectively recalled facts of life. In his enduring experience of being "caught in the nets of his "'discipline'" (DeCerteau 1984: xiv-xv), Steve struggled to combat the solitude of the city both from "the heights," where he spent most of his days, and from the mesh of Brooklyn streets.

In the account that follows, this elaborate cultural experience is restored by narrativized moments of description, digression, an incessant compulsion to story things that happen through a process of remembering, and retelling, all of which make us understand better what the city is all about according to one Mohawk's individual perspective. The ethnographer uses the process of "crude translation"—from the oral narrative to the written ethnography. Mohawk values, such as daring, courage, and cooperation are captured here as a series of experiences, through an adventuresome and dangerous occupation, allowing the main protagonist to express his memories and thus become a part of the ironworkers' historical and cultural heritage.

## Olden Days or the Long Tradition of Ironworking

Like most ironworkers, Steve was introduced to ironworking through his immediate family:

> My father-in-law was a foreman for the Rising Gang, which is the guys who connect and who put up the structure. They are also called Foreman Pushers, so he was a Pusher. I moved on to New York because my father-in-law at that time didn't like the fact that I was working a non-union job. I was working Saturday in Massachusetts and on Wednesday my father-in-law called and said, why don't you come and work at the Union job in New York. I said doing what, you know, I don't have any experience, and he said look, I get you to shoot studs and basically it's this large studs, maybe 6 inches, that you have this gun and you shoot into the deck. It stabilizes the deck so when they pour the cement if you have a strong stud and a bunch of studs on the beam, when you pour the cement, it holds easier. So I said ok, you know, it sounds interesting. He told me that on Wednesday night, so I had to work on Saturday 'cause I already said I was going to work and he said ok, work Saturday, come home, and we will leave on Sunday. That's what I did, I worked half day, Saturday, I got home Saturday night, Sunday night ironworking traditionally we leave at midnight so, we left at midnight and I started in New York.

And when speaking about how the "work" came to him, Steve stated:

> I started to look seriously at ironworking, and even if I didn't have any
> experience, I knew that the only thing that I had was the legacy of the
> Mohawk ironworkers.

This legacy started in the decade of the 1850s when the Caughnawaga
community had its introduction to construction work with their participation
in the building of The Victoria Bridge, which abutted on reservation land
across the Saint Laurence River in Montreal. The Dominion Bridge
Company hired some Mohawks in 1886 to work as unskilled labourers on
the Victoria Tubelar Bridge and was quickly persuaded to train several
crews for the more demanding high steel erection work (Mitchell 1949).
Of the two kinds of employment available for the Dominion Bridge
Company, fabrication and erection, Caughnawaga men overwhelmingly
opted for the latter. They made up their own crews, usually of family
members and trained apprentices who could be sent to other construction
sites. In the early years of Caughnawaga's participation in high steel work,
a single job would often have more than one Mohawk crew on site,
sometimes with a total of one hundred or more. The tragic collapse of the
Quebec Bridge that same year, in which a total of 96 men died, 33 from
Caughnawaga, didn't affect the Caughnawaga's devotion to the job and
increased the prestige of ironwork in the community. While the incident
stays today well alive in the collective memory of the community, the
disaster encouraged many men to take up this occupation (Mitchell 1949).

Pretty soon, there weren't enough bridge jobs and the Mohawk crews
began working on all types of high steel factories, office buildings,
department stores, hospitals, hotels, apartment houses, schools, breweries,
distilleries, powerhouses, piers, railroad stations, and grain elevators in the
growing city of Montreal. Mohawk ironworkers began to look for work in
larger geographical areas. At the same time, they expanded the kind of
work to include a new type of building—the skyscrapers. The migrations
that began about 1912 sent people not only to larger cities in eastern and
central Canada, like Toronto, but also to the United States–to New York
City, Detroit, Buffalo, Syracuse, Boston, and Chicago (Katzer 1972).
Increasing numbers of young ironworkers found work in the western parts
of the United States as well: Texas (Houston), Arizona, up to the Sun Belt,
in California (San Diego and Los Angeles). The Golden Gate Bridge in
San Francisco received some groups of Mohawks ironworkers too.

The earliest settlement in Brooklyn, according to Katzer (1972: 163)
was started in 1916, when a Caughnawaga bridge man named John Diabo,
came down to New York City and got a job on Hell's Gate Bridge.

Another family moved in 1920 and opened a boarding house for ironworkers near Tillary, Adams, and Pearl Streets. In 1926, attracted by the building boom, three to four Caughnawaga groups came down and worked first on the Fred F. French Building and the Graybar Building, both on Fifth Avenue in Manhattan. Around 1927, these families were among the first to move into the area bounded by Warren, Court, Schermerhorn Streets and Fourth Avenue—the new center of Caughnawaga residences. In 1928, three more families came down. The men worked first on the George Washington Bridge. In the thirties, when Rockefeller Center was the biggest steel job in the country, at least seven additional Caughnawaga crews enrolled in the local high-steel union in Brooklyn—the International Association of Bridge, Structural, and Ornamental Iron Workers—as well as in the American Federation of Labor.

During the Depression, the decline in building construction weighed heavily on the Caughnawaga ironworkers and many of them returned to Montreal, to the reservation, where there was housing and family support. Previously, when families settled in Brooklyn, their children went home to Caughnawaga (Kahnawake) for their schooling, and visited Brooklyn for the summer. After 1937, however, the pattern was reversed. Children stayed in Brooklyn with their parents, returning to Kahnawake, to visit the reserve, in the summer. Between 1938-1939, and again between 1941-45, there was a large scale migration of Mohawk families to Brooklyn, who ended up serving as hosts, providing accommodations for single ironworkers coming from the reserve.[2]

The Caughnawaga all lived within ten blocks of each other in the neighborhood of Northern Gawanus, "Little Caughnawaga," bounded by Court Street on the west, Schemerhorn Street on the north, Fourth Avenue on the east, and Warren Street on the south, in spacious apartments occupied by five to eight ironworkers, or a family.[3] These apartments

---

[2] In New York City, the Caughnawagas worked mostly for the big companies—Betlehem, American Bridge, the Lehigh Structural Steel Company. Among the structures in and around the city on which they worked in numbers are the RCA Building, the City's Service Building, the Empire State Building, the Daily News Building, the Chanin Building, the Bank of the Manhattan Company Building, the City Bank Farmers Trust Building, the George Washington Bridge, the Bayonne Bridge, the Passaic River Bridge, the Triborough Bridge, the Henry Hudson Bridge, the Little Hell Gate Bridge, the Whitestone Bridge, the Marine Parkway Bridge, the Pulaski Skyway, the West Side Highway, the Waldorf-Astoria, London Terrace, and Knickerbocker Village.

[3] A typical family group consists of a husband and wife, a couple of children and a female relative or two.

maintained the distinctive look of a Mohawk home, with mementos, pictures, beadwork, and other crafts decorating the walls and mantles. They also had their Mohawk hangouts: the Spar Bar, the Wigwam bar, The Nevins Bar and Grill, the Thompson Boarding House, and the Cuyler Presbyterian Church (Katzer 1972). Soon people began to think of their sojourn in Brooklyn as a lifetime commitment and not a temporary stay while more and more Mohawk ironworkers' children joined New York City's public schools.

Thus began a process of migration to and from the reservation that continued until the 1980s. Many individuals eventually returned to the reservation while keeping in contact with families that were maintaining the sense of community alive in Brooklyn. Even in 2001, when Steve worked as an ironworker and lived in Brooklyn, the Mohawk ironworking activity was significant:

> Back then in 2001, there was a huge boom in New York City; I mean, there have to be 5-600 ironworkers from Kahnawake that worked in New York City at that time and that's a lot. There are only 8000 people here in Kahnawake. All my layout guys were from Kahnawake and in decking, I would say mostly Kahnawake guys.

## The City of Labor

Michel de Certeau, philosopher of everyday life, wrote that when the walker of New York is lifted up above the city street in an elevator or by taking stairs, "he leaves behind the mass that carries off and mixes up in itself any identity of authors and spectators … His elevation transfigures him into a voyeur" (De Certeau 1984: 92). Mohawk ironworkers spent most of their times in the city *way up*. And from this totalizing, voyeuristic position, far above the streets and traffic, they comprehended the city in a very specific way—"from the heights," as Steve suggests, where it is only work and not much time to enjoy the city:

> So everything you were doing whether it was shooting studs, dragging deck, patching, flashing, which is putting, some people call it flashing, some people call it poor stop. It's on the edge of the building and it goes underneath the steel and it's a lip and it holds all the cement in. All of that, everything you re doing is for the cement. And so you can pour the cement and none of it overflows into the holes or on, off the side and so it has a lot of support with the studs and everything else.

Concrete and cement, with their appealing density and strength, are the basic materials of the urban built environment, coming from those big mixing trucks that thump down the street on their way to the building site. In the world of the ironworker, there is no such thing as form without matter or matter without form, and cement is the necessary conjunction of pure form and primary matter. The cement plays with the material palette of any city and its transformation principles and when the mixture of water, cement, and gravel is set, the form is fixed. All construction is linked in some way to the everyday expression of human aspiration and commitment. Buildings, then, are more than edifices; they are locations and places that gather common human competence, skill, experience:

> So, within the first little bit less than a month I was shooting, I became the primary shooter. I started to lay on my own furrows but then they gave me a layout guy. So then it was good because, you know, I basically went in a month from having no experience to be able to read prints and then be able to, you know, run the show, basically: I was the shooter, there was a guy under me who was laying out, I read the prints, one guy who had to lay out for me didn't know how to read prints at all, so I had to go to the beams and write the number of furrows that you should have on this specific beam which is more work but it's just that he didn't know how to read the prints.

Even the simplest building entails the creation of space, and thus, of *meaning* in shared competence and cooperative values:

> Basically what happens in ironworking is, there is connectors, who connect the beams, just with one bolt. Ok, a beam's set, you move on to another beam. They are building the structure. Then there are those who come in and they bolt the beams together so there are safe. Then there was us, the connectors and the deckers; we deck, grab a big corrugated steel, we drag it along the beams to make a floor, for anybody else to come up, and for them to land more iron … sometimes, the bolt is up to get there before, sometimes, the stuff that we are putting corrugated steel onto, is not totally bolted down, so we have to leave a space for them to get in there and bolt it down.

The mastering of cement used in everyday construction by Mohawk ironworkers is also expressive of cultural values, shaping manhood through physical strength, the absence of fear from heights, cooperation, and courage:

> You know decking was one of the hardest jobs for sure. Probably the initial job of connecting was the hardest and then you had decking because you're constantly bending down, you're dragging what ends up being one hundred or something pounds of corrugated steel across open beams, it's a tough job…

# The City of Leisure

According to Steve, ironwork, then, leaves little to no space for the domestic sphere of existence:

> An ironworker's life, you don't live, you just work ... we were in bed usually...the latest was 9. We were very tired, I mean, I get home around 3:30 or 4 depending on the traffic, get something to eat, call my girlfriend, read the paper, and then soon enough, 9 o'clock, I was in bed ... sometimes earlier. Depending on how big the day was, you were asleep ... you don't really live, you know ... I would say, the ironworker's life consisted of getting up early, going to work, working hard.

The harshness of ironworking is encoded in Steve's memory not only in feelings but also in scents that haunted the place where workers rested:

> I was living on a couch in the living room and it was an old ironworker's couch, it smells like ironworkers, and it's that smell of steel, I don't know if you know that smell but it's a very strong smell and I put a sheet over the couch because it was such a strong smell that I could still smell it.

Apart from its temporary nature, the ironworker's dwelling place is as if an extension to the construction site, with shared experiences that belong only to men:

> When I lived in Brooklyn, I think it was 85 street or 84 street something like that. I don't remember the cross street but it was in Bay Ridge, which was a nice neighbourhood for us, you know. When I first got there, we were 8 of us in a house, all guys from Kahnawake. Where we lived was a little further away from the other families, the other houses were about 10 streets away. There were like little clusters, apartments and houses, and like I said, there had to be 600 ironworkers, easily ironworkers from Kahnawake. Some lived in Brooklyn, some were lucky enough to live in Manhattan, we would see them all the time.

Social life emerges through the few distractions the workers had in the neighbourhood where bars, for example, were the main place to reconstitute the Mohawk network in New York.

> There was a place called "The Snook" (it's closed down now); but it was a place people would go to, and it was mostly about drinking, so I wouldn't go all the time but a lot of guys would go everyday. I popped in once in a while, they had special things, like Wednesday was pay day, so they had a free barbecue, go eat whatever and put down their check. It was another bar called "Killarney's" that we'd go to sometimes. It was 12 to 15 streets

away, and that's where those guys would go because they were new there. Sometimes we do things like go to Coney Island, I remember, with a few of the guys from Kahnawake, we took a drive to Coney Island, the Holocaust Museum, we hung out on the beach, we ate there. It was like the New York experience, you know. Off days I would go to the Empire State Building, just to do different things.

This geography of the ironworker's social life extends out of the city to places that Steve has tracked down from his memory:

> There were other clusters where they were living—in Jersey so one time we went to visit them. I don't even remember where it was in Jersey, and there were little clusters of Kahnawake ironworkers and they had their own bar locally where they'd go, so we went to visit them. There was this guy who stays in Nayak which is about maybe 40 minutes outside of New York City and there were a cluster there, so one night I had to sleep there because I was travelling with them before going to the city, so you know, there were always these little clusters of people that we went sometimes for visit during a day.

## The City of Constant Return

To show how ironworkers are "being in the world" of the city is to rely on the existential and phenomenological reality of the place where they worked (the city of labor), the place where they lived (the city of leisure), and the place that they would leave on Friday night for Kahnawake, and then return to on Sunday night – New York City. Back in the old days, it was difficult for the ironworkers to return to Kahnawake while cars were slow and gas was expensive. Nowadays, some ironworkers, like Steve, easily make the trip back to the community almost every weekend:

> Because we were deckers, sometimes we get off at noon on Friday, usually getting off around 2. We wait for the guys to get off at three, and we were home (in Kahnawake) at 9; but we were so full of energy, do what we have to do for the weekend, and then back at midnight on Sunday for the trip to New York, every single weekend. So when I get home Friday night, I call my buddies, "what are we doing?" We end up going out for dinner, bar, whatever, Saturday, same thing, with my girlfriend. I had to fit in all these people in two days, and leave Sunday at midnight.

The journey back to New York is another memorable aspect for Steve:

> But then comes Sunday, you have to take a nap in the daytime, because you leave at midnight, and sometimes you are the first person driving, sometimes you are the second, if you are the second, you'll drive and then

you'll sleep, and then you'll take over in Albany, and it's 3 hours. So you're driving at midnight and then you're getting in Albany at 3-3:30 in the morning. It's long ... and then you'll drive and to work. So whoever was driving you, they drop you off at the worksite. And Monday is the worst day of the week because you didn't get enough sleep.

The borough of Brooklyn finds itself captured in an alternate way of life that stretches people between the return to the community and their presence, sometimes inevitable, in the iron arcane of the Big Apple. This process of the constant movement of people creates new trans-local spaces and forms of culture that dissolve notions of community (Gupta and Ferguson 1992; Appadurai 1996), where people restructure their everyday lives and localities, and re-territorialize in other landscapes, re-creating meanings and community in another context. In the native world, this tendency to trans-locality and diaspora challenges the power of the community's existence and the treasured territorial sovereignty. From new forms of spatial commitment (Gupta 1992) comes a new form of mobility and linkage, new itineraries based on circuits and network, and contiguously new feelings that traduce a sense of being far from home, and the wish "to come back, someday." Or, as Steve promised to himself:

I will be here for a couple of years, maybe less, and then I am done.

In fact, Steve remembers well his first and last jobs in New York City.

I started off in Spanish Harlem, I ended up, my last job was in Washington Heights!? And 166, and I think it was on Broadway: it was way up ... December 23$^{rd}$ wherever the last day before, the Friday before Christmas was, that was my last day in 2001.

Interestingly, the memory of that is intertwined with another one—that of September 11, 2001, and the fall of the Twin Towers, which Steve could observe from the high vantage point of his work place. As his account shows, memory allows for the uncanny collision of disparate city places, with the real distance among them totally gone:

And I could see the World Trade Center when it happened from where we were, we were high enough, it was the Presbyterian Hospital, and we could see, I didn't see the plane, but we could see the smoke and everything.

# The City of Memories

To grasp the nature of Steve's ironworking experience in New York City, which lasted one year, there is a need to investigate the processes of place making, and how feelings of de-centralized belonging to a fluid and fragmented community organized around ironworking bind identity to spatial locations, where seasonal or temporary workers are "suspended," never fully in the new place, never really in their place of origin. But while ironworking requires constant mobility and transportation, it is still a glamorous occupation that shapes Mohawk manhood and plays a significant cultural role in contemporary Mohawk culture.

Constructing intricate relations with place through the specific trade of ironworking, which became formative for Mohawks, is indicative of the meaning of place within that particular culture. Place, be it temporary or permanent, becomes essential in shaping Mohawk identity as well as in holding personal and collective memory. Places host actions, concerns, communities, and goals, as well as the memories of all these. As fragments of speech and stories, Steve's memories are infused with his aspirations and beliefs, and juxtaposed with his personal trajectories—themselves governed by the corporeal experiences of being in and moving through spaces, while interacting with the multitude of identities that New York City has to offer: sometimes dominating, sometimes being dominated by them, as Baudrillard suggests in *America*:

> In New York there is this double miracle: each of the great buildings and each of the ethnic groups dominates or has dominated the city—after its own fashion. Here crowdedness lends sparkle to each of the ingredients in the mix whereas elsewhere it tends to cancel out differences. (Baudrillard 1986: 14)

Steve's experience of the city then, although limited to his work site and his shared Brooklyn rental, is one charged with a double meaning, or "miracle": as a temporary worker, he is both within and outside the grasp of the city; both partaking in the progress of constructing skyscrapers and in the nostalgia of returning to his home community; both pulled into this vibrant new city and pushed away to the reserve … indeed, the human embodiment of suspension, just like the bridges he helped built, and which, despite being in-between places, like Steve, or other Mohawk ironworkers, are the crucial connective tissue in any functioning city.

# Bibliography

Appadurai, A. (1996). *Modernity at Large: Cultural Dimensions of Globalizations.* Minneapolis: University of Minnesota Press.

Baudrillard, J. (1986). *Amérique.* Paris: Grasset.

Blanchard, D. S. (1982). "Pattern of Tradition and Change: the Recreation of Iroquois Culture at Kahnawake." PhD Dissertation. University of Chicago.

Blanchard, D. S. (1983). "High Steel! The Kahnawake Mohawks and the High Construction trade" in *Journal of Ethnic Studies* 11 (2) 41-60.

De Certeau, M. (1984). *The Practice of Everyday Life.* Berkeley: University of California Press.

Feld, S. and K. H. Basso. (1996). *Senses of Place.* Santa Fe, Mexico: School of American Research Press.

Freilich, M. (1958). "Cultural Persistence Among the Modern Iroquois" in *Cultural Anthropology* 53: 473-483.

Gupta, A. and J. Ferguson. (1992). "Beyond Culture: Space, Identity and the Politics of Difference" in *Cultural Anthopology,* 7 (1), 6-23.

—. (1992). "The Song of the Non-aligned World: Transnational Identities and the Reinscription of Space in Late Capitalism" in *Cultural Anthopology,* 13 (3), 63-79.

Hubard, P. (2006). *City.* London and New York: Routledge.

Katzer, B. (1972). "The Caughnawaga Mohawks: Occupations, Residence, and the Maintenance of Community Membership." Ph.D. Dissertation, Columbia University.

—. (1988). "The Caughnawaga Mohawks: the Other Side of Ironwork" in *Journal of Ethnic Studies* 15 (4) 39-55.

Kingwell, M. (2008). *Concrete Reveries. Consciousness and the City.* Viking Canada.

Mitchell, J. (1949). "Mohawks in High Steel" in *The New Yorker, Vol 28, n30.*

# Acknowledgments

I would like to thank Steve Bonspiel for his collaborative spirit and availability; for always finding the time to answer questions and contributing to this research while being one of the busiest and most successful editors-in-chief in Canada. My gratitude goes also to Dr. Blagovesta Momchedjikova's patience, guidance, and encouragement.

# CHAPTER TWELVE

## STAMP AND GO:
## LIFE AS AN URBAN NOMAD

## KEISHA-GAYE ANDERSON

Several generations of Afro-Caribbean people see migration as an inevitable reality of their condition and understand the economic and political "pull/push" factors that continue to govern their movements—factors that are a direct result of the way these small island developing states came into being. How this urban nomadic existence impacts cultural production, artistic expression, and socio-economic patterns is of great interest to me because of the potential of this information to unify these Diaspora communities and to bring a sense of healing to a people who have scarcely had the opportunity to acknowledge or process the psychic trauma of slavery. Both Caribbean Studies and African American Studies provide a useful lens through which to examine the aesthetics and challenges of assimilation met by those born in post-colonial Caribbean societies, of which I am also a product.

I seek, within my fiction and poetry, to articulate and examine the challenges and realizations that derive from the particular patterns of migration that exist between the English-speaking Caribbean region and the United States, Canada, and the United Kingdom. These Caribbean immigrants, who are usually drawn to urban centers in the West, and simultaneously pushed from urban centers in the Caribbean, mainly because of economic opportunities in the former and lack of viable opportunities in the latter, tend to hold fast to their cultures wherever they settle, creating pan-Caribbean connections, both social and economic, based on those shared experiences. My interest lies in the wider discourse about urban primacy and cultural retention that can be cultivated via these geographically disparate, but largely uniform, urban experiences. How does migration enhance our understanding of ourselves, our culture, and our place historically and presently in Western, urban societies?

I sat in the large bay window, making shapes in the canvas of condensation that I'd formed by breathing my four year-old breath onto the glass. It was one of those old buildings that whispered its stories through the creaky wooden floor, splintered molding, over-painted tin ceiling, and hissing radiators. If it could speak words, it would shuffle through Yiddish, Irish, Sicilian, and southern African American speech. Today, it was learning Jamaican patois—a sturdy and musical language, singularly equipped to articulate the humor in the chain of events that created it in the first place.

"Midey yah" (I am here) was a common expression of my mother's. It was not only a literal description of physical location, it also implied that we had come through hard times, and that we would cope with, tackle, and confront our circumstances—that's all there was to it. And urban nomads need that sort of attitude to survive wherever they happen to land.

So, I was here. In Brooklyn, in the late 1970s. We'd left one large city, Kingston, Jamaica, for another, New York, United States. My scant childhood memories included cozy and closely situated concrete houses with verandahs, colorful clusters of potted tropical plants amidst the concrete, and my cat eyeglass-wearing grandmother bent perpetually over her sewing machine to earn her bread and butter. That one-way stream of people from Kingston to New York City was nothing new, and stretched continuously all way the way back to the 18$^{th}$ century, when enslaved Africans in Jamaica were regularly shipped up to the US, alongside other cargo. But the American collective memory is notoriously short, and purposely intolerant of facts that threaten to crack the carefully crafted image of the melting pot. Dissonance is bad for business, especially when the workforce from countries like mine only legally began to receive wages during the 19$^{th}$ century. So, my family and their friends would be defined as part of that wave of Jamaican immigrants who left the island during its "socialist experiment" period. But, truth be told, people left for a myriad of different reasons, the need to make a living usually being the common push factor.

My grand aunt Hyacinth MacFarlane was short, pale, with wavy black hair that flowed down to the middle of her back. This, plus the fact that she legitimately used the surname of her Irish father, was a source of pride for her. Whether or not our paternal Irish ancestors living in Jamaica were landed gentry or indentured servants didn't really matter. The complexion was a sort of currency, especially during the 1920s, when she was born.

Aunt Hyacinth owned the brownstone, with its red painted front steps, flanked by empty cement planters. She stirred a pot of curry goat as I watched cars pass by the bay window. Someone else transferred the rice and peas onto the counter and took out the serving crockery. The ladies laughed and chided each other, traded gossip from home and from here in 'foreign,' which contained at least one account of a "worthless" man with children that his wife didn't know about. Then, there was the knock at the front door.

My mother walked in, all smiles and youthful curves. I thought she was so beautiful. As she entered, the ladies all complimented her. But I began to cry. Loud, hysterical, bawling, in fact. My mother was somehow transformed, different from the woman who'd left me in this house with these ladies while she ran out to do her errands. That huge chestnut Afro I'd seen since I knew my own self had been flattened and pressed into shiny curls that didn't move and took on a helmet-like shape round her angular face.

"Never mind, baby," one of the ladies said, as she comforted me and chucked. "Don't cry," said another, as she whispered a question to my mother, who responded with a shrug.

To a four year-old, change can be jarring, especially for one recently uprooted from the warmth of the tropics to the cold grit of New York. But in that moment, I just remember feeling as if my mother had put on a mask that I didn't recognize or like. As I grew, she would teach me to wear that mask as well.

"Whayu ah go do?" my mother would say when I probed her on why she'd changed her appearance back then in order to find a so-called good job. The house cleaning work she took when we first arrived, to which I'd sometimes tag along, did not qualify as good. "What yu ah go do?"

That same refrain brought my great grandmother from her rural town of Alexandria, St. Ann to Kingston to work as a domestic and nanny for a British family in the early 1900s. Like most colonial cities, Kingston was a sprawling mercantile cog that took from the local workers and gave and gave to the Crown—in that direction only. The people were the levers that kept the machine spinning, and just as during slavery, they were expendable and transferrable. When all you own is your labor, home is wherever you can find a regular meal.

This was, of course, as true for us as it was for my classmate Maria Castellano, whose family changed their Italian surname to 'Castel' in order to blend in and be more anonymously Anglophone. Blending in over time is easier when America agrees that you're white. On the other hand, when you fit the description of those in the historically and permanent subordinate status in the nation, very few keys unlock the door to a certain type of unencumbered existence and freedom of movement that the

Castels of the world can take advantage of. But that didn't mean my mother wasn't going to try.

"What a way her hair plenty!" said the hairdresser to my mother. I sat perfectly still as the sizzling hot comb was pulled through the hair closest to my ears. I hated that part. A burn and ugly boil on the top of the ear was almost a given during his ritual, along with the lingering smell of grease and burnt hair. Forget playing in the rain—that would render the whole process a waste of time and money, as the water quickly reverted your hair to its natural curl pattern.

I was twelve, and told I was beautiful, especially when my long, wavy hair was straightened. It was all a part of the blending in, which when combined with that Jamaican "ambition," was believed to lead to that long sought after material success.

"It's a white man's world; we just live in it," my mother would always say, clarifying the parameters of my actions and modifying my expectations. Afterward, she would exhale the same sigh she sighed when the rice was accidentally burnt or if a red sock got into the white laundry.

I can't say that I blamed her, when some of her early memories in Jamaica—an island where 90% of the people are visibly of African descendent—involved pressing her nose up against the window of a dancing school that only admitted British expatriate children into its classes.

"Stay away from this black business," another aunt cautioned, as I began to voice questions about the necessity of using chemical hair strengtheners and why bleaching creams were still being marketed to perfectly beautiful dark skinned women like the ones in my family who I admired and loved so much, just as they were.

But I was given my manual and my marching orders. The wealthy had time to sit and think. We had to survive. Hadn't we always? If your great-great-grandmother didn't legally own her own body, how far could you expect to go without great effort and minimal conflict? The instructions were clear. Study hard and focus on school and a career. Do play up the much-lauded Jamaican work ethic. "After all, you have brought-upsy" (good home training). Do play up your Scottish and Irish mixture; after all, you'd really be considered brown, not black, if you were back home, because of your light reddish brown skin color. And do *not*, under any circumstances, get involved in this "black business," which had caused riots and fire hoses to be used on people. Those pursuits would prove you had no ambition and that you would likely find company with those broom-making, ganja-smoking rasta types, according to the likes of my mother and other well meaning Christian ladies from my part of the globe. The choice was clear.

But even if I had chosen not to get involved with this black business, it got involved with me, which is what my fellow working class Caribbean urban nomads didn't always understand upon first landing here.

I understood it clearly the day I walked into the senior producer's office at the TV network where I was tenaciously working my way up the professional ladder. A Syracuse University graduate, I'd put in a good seven years in the field and had no plans of staying in the proverbial lobby for the rest of my career.

I'd only communicated with the producer by email and was thrilled when he agreed to seem me for an informational interview. I was good at socializing. I made sure my hair was straightened and brushed back into a neat bun, donned conservative slacks and shirt, and whipped out the classy heels that put me right at six feet tall. I wanted to convey, "I'm affable and disarming, but don't mess with me 'cause I'm not big-for-nothing."

As I walked back to the office from lunch, mentally preparing myself for the meeting, I took comfort in midtown Manhattan's frenetic pace. Everyone was after something. They came from all corners of the world and moved through the arteries of the city in regular patterns. The loading dock guys at the building across the street gracefully moved packages along, testing their most creative lines on passing women. In the café down the block, ladies lunched, people-watched, and enjoyed being watched while feigning aloofness. There was a place for everyone in New York City, if you had the savvy and stamina to carve one out, I thought.

I stepped into the building while studying my reflection on the revolving door. When the producer called me into his office, I shook his hand and sat down, reigning in the smile that was growing too wide with excitement about the professional possibilities that could take root in this very moment. I was bursting with story ideas. I was willing to work as much as it took to get the job done. I was the one he needed on his team, and I would prove it. I'd paid some dues and wanted to move forward in my journey toward a career that the whole extended family had somehow supported me in attaining.

Whether it was the stamp-and-go (codfish fritters—the original "fast food") sent to my college dorm room by my Aunt Bev or the underwear and socks my mom found cheap on Fulton Street, they all aided me on a journey that was often quite lonely, but which I knew was essential. In many ways, I was the caboose, holding the precious dream cargo amassed by all the preceding train cars on this life journey. All of it love, and a collective desire to root us somewhere, help us find a yard where we could park and rest our wheels.

The producer glanced at my resume and then pushed it to the side, like a bill you've decided it's okay to skip this month. He clasped his fingers and looked at me over his glasses, giving me that smile that usually precedes a stock rejection talk from the upper management handbook.

"Look, I don't think we have anything here for you at the moment," he said.

I then went into a not-too-desperate, but spirited, summary of my skills and praise for his show. He cut me off.

"Besides, you probably want to do black stories," he said, "and that's just not our audience." He looked away, rifled through some papers. This was my cue that the conversation was now over.

Silence. Brain freeze. Lucid dreaming?

No. This was all too real. My mind raced and bubbled with explicative after explicative. This was a major television network, a nationally syndicated, prime-time show. You mean to tell me that they didn't have one black audience member? Or maybe they did, but you didn't really want to encourage them and so avoided those "black stories"?

But mostly, I wondered what exactly are these "black stories"? My resume was filled all types of writing—from business to wellness—but clearly, according to this producer, my physical appearance led invariably to an insatiable hunger to write about all things black.

I knew that anything I said would elicit a polite chuckle and then a cue that it was time for me to leave the office. He checked his watch, he had other meetings, it was nice to meet me, please stay in touch. Best of luck.

I also knew that if I shared this incident, I would be branded as either the sensitive or angry black woman who sees racism everywhere. Not a good look. I decided never to tell anyone. I just took a walk to a nearby coffee shop after work and stared into my paper tea cup. I watched the suits come and go, observed the unhurried gait of the same homeless guy I passed every day when hopping on a Brooklyn-bound train, and wondered if I would ever be able to carve out my distinct path in this city that was beautifully chaotic but hopelessly segregated and rigid, all at the same time.

What I knew since childhood had been confirmed in that one crushing moment: No status or material acquisition erases blackness in America, and blackness was and still remains the thread dangling from the ballroom gown; no one wants to unravel it, lest the gown fall apart and leave the queen naked.

I realized that my mother, my relatives, my friends could often not see the big picture. Survival mode put blinders on them. And in my family, our generational history as urban nomads insulated them from the broader understanding of the entire framework of industry responsible for their very existence. In which other crossroads on the globe can Africa, Hong Kong, Madras, and Glasgow mingle together in one individual's veins?

That's the one thing that many of my fellow Jamaican urban nomads didn't quite understand. "Clear skin" (light skin) did not make one almost white, not in America. Evidence for me was this producer wanting to close the gates to his franchise before I even began knocking. And there would be many more professional and personal experiences that would play out in the same way. Luckily for me, New York is also a place that draws forward thinking artists and activists, some of them with wealth and influence. And if it weren't for those sort of people, who were able to recognize my talents and my passion, I would not be writing this essay today. For those friendships and mentors, I'm forever grateful.

And those moments, which were stinging and disappointing were ultimately useful. It was good to see through the glass clearly and understand my true self and my desires, as well as the self that I needed to project into this urban domain I inhabited in order to survive and to allay the inherited fears of the gatekeepers. And with that type of enhanced vision, I was in a far better position to paint what I wanted on the canvas of my life, make my way through the maze, and see the big picture.

I was more than an identity group, a collection of experiences filtered through the legacy of slavery, a stew of DNA forcibly planted in the archipelago. I was a chameleon, equipped with the wisdom to survive in any urban jungle we happened to find ourselves. An eternal navigator of the shifting sands of global commerce and politics makes one skilled at rooting out the human factor in every polarized situation.

Life as an urban nomad is challenging, but refreshing. It reminds that we live on this planet, and that wherever we end up, we are ultimately human beings, doing the best we can to thrive. The bigotry, the ignorance, the invisibility is almost always masking an intense fear of the "other." To wear the shoes of the "other" can be liberating in a different sense—we can see. We immediately see through the fear, know how it operates, recognize the ugly mask it wears, even when the bearer of the mask believes he is acting instinctively. We learn that there's a person behind that fear who is like a brittle branch, who can't bend with the wind, could never be a nomad, and could never live as deeply as our predicament has forced us to.

# PART III

## PERFORMING THE CITY: VOICES AND PRACTICES

# CHAPTER THIRTEEN

# EVERY CITY HAS A VOICE:
# PUTTING THE URBAN IN URBAN
# DIALECTOLOGY

# JOE TROTTA

Urban dialectology, a sub discipline of linguistics, arose out of the need to understand the linguistic behavior of urban residents. Urban dialects had been mostly ignored by early dialectologists since the language used in cities was felt to be chaotic, ephemeral and unpredictable because of the complex interplay of shifting immigration trends and seemingly irrelevant social variables like ethnicity, education, socioeconomic status, age, gender, etc. Despite the problems involved, studies in urban dialectology have provided interesting perspectives on city life and the urban experience; it not only informs us on linguistic variations connected to social factors, it also reflects the values, multiple identities and group memberships of city dwellers and is thus invaluable for urban theorists in understanding the complexion and social mechanics of a city.

However, as the first studies of urban dialectology proved their usefulness, it became clear that its approach to language was not only limited to the city, but rather was applicable in almost any communicative situation, thus downplaying the urban factor and evolving into the broader field of sociolinguistics. Against this background, the present study examines the questions: what elements play a part in the creation of an urban dialect? What makes urban areas unique in studying dialect phenomena? And finally, what is so urban about urban dialects?

I have a fancy that every city has a voice. Each one has something to say to
the one who can hear it. (O. Henry)

# The Voice on the Map

Traditionally speaking, dialectology was a self-contained branch of
linguistics whose primary aims were to correlate dialect variations with
geographical locations, thus it could be seen as a type of dialect geography
(in accordance with the term as it is used by Chambers & Trudgill 1998)
with an emphasis on the physical charting of dialect features into actual
maps. In this approach, which necessarily focused on relatively conservative
speakers and stable linguistic features, rural speech represented pure,
unadulterated, "genuine" dialects whereas the language of cities was
considered to be too complex and shifting for consideration. Furthermore,
cities and other urban areas were not systematically investigated because
many urban speakers were frustratingly inconsistent in the use of their
dialect features and appeared to vary them in apparently unpredictable
ways (so-called "free variation"); with very few exceptions, early
dialectologists simply did not have the necessary knowledge, tools or
techniques to understand and make insightful generalizations about urban
vernaculars.

When new studies of urban dialects started to gain recognition in the
1960s and 70s, primarily due to the work of ground-breaking linguists like
William Labov, new analytical tools were created involving so-called
"variationalist" methods, i.e. methods that could account for the
problematic nature of free variation and the complex make-up of speech
communities in urban areas. Labov showed that it was possible to
investigate more systematically the dialect variations found in urban
centers by proving that they were not haphazard at all but rather correlated
to social, contextual, stylistic and situational variables.

Though urban areas were clearly in focus for these early studies, there
was (and still is) a peculiar terminological dilemma involved in so-called
urban dialectology (henceforward also referred to as UD). Whereas
traditional dialectology is very much about geographical location and
dialect features, urban dialectology, despite its name, is only ostensibly
about urban locations. UD was, of course, a necessary advance in tackling
the problem of describing and analyzing linguistic phenomena in the city
and it represented a major shift in theoretical assumptions and
methodology. However, on closer inspection, nothing about UD
(historically or at the present moment) situates it exclusively in urban
areas. In other words, though it is well-suited in understanding the

complex nature of communicative behavior in urban areas it can be (and is) just as successfully applied to non-urban areas (cf. Britain 2009). In this sense, UD is more or less a synonym for what most people today would refer to as *sociolinguistics*, the study of language in which speech variations are understood in relation to social variables, style and situation, among others.

## Locating the Urbanity in Urban Dialectology

Against the above background, the present work is mainly a qualitative discussion of some of the most salient assumptions and practices of urban dialectology with a specific emphasis on situating these in the urban world; it attempts to spell out the reasons why urban areas have been important for linguistic studies while asking the question "what is so important about urban dialects and what is 'urban' about urban dialectology"? Alongside these issues, it also touches upon some micro-level questions such as "how does a city map itself onto us linguistically"? And, conversely, "how do individuals (with various group and subcultural memberships) map themselves linguistically onto their urban identities"?

Within the context of this volume, this work illustrates how the discipline of linguistics deals with issues concerning the complexities of urban life, the verbal behavior associated with it, how behavior can be disseminated from it, and how these issues have become central elements in the study of sociolinguistics.

## At the Intersection of Urban Studies and Linguistics

As readers of this collection will be well aware, urban studies (US) is something of an umbrella term and there are a number of different research traditions that participate in the discursive space that US provides. Scholars in this area may draw on the conceptual units, analytical tools and methodologies of many disciplines, including (but not exclusively), urban planning/development, ethnology, economics, architecture, ecology, anthropology, transportation and infrastructure studies, politics, sociology, history, media studies, literary theory and so on. However, whatever the angle of approach, urban studies focus on making sense of the urban world, unraveling its intricacies by scrutinizing its structures, functions, problems, trends as well as the practices of its inhabitants.

Urban dialectology is, at least nominally, an area that could easily be subsumed under this same umbrella, but few studies make explicit reference to the relevance of the urban setting to the dialect under investigation. Naturally, sociolinguistics and urban dialectology have contributed significantly to the understanding of linguistic practices in cities, but if urban dialectology is to properly contribute to urban studies, it should, to my mind, ideally include the special relation that obtains from a dialect being physically sited in an urban area. In other words, it is all well and good to study, say, code-switching, accommodation or linguistic identity as urban phenomena, but what is it about the interrelation of said phenomena and urban life that differentiates their manifestation here from other environments? What is it about urban life that creates the prerequisites for specific linguistic behaviors?[1]

With this context in mind, research that truly emphasizes urban dialectology in relation to urban studies would be broad in scope, investigating language as its starting point, but necessarily including factors such as identity, public "face," and the urban-sited perspective. Borrowing from the methods of ethnography, this would necessarily involve understanding, at a minimum, the following elements and interactions (modified below from Rampton 2007):

- *individuals*: their motivations, their sensibilities and worldviews; their cultural and linguistic repertoires; their habitual practices and dispositions; their likes, dislikes, commitments, and personalities; their social status and category memberships;
- *situated encounters*: the events and types of activities in which people interact together; actions, routines and the use of semiotic materials (signs, language, texts, media); interpretations, implicatures and the efforts of participants to understand or influence each other; the physical location and organization of the participants; how verbal behavior, actions and encounters fit with interactional and institutional processes over longer and broader stretches of time and space;
- *identities, networks and communities of practice*: varying in scope from e.g. the playground to clubs to schools, mass media and government policy: how linguistic identities, dialects, etc., get shaped, sustained, and reproduced through texts, objects, media, genres and practices, etc.; how individual and group identities influence linguistic behavior and contribute to specific discursive practices and the linguistic embodiment of shared life

---

[1] We know, to take just one example, that ethnic background can be relevant in urban areas, does this differ, and if so how, from the influence of ethnic background in non-urban areas?

worlds as well as the subsequent representations of those linguistic features.

In this approach, individuals, encounters and networks are intensely intersected and interrelated; they engage in a hermeneutic dynamic in which understanding any one element contributes to understand the whole and vice versa. The situated encounter is particularly important since it is here that what is uniquely contributed by the urban setting can be taken into account. The relevant communicative practices are established in these situated encounters, which in turn create and reinforce group memberships and (sub) cultural identities; these identities then produce and solidify the typical discursive behaviors, dialect features and linguistic repertoires of the group, which in turn are regularly mediated and supported through the encounters.[2]

# All Roads Lead to the Urban Hub?

Considering the range and geographical distribution of languages, language varieties and dialects, and considering that the above mentioned interplay of individuals, encounters and networks is not exclusive to urban life, one could reasonably ask why cities and urban areas should be so significant in the study of language. The remainder of this section sketches out, point-by-point but in no specific order, the factors that make urban areas important not only for the study of dialects, but also for linguistics in general.

# Population

Consider the following statistics taken from the *Population Reference Bureau*:

The world has experienced unprecedented urban growth in recent decades. In 2008, for the first time, the world's population was evenly split between urban and rural areas. There were more than 400 cities over 1 million and 19 over 10 million. More developed nations were about 74 percent urban,

---

[2] These interrelations resemble a mutual feedback dynamic, the significance of which is discussed below in connection with diffusion models.

while 44 percent of residents of less developed countries lived in urban areas.[3] (*Human Population: Urbanization*, n.d., online)

This fact alone makes the urban environment extremely interesting for any linguistic study; in the UK, for example, the figure is roughly 90% at the time of this writing, in Germany it is 88%, the USA 80%, France 76%, and Spain 76%. With these selected countries representing major world languages, how can one avoid urban dialects in describing and understanding them?

## The City as a Center of Knowledge and Power

The city typically embodies a culture of expertise, knowledge, economic power and cultural influence and people who live and work in city centers are usually highly educated and highly skilled. In urban areas there is typically an array of universities, financial centers, government organizations and major cultural institutions all in relatively close proximity. As a result, city residents typically include relatively large numbers of students and professionals, as well as leaders in business, finance, academia, and the arts, who form networks and alliances to run the major cultural institutions of society.

Many new innovations, inventions, technologies, trends, academic paradigms, etc., will invariably be described and articulated first from urban centers, occasionally leaving the fingerprint of the urban on them. In addition, the very fact some urban dialect variants are associated with key literary texts, cultural traditions or respected individuals from influential groups (take for example, the so-called Oxbridge dialect of South-East England, the French of upper-class Parisians, or the Florence dialect in Italy) will bestow a certain prestige to these forms and thus they can readily serve as models for codification in textbooks and consequently become targets for imitation by others.

## Employment and the Linguistic Marketplace in Urban Areas

Cities generally offer more and better employment opportunities than other areas and certain types of jobs exist only in urban areas. When

---

[3] A precise definition of what constitutes an "urban area" is not given by this resource, however the numbers and locations used here are not controversial and do not need a rigorous definition to be useful in this context.

people need to relocate to cities for the purposes of employment, they encounter market pressures to conform to the standardized speech of urban professionals (see Chambers 2009: 190-197). Hence they will accommodate or remodel their language use to show awareness of and respect for the linguistic norms of the workplace, which in turn are influenced by the dialect and speech of the relevant urban area.

## Diversity and Multiculturalism in the Urban World

Urban areas are where diversity and multiculturalism are mainly concentrated, giving urban areas a rich variety of social, cultural, and religious traditions. Cities provide a space for new immigrant families and their second-generation children who typically identify both with their cultural background as well as their new national and urban identities. In the US in particular, city residents, no matter how far removed they are from their immigrant roots, often identify with and see themselves as members of well-established categories of ethnicity or ancestry (e.g. Irish, Italian, Jewish, African-American), and this is still a factor in the social networks and neighborhood structure of the city.[4]

In this connection, there has been a great deal of research in recent years on so-called heteroglossic speech as examples of stylized performances of identity.[5] Such behavior is particularly noticeable in US cities (in, e.g., the Hispanic residents of Los Angeles, Miami, New York or the African-American speakers of Baltimore, New York and Atlanta, to name only a few), but this is far from a strictly American or even an English-speaking phenomenon. Other world metropolises, such as Berlin (with its *Kiezdeutsch*), Amsterdam (with *Straattaal*), Oslo (with *Jallanorsk*) and Paris (with Arabic-influenced or multicultural French) have witnessed the same phenomenon. For present purposes, so-called "Rinkeby Swedish," which originated in the greater Stockholm area of Sweden, can serve as a representative example. The dialect is clearly Swedish, but with strong features of immigrant language; it signals not only ethnic difference but

---

[4] For example, the impact of immigration and ethnic diversity on the stereotypical New York dialect has been enormous and influential; the "oi" pronunciation of the stigmatized "thoity thoid street" (*thirty-third street*), the "aw" pronunciation of "cawfee" and "tawk" (*coffee* and *talk*) along with the "dese" and "dose" of *these* and *those* are all contributions from previous waves of immigration from Irish, Italian, Jewish and Dutch immigrants.

[5] The term *heteroglossia* in this context is meant to cover not only the language of multilingual immigrants, but also the coexistence of distinct varieties, such as African-American Vernacular English (or AAVE), within a single linguistic code.

also carries covert prestige through an identification with otherness, outsiderness and, in some contexts, masculinity and male toughness (for further discussion, see Milani & Jonsson 2012).

Because of the semiotic potential of such immigrant dialects (sometimes referred to as multiethnolects, see Jaspers 2011 and Rampton 2011), other ethnicities and even non-migrant peers may imitate this dialect using it as a source of symbolic capital. This kind of dialect appropriation, or incorporation of dialectal features into one's routine register, has been a salient issue in sociolinguistic research. In such work, the focus is often placed on the attempts of young white speakers to use these non-standard dialects as ways of showing identity and rebelliousness against mainstream society or as a way of associating themselves with gang culture or popular culture in general (see e.g. Auer and Dirim 2003; Bucholtz 1999; Cutler 1999; Hewitt 1986; Nortier and Dorleijn 2008; Rampton 1995).

These appropriations of multiethnolects and non-standard dialects are most typically attributed to young people, so much so that they are often described as "youth language" (cf. Rampton 2011; Quist 2008). It is surely no coincidence that this speech style is more commonly evidenced among young people, but as the next section shows, a more important factor in these stylizations is their role in the performance of (linguistic) identity.

## Identity: "You are Here" on the Urban Map

For many people, urban areas are places of transformation and self-discovery. Whereas identity has traditionally been realized through one's role in the family and community, modern and postmodern culture typically encourages individuality, mobility and self-actualization. The urban environment, with its relative anonymity and looser ties to community and family, can free individuals to create their own identities and achieve their own significance. Consequently, many people move to cities, either temporarily or permanently, to work out who they are and explore the lifestyles and subcultures with which they have had no direct contact in their birthplace.

So far, I have only mentioned identity as an important variable in the communicative practices of heteroglossic discourse communities. However, linguistic identity is a more influential and pervasive force and it has many other consequences for the language of urban residents. The main principle of linguistic identity stems from the work of LePage & Tabouret-Keller in their "acts of identity" theory and stated succinctly is when "the individual creates for himself [sic] the patterns of his [sic] linguistic behavior so as to resemble those of the groups with which from time to time he [sic] wishes to be identified or so as to be unlike those from whom he [sic] wishes to be distinguished" (1985: 181).

A full examination of linguistic identity is beyond the scope of the present study, but two short examples show the basic gist of the principle. Labov's 1961 classic study of the dialect used on Martha's Vineyard showed that a small group of fishermen began to adjust their pronunciations in a (presumably subconscious) attempt to establish themselves as an independent social group with superior status to the despised summer visitors. In turn, other residents imitated the fisherman to identify themselves as true islanders. In this case, the identity was a reaction against urban residents; it signaled a distancing from the lifestyle of the city dwellers who were tourists in their village (see Labov 1963).

In another case, Preisler (1999), found English (in particular, non-standard English) to be an important status symbol in some Danish subcultures such as hip-hoppers, death metal fans and computer nerds. The motivation of learning and using this variety of English is the desire to identify with the subculture and to find peer group solidarity. Even if the sub group consists of Danish boys only, Preisler found frequent code-switching to be a speech style which marks superior status within the group.

Thus, using one's linguistic repertoire to establish or reinforce an identity can be achieved through standard prestige dialects as well through the use of stigmatized variants. Depending on one's profession, background, ethnicity, etc., one may shift seamlessly across a number of identities, either to signal convergence and solidarity with a particular allegiance or group membership or to demonstrate disapproval or distancing from it. The urban setting is a vital element in understanding what identities can be enacted, why they are relevant and how they are performed; e.g. an Irish identity can manifest itself and make one kind of sense in the context of, say Boston or New York, but in different ways with different effects in London or Bombay.

## Urban Areas as Centers of Entertainment and Media

Cities, especially large ones, are typical centers of the entertainment industry, e.g. TV, film and the print media, among others. Aside from being areas in which entertainment is produced for consumption outside the city, urban areas themselves also offer their own diversions, entertainments and attractions for residents as well as tourists. The relationship between cities and entertainment has three relevant dimensions for linguistic behavior:

1. the city draws to it both occasional and regular visitors, enabling an exposure to the dialect and allowing the crucial element of language contact to occur;
2. city life is regularly portrayed in popular culture, often making the cities themselves key elements in the narrative;[6] and
3. because of points 1 and 2, cities have the potential to act as channels of diffusion for urban dialects and the language innovations which stem from and are associated with the city.

## Diffusion Models: We Map the City, then the City Maps Us

Urban areas are, therefore, unique spaces, which provide the prerequisites that make them centers of linguistic creativity as well as models for imitation. The following covers a few conceptualizations of linguistic diffusion that emphasize the importance of urban areas, not only as sources of innovations, but also as vital links in transmitting change through a speech community.

## The Gravity Model

As early as the 19th century, some linguists had entertained the notion that language change might spread in waves from a center of innovation, an idea (known as the "wave" theory) that is at the base of many models of the spread of linguistic changes (see Wolfram & Schilling-Estes 2003: 721; Labov 2001: 285; Haynes & Fotheringham 1984). Trudgill (1974) improved on this model by suggesting the use of a so-called "gravity" model, which, drawing on a metaphorical comparison to the Newtonian laws of gravity, had been used previously by social scientists to understand

---

[6] A list here would be subjective and extremely lengthy, but using New York as an example, it could include immensely popular TV shows like *Friends, Seinfeld, Sex and the City, Law and Order*, not to mention innumerable films such as *Taxi Driver, The French Connection, Manhattan* (or any number of Woody Allen films), *Do the Right Thing, Saturday Night Fever*, which all feature New York City as a major plot device. Interestingly, even the fictional home of many superheroes like Spiderman, Superman, and Batman, is literally or metaphorically understood as New York; this too gives the city an almost magical, supernatural quality that is disseminated through the stories.

the relative "pull" of certain areas in analyzing demographic trends and the distribution of information and goods. In the gravity model, population size (in correlation with socioeconomic strength) acts as an attractor in a network of influence; larger places have a greater attraction than smaller places and places closer together have a greater attraction than places which are isolated. With the proper understanding of these factors, a predictive formula can be devised to interpret and anticipate the movement of people, ideas, information, and commodities between cities and even continents.

In a typical case, a linguistic innovation spreads down the urban hierarchy from a large population center directly to another of intermediate size, often skipping over smaller, geographically neighboring sites. From there, it disseminates to even smaller areas, then to smaller ones still, and so on. This seems to indicate that each city, town, village has its own sphere of influence and the linguistic behavior within it is best studied with respect to the locally influential center (cf. Anderwald & Szmrecsanyi 2009; Chambers & Trudgill 1998: 197-202; Labov 2001: 285). The model is not exceptionless, however, and arguments have been raised for the need to integrate social-psychological factors (e.g. attitudes towards the urban centers in question) and structural-linguistic factors, i.e. how potential changes from one area may disturb or conflict with the system in the area on which it should exert influence (cf. Taeldeman 2005).

## The Effect of Popular Culture

Despite the prevalence of potential urban language influence through the media, the effect of Popular Culture on language use is a contested area. Few would dispute that conscious adjustments in linguistic behavior can result from media influence, e.g. the intentional use of vocabulary one has encountered in films, TV, the internet, etc. However, in the received wisdom of mainstream sociolinguistics, the effect of the media on "real," deep-seated language change is minimal. The main tenet, repeated in research articles and textbooks, is that language change primarily takes place through face-to-face interaction (dialect contact), and though the media may influence vocabulary, it does not affect core features of language, e.g. pronunciation and grammar; in other words,"[…] at the deeper reaches of language change—sound changes and grammatical changes—the media have no significant effect at all" (Chambers 1998: 124; Trudgill 1986; see also *Do you speak American?* n.d, online). Additionally, in line with this view, the broadcast media may increase awareness of linguistic varieties and/or affect attitudes towards other varieties (e.g. Milroy and Milroy 1985), but if features of grammar are affected, this results from voluntary orientation towards media and conscious copying from media models (Trudgill 1986; Carvalho 2004).

If the media in general are assumed to affect other social behaviors (see, for example, McQuail 2005; Klapper 1960: 8; Abercrombie 1996; Philo 1999), then why should Popular Culture phenomena be an exception to this? The question is vast and worthy of investigation in its own right and cannot be duly examined within the limits of the present study. For present purposes, this issue can remain unsettled, since the conscious adjustment of language toward media representations of dialects is more than sufficient for the points at hand. It is interesting to note, however, that several recent studies, such as Stuart-Smith (1999, 2005, 2007), Muhr (2003), Carvalho (2004) and Trotta (2003, 2010, 2011) have been challenging the claim that broadcast media do not influence language change significantly. What such studies are showing is that one must take into account the level of engagement that speakers can have with TV programs, films, music artists, etc. If the level is sufficiently high in combination with attitudes towards social groupings and issues of identity construction (Eckert 2000), it could constitute a type of language contact that may affect not only vocabulary, but also other elements of language use (cf. Stuart-Smith 2005; Carvalho 2004).

## Mutual Feedback

As a final model for the possible influence of urban areas on dialects in general, let's examine the notion of linguistic mutual feedback (from Trotta 1997) as a viable model in supplementing wave and gravity theories of diffusion, while at the same time taking into account the possible influence of Popular Culture and the media. Consider the relations in Figure 13-1:

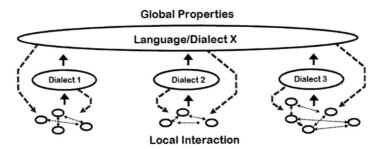

Fig. 13-1. The mutual feedback model (from Trotta 1997)

The underlying idea of this model is that the output of the local interaction, i.e. the situated verbal interaction of individuals, results in a linguistic epiphenomenon on different levels,[7] one level being particular dialects (1, 2 and 3 in Fig. 13-1) and another level being the language or super dialect to which 1, 2 and 3 belong. These dialects can be understood in terms of regions, e.g. the dialects of New York, Philadelphia and Boston; they could also be understood in terms of different ethnic or social dialects in the same speech community, e.g. Brooklynese, Oxbridge, Cockney, Rinkeby Swedish, and so on. They could also, for example, be understood in terms of supra-regional dialects such as African-American Vernacular English, i.e. Dialect 1 could be Los Angeles AAVE; Dialect 2 could represent Chicago AAVE; and Dialect 3 could be NYC AAVE.

In this model, the output of individuals does not only serve to shape a particular dialect; if these dialects have an established status as indicators of a particular group, they can feed back (the shaded downward arrows in Fig. 13-1) to the level of local interaction and function as a kind of 'attractor' which affects the linguistic choices of individuals. For example, an urban dialect such as say, New York English, is the result of the aggregate linguistic behavior of individual New Yorkers; once associated with that specific location or the perceived typical qualities of people from that location, it then becomes not only a dialect but it acquires symbolic capital and usefulness as a tool in signaling and reinforcing one's identity (or attitude to one's identity), and as such determines to some extent what one can or cannot say in order to align oneself with the received linguistic stereotypes of that group.[8]

---

[7] For the sake of simplicity, the figure only illustrates two levels, but a far more sophisticated figure is not difficult to imagine.
[8] Naturally, I am not claiming or implying that African-Americans must use AAVE to assert ethnicity.

If such a relationship obtains for some geographically non-contiguous speech communities, then the model predicts that these dialects should logically be able to exert an influence on each other regardless of the fact that there is little or no face-to-face social contact between speakers of the different dialects. This prediction presupposes the following conditions: (i) that widely accessed, popular media, e.g. television, film, radio, etc., provide opportunities for the relevant features to feedback to individuals across regions and (ii) that there is a strong enough reason for individuals to use these features as a guide in their linguistic productions and (iii) they are sufficiently engaged with the Popular Culture phenomenon in question to accept it as a model for imitation.

## Pulling it All Together: Final Notes and Comments

The need to understand the intricacies of urban dialects forced necessary changes in the theory and methods of dialectology and gave birth to present-day sociolinguistics. However well sociolinguistic research helps us understand the nature of verbal interaction in the city environment, the urbanity of urban dialects is still largely an underrepresented element in the work of most sociolinguists, general linguists and urban studies scholars as well. If the study of urban dialects is to help us understand them as situated specifically in the unique mix of any particular urban area, then more emphasis needs to be put on what that specific urban area actually brings to the table in creating and influencing specific linguistic behaviors.

In the discussion above, I have endeavored to map out, however sketchily, the significance of urban areas in the study of linguistics. I have made assumptions and connections using conceptual units, theoretical constructs and categories that are not watertight and a great deal of overlap is possible between two or several of these notions; for example, identity can easily converge with multiculturalism, population correlates with cultural and economic power, and so on. However, it is exactly this kind of complex interplay and overlap that makes the city a fascinating space of potentiality, and it is its multiple voices and what they tell us that makes it invaluable for urban scholars and linguistics alike.

## Bibliography

Auer, P., & Dirim, I. (2003). "Socio-cultural orientation, urban youth styles and the spontaneous acquisition of Turkish by non-Turkish adolescents in Germany" in J. Androutsopoulos & A. Georgakopoulou (eds.), *Discourse Constructions of Youth Identities* Amsterdam/ Philadelphia: John Benjamins, 223-246.

Abercrombie, N. (1996). *Television and Society*, Cambridge: Polity.

Anderwald, L., & Szmrecsanyi, B. (2009). "Corpus Linguistics and Dialectology" in *Corpus Linguistics: An International Handbook. Handbücher zur Sprache und Kommunikationswissenschaft/ Handbooks of Linguistics and Communication Science. Berlin/New York: Mouton de Gruyter.* http://www.benszm.net/omnibuslit/Ander wald_Szmrecsanyi_HSK_webversion.pdf

Britain, David J. (2009.) "'Big Bright Lights' Versus 'Green and Pleasant Land'? The Unhelpful Dichotomy of 'Urban' versus 'Rural' in Dialectology" in Brill, L. (ed.), *Arabic Dialectology: Studies in Semitic Languages and Linguistics* (53). 223-248.

Bucholtz, M. (1999). "You da Man: Narrating the Racial Other in the Production of White Masculinity" in *Journal of Sociolinguistics*, 3(4), 443-460.

Carvalho, A.M. (2004). "I Speak Like the Guys on TV: Palatalization and the Urbanization of Uruguayan Portuguese" in *Language, Variation and Change*, 16, 127-51.

Chambers, J. K. (1998). "TV Makes People Sound the Same" in L. Bauer and P. Trudgill (eds.), *Language Myths*, New York: Penguin, 123-31.

Chambers, J. K. (2009). *Sociolinguistic Theory: Linguistic Variation and its Social Significance.* Chichester, U.K.; Malden, MA: Blackwell.

Chambers, J. K., & Trudgill, P. (1998). *Dialectology.* Cambridge, New York: Cambridge University Press.

Cutler, C. (1999). "Yorkville Crossing: White Teens, Hip Hop and African American English" in *Journal of Sociolinguistics*, 3(4), 428-442.

Do You Speak American. What Lies Ahead? Media Power. Media|PBS. (n.d.). Retrieved August 15, 2012, from http://www.pbs.org/ speak/ ahead/mediapower/media/

Eckert, P. (2000). *Linguistic Variation as Social Practice.* Oxford: Blackwell.

Haynes, K. E., & Fotheringham, A. S. (1984). *Gravity and Spatial Interaction Models.* Beverly Hills: Sage Publications. http://web.pdx.edu/~stipakb/download/PA557/ReadingsPA557sec1-2.pdf

Hewitt, R. (1986). *White Talk Black Talk.* Cambridge: Cambridge University Press.

Human Population: Urbanization—Population Reference Bureau. (n.d.). Retrieved September 2, 2012. http://www.prb.org/Educators/TeachersGuides/HumanPopulation/

Jaspers, J. (2011). "Strange Bedfellows: Appropriations of a Tainted Urban Dialect" in *Journal of Sociolinguistics*, *15* (4), 493–524.

Klapper, T. (1960). *The Effects of Mass Communication*, Glencoe: Free Press.

Le Page, R.B. and Tabouret-Keller, A. (1985). *Acts of Identity: Creole-Based Approaches to Language and Ethnicity*. Cambridge: Cambridge University Press.

Labov, W. (1963). The Social Motivation of a Sound Change. *Word* 19: 273-309.

—. (2001). *Principles of Linguistic Dhange. Vol. 2, Social Factors*. Oxford: Blackwell.

McQuail, D. (2005). *McQuail's Mass Communication Theory*, Fifth Edition, London: Sage.

Milani, T. M., & Jonsson, R. (2012). "Who's Afraid of Rinkeby Swedish? Stylization, Complicity, Resistance" in *Journal of Linguistic Anthropology*, *22* (1), 44–63.

Milroy, J. and Milroy, L. (1985). *Authority in Language: Investigating Language Prescription & Standardisation*, London: Routledge.

Muhr, R. (2003). "Language Change via Satellite: The Influence of German Television Broadcasting on Austrian German" in *Journal of Historical Pragmatics*, 4, 103-27.

Naro, A. and Scherre, M.M.P. (1996). "Contact with Media and Linguistic Variation" in J. Arnold, R. Blake, B. Davidson, S. Schwenter, and J. Solomon (eds.), *Sociolinguistic Variation: Data, Theory and Analysis. Selected papers from NWAV 23 at Stanford*, CSLI Publications.

Philo, G. (1999). "Children and Film/Video/TV Violence" in G. Philo (ed.), *Message received: Glasgow Media Group research 1993-1998*, London: Longman.

Nortier, J., & Dorleijn, M. (2008). "A Moroccan Accent in Dutch: A Socio-cultural Style Restricted to the Moroccan Community?" in *International Journal of Bilingualism*, 12(1,2), 125-142.

Preisler, B. (1999). "Functions and Forms of English in a European EFL Country" in T. Bex and R. J. Watts (eds.) *Standard English: the Widening Debate*, London: Routledge, 239-267.

Quist, P. (2008). "Sociolinguistic Approaches to Multiethnolect: Language Variety and Stylistic Practice" in *International Journal of Bilingualism* 12 (1 & 2): 43-61.

Rampton, B. (1995). *Crossing: Language and Ethnicity Among Adolescents*. London: Longman.

—. (2007). "Linguistic Ethnography, Interactional Sociolinguistics and the Study of Identities" in *Investigating Language in Action: Tools for Analysis*. *Milton Keynes, UK: Open University*. http://www.kcl.ac.uk/projects/ldc/LDCPublications/workingpapers/43. pdf

—. (2011). "From Multi-ethnic Adolescent Heteroglossia to Contemporary Urban Vernaculars" in *Language & Communication*. http://www.sciencedirect.com/science/article/pii/S0271530911000024

Stuart-Smith, J. (1999). "Glasgow: Accent and Voice Quality" in P. Foulkes and G. Docherty (eds.), *Urban Voices*, London: Arnold, 203-222.

—. (2005). "Is TV a Contributory Factor in Accent Change in Adolescents?" Final Report on ESRC Grant No. R000239757.

—. (2007). "The Influence of Media on Language" in C. Llamas, P. Stockwell and L. Mullany (eds.), *The Routledge Companion to Sociolinguistics*, London: Routledge. http://www.arts.gla.ac.uk/SESLL/EngLang/phonetics/

Taeldeman, J. (2005). "The Influence of Urban Centres on the Spatial Difusion of Dialect Phenomena" in P. Auer, F. Hinskens & P. Kerswill (eds.), *Dialect Change: Convergence and Divergence in European Languages*. Cambridge: Cambridge University Press, 263–283.

Trotta, J. (1997). "Ethnolinguistic Identity in Non-standard Metropolitan New York Dialects" in H. Lindquist, S. Klintborg, M. Levin & M. Estling (eds.). *The Major Varieties of English. Papers from MAVEN 97*, Växjö: Acta Wexionensis.

—. (2003). "Bada-Bing! Looking at Language in *The Sopranos*". *Moderna Språk*, XCVII, 17-36.

—. (2010). "Whose Rules Rule?: Grammar Controversies, Popular Culture and the Fear of English from Below." *Nordic Journal of English Studies*, 9 (3), 41-65.

—. (2011). "Game Done Changed: A look at selected AAVE features in the TV series The Wire." *Moderna Språk*. 105 (1), 15-42.

Trudgill, P. (1974). *The Social Differentiation of English in Norwich*. Cambridge: Cambridge University Press.

Trudgill, P. (1986). *Dialects in Contact*, Oxford: Blackwell.

Wolfram, W., & Schilling-Estes, N. (2003). "Dialectology and Linguistic Diffusion" in B. Joseph and R. Janda (eds.), *The Handbook of Historical Linguistics*, Oxford: Blackwell, 713-35.

# Chapter Fourteen

# Flambeau:
# Orality as Reflexive Flame
# of New Orleans

# Ronald Dorris

The interdisciplinary field of American Studies, among other approaches, fosters examination of cultural and intellectual history—the impact of ideas on our lives, and how the populace attempts to introduce counter ideas to offset aspects of social control. American Studies augments examination of Urban Studies, given the United States was ushered onto the world stage as an urban nation by 1920 when 52 % of the population lived in cities. This development gave rise to myriad voices that continue to sound the various notes of life that serve as signature for the intersection of urban culture in the context of ethnic inclusion in the United States.

This essay recounts how New Orleans, as a cosmopolitan city, generates its sound via orality. The investigation shows how command of the spoken word has been passed on from generation to generation to empower inhabitants with a sense of identity and purpose when economic and political power has not been forthcoming. In New Orleans orality continues to link the people with the past as they reach to the future in the Everlasting Present, given their interest in perpetuating life in a circular as opposed to a linear frame of reference.

To touch the pulse of a city, one must hear its sound; one must hear its heartbeat—the drum, dance and song that signs its signature. In traditional African societies, the heart is a drum that beats the dance of a song. How does one hear a city like New Orleans, Louisiana, an urban land space that since 1712 when founded has retained a large presence of people of African descent, and who have attempted to offset control of their lives as politically they have been defined on the basis of race as a social construct? Here, I examine how in New Orleans cultural and intellectual history relative to place, people and performance is reinforced and sustained by orality in continual command and exchange among the people.

In *Africans in Colonial Louisiana* Gwendolyn Midlo Hall informs that under initial French rule, and given the 13 slave ships brought to Louisiana from 1726-1731, all but one of these came from Senegambia, which contributed to Louisiana being highly Africanized (Hall 1992: 34). Such a close-knit body of people from Africa sustained their sense of well-being, history and family and ancestral ties in oral discourse which continues to this day. Thrown in with marginal peoples who in Europe had been kidnapped for a New World labor arrangement as well, the Africans were on their own in generating language usage, and therefore executed performance that enabled them to speak the truth to educate.

Given its water outlets to the Gulf of Mexico, and proximity to the Caribbean, Mexico, Central, Latin and South America, for three hundred years New Orleans has projected a cosmopolitan setting and flavor. Initially, New Orleans was the domicile of Native Americans, Africans, French, Spanish, Swedish, Austrian, Belgian, Italian, and Irish inhabitants, among others. Since the 1700s, family names such as Cola, Doré, Gonzales, Senegal and Schexnayder remain on the Louisiana registry.

Europeans in New Orleans were surrounded by scores of people of African descent, who immediately began to seek their recognition by sounding a call for redress of their captivity. Drummers in maroon enclaves in the surrounding swamps, and in Congo Square, the center of cultural New Orleans, were inspired by grapevine news filtering in from the Atlantic corridor. Across the water from Florida, on the island of Hispaniola, African slaves began to engage in armed struggle in 1791. By 1803 they had captured the western half of the island and declared Haiti an independent republic. Now a nation politically defined as *black* was on the doorsteps of the United States, and the government was concerned with Louisiana being peopled by whom congressmen designated as a "polyglot nation of half-breeds," and feared Africans could form an alliance with Haiti (*American Historical Review* 22, 1917: 235). Thus the U.S. decided secretly to buy Louisiana. Although all of Louisiana (828,000 square miles) was purchased in 1803, the present site land mass was not granted statehood until 1812 when Congress had a sense of assurance that the polyglot half-breeds would embrace being politically defined as *white.*

Given slaves from Africa were still being transported after the Louisiana Purchase, the mixed population of New Orleans continued to be immersed and reinforced in oral history. Hence keepers of the flame, descendants among the communal collective in New Orleans, have preserved cultural and intellectual history through the power of the WORD. Messages have been passed down through proverbs, story-telling, visual art, and drum, dance and song, among other forms of expression. Without waiting for technology to be invented, spared from catastrophe, or restored in the aftermath of disaster, inhabitants in New Orleans continue to transcend adversity to get the message through by sending up an oral call in life and the arts, and waiting for an oral response. For example, when the people feel there is injustice emanating from police brutality, they issue a public call for redress, generally answered by a preacher and/or social activist who answer by helping the multitude to shape the response by "taking it to the street." The sound of the call as protest melds into the response as communal celebration for redress once singing and dancing is added.

When printed material is not available and/or is destroyed, culture is not arrested if the intellectual base of a people is rooted in oral history. Life continues *ad infinitum.* Orality sustains the culture because people continue to talk, and ritual sustains the talk, which is transmitted and performed. In this respect, New Orleans is in the forefront of cultural and intellectual history whereby "individual subjects tend to be both distinctly themselves, and members of generational cohorts with characteristic assumptions, values, and patterns for communication" (Chandler 2005: 48). Hence oral culture is produced, maintained, repaired, and transformed to allow participants to sit in communion each with the other because "subjectivity evolves as a dynamic entity shaped by complex interactions among dominant cultural discourses as scripts, local variants of those scripts and individual psychological and social experiences within a particular social context" (49). This is important to sounding the voice of the city among those who seek a sense of belonging when economic and political power does not seem forthcoming.

Historically, before the invention of technology to advance transmission, citizens relied on the spoken word to participate in the affairs of the city-state, and needed to be within walking range of social activity to participate. From a knock on the door at City Hall to a jazz funeral on the way to the cemetery, inhabitants in New Orleans *take-it-to-the-street,* where what matters is the spoken word. "Throw me something, mister," sounded by revelers reaching for beads tossed from Mardi Gras floats, refers to *lagniappe* (a little something extra in life). New Orleans cultural and intellectual history is replete with entertainment in order to teach by way of oral traditions.

In fact, the African fabric of New Orleans has remained constant despite the political change of hands—from French, to Spanish, and then to the United States. The Africanized population consisted during the colonial 1700s of large numbers of slaves and free blacks—*les gens de coleur*. Documentation and advertisement in various legal documents and newspapers about those who ran away confirm a number of people of African descent could speak five languages—Wolof, French, Spanish, English and Creole. Unlike English common law, under French civil law governed by the Napoleonic code, the *Code Noir* drafted at Versailles in March 1685 stipulated no child designated a slave could be sold from their parent(s) under the age of 10, nor could slaves be worked past age 65 and had to be cared for and put to other use (*Code Noir* 1685). To augment this base of operation, Catholicism was the only religion sanctioned in colonial Louisiana (Baudier 1939: 41). Hence language and religion served to account for New Orleans being sustained as a highly Africanized open culture.

Orality in New Orleans is sounded and reinforced by voices emanating from a mixed population. Among these voices is a language pattern referred to as Black Speech. Antonio Brown in "Performing "Truth": Black Speech Arts," declares, "I posit that the form of "truth" asserted by the invocation of Black Speak is based in the sense of community evoked by and attributed to the cultural/communicative form. Black Speech communicates a "truth" by infusing its messages with the linguistic style that formulates and informs cultural identities and communities" (Brown 2002: 213). Brown further informs that "For those individuals whose daily demands require a reliance on 'mainstream,' standardized speech acts, the purposeful invocation of Black Speak can be a powerful statement about identity, community, connectedness to the counter/alternative culture, and the oration as well as the perception of a 'truth'" (214).

Orality generating response relative to context can be aligned with theory advanced by George Brandon in *Santeria from Africa to the New World: The Dead Sell Memories*. He informs that "To get a better understanding of collective memory we will have to study acts that transfer memory and keep the images memory contains circulating within the group, for it is these acts that make it possible for a tradition to persist and for a group to have a common memory" (Brandon 1993: 143). If we take the position that the function of orality is central to personal memory, we may declare from Brandon's perspective that "events successfully evoked come located in a context in which the persons, places, things, and events gained their meaning. Personal memory is also concerned with the self that was involved in the past events as well as the self that is recalling these events in the present" (130).

Culture thrives on permanence and change; hence spontaneity never is ruled out. Parallelism also is central to orality, involving systematically repeated elements of language: sounds, grammar, meaning and/or structure. We can get a sense of the spontaneity of language as performance by referencing Michelle Rosaldo's case study on the Ilongots of the northern Philippines who traditionally value oratory and a speech style regarded as "crooked language," rich in art, wit, and indirection in certain situations. When using crooked language, the Ilongots say they hide behind the wit and beauty of their words. "Straight speech," they say, is speech equal to one's fellow-equal-to me-man, and is forthright, open, sincere and kind" (Rosaldo 1973: 197-98).

Similar to the Ilongot, people descended from the inaugural inhabitant base of New Orleans speak in "degrees" and with "local color." In addition to music, this command of language continues to sound a powerful note that is New Orleans, and which enables us to hear the city as sound. When speaking in the *first degree* to address something negative being advanced against someone an adversary wants to victimize, the response would be, "Don't do me nuttin." The warning is issued to the adversary to back off because they (he/she) already have (has) struck out, given that two negatives have been sounded, "don't-do-nuttin." Should the adversary continue to be negative, the *second degree* declares, 'Don't do me nuttin', no." These three negatives confirm that a warning has been issued to cover every direction of the universe. The *third degree*, "Don't do me nuttin', no, yeah," comes with action. The three warnings and one positive means that yes, the adversary was told to behave, and yes the adversary has been struck with a fist, which landed in a split second before the "yeah" was uttered at the end of the sentence. In terms of conjugating a verb that connotes movement, one might say, "If'n I go; if'n you go; if'n us go two gezzer." The coloring of the language in New Orleans is an art in exercise: the more color, the stronger the language; the stronger the language, the more color.

The sounding of New Orleans as local color is heard also in the way food is described. When asked what one will have for supper, the answer might be *alligator swamp water* (gumbo) *et ris* (and rice). One might choose to wash down the gumbo with *yeast and water* (beer), also referred to as *flack*, skillfully uttered as "'guzzling'" (drinking) dat flack." On another day the meal might consist of *bullets* (red beans) and rice.

The experience of movers and shakers in sounding the cultural and intellectual history of New Orleans is cloaked in "primary orality" which, according to work by Walter J. Ong, is a culture untouched by reading and writing. Ong calls attention to several characteristics of "oral based expression" specifically devalued in writing: non-stop talk, stock phrases, connectors, and concreteness. Ong frames non-stop talk as repetition and redundancy, the orator's ability to talk without hesitations, long pauses, while thinking on his feet is highly valued (Ong 2002: 31-40).

One who demonstrates non-stop pattern of communication is accorded the honor of being a master of signing their signature with their speech. Today this is carried on in a form of art referred to as *rap*. Ong frames stock phrases, word clusters and formulas as writing, which highlights "clichés." In New Orleans one could be heard saying, "Don't be pushin' up on me, no, yeah, now, 'fo I finger yah fine width ah poke in dah eye." Ong directs attention to the originality in oral cultures as stemming from new uses of applications of traditional materials. For example, in New Orleans one might say, "I be feelin' yah," in place of the earlier, "Ah be hearin' yah." Another example would be the current phrase, "check yah later," in place of the earlier, "plant yah now, an' dig yah later."

Ong also points out how oral expression tends to connect thoughts additively through use of the word "and." New Orleans is sounded in language with connectors, particularly the phrase, "An' sho' nuff, yeah," uttered to express by the listener that they agree with the speaker without hesitation or reservation. When it comes to concreteness, Ong posits that oral expression is close to the human life world, given proverbs are full of real tangible things—peoples, animals, nature. In New Orleans, "him an' her be flip" means that both have a disposition so nasty it seems as though they were reared without home training. "The squirrel gets the rabbit" refers to the scout who has the elevated lookout post. "Mud puddle ain't got no bleach" refers to someone who has messed up so badly they cannot remove the stains from the damage done.

In New Orleans those against whom government restricted the use of written text, were not sanctioned to import information from outside their delivery, given reading and writing was outlawed under slavery. Such non-interference left people under domination in New Orleans free to strengthen orality. To this day such orators have a command of "double-speak," whereby they say one thing, but mean something else. This shields them from direct confrontation with adversaries, a practice transmitted from generation to generation.

The ability to speak well brings prestige to an individual, his family and community. In New Orleans, one of the higher compliments a speaker can receive is the pronouncement, "He speaks with his "hot" [heart] and soul." As with many other societies throughout the world, in New Orleans great orators must be in command of delivering a speech to fit the occasion. Whatever is involved—goods, services, participation relative to people, place and performance—a careful balance of give-and-take, of rights and obligations, of "basic compensation" is maintained. Orality provides a unifying bond between individual and family, community identity, people and place. It provides local color for commonplace lives. This is the fabric of sounding New Orleans. Here it is said, "if one ain't got WORD, one don't got squat."

In "Aging and Slavery: A Gerontological Perspective," Leslie J. Pollard informs: "In Africa, the elderly performed special roles and functions that continued in slavery. They were the storytellers, the advisors, the links between the past and present, and the historians of a non-literate people" (Pollard 1961: 228). For those among the governing body who wished to lessen empowerment in the hands of the populace, traditional healers were a commanding force not easily downplayed, given their contact situation was without conflict. Relative to role performance, medicine was its own call and response. Practitioners shared a common language with the people they served and was part of their world view, a course of action which holds true to this day.

Psychological healing was reinforced by drawing from fusion of the sacred and secular base. John Mbiti's description of the role of medical practitioners in Africa mirrors what once was open practice of medicine by Africans in New Orleans. Practitioners were regarded as "specialists," who could dispense the greatest gift as the most useful source of divine help. They addressed illness as partly physical and partly psychological, and applied both physical and "spiritual" (psychological) treatment. They cured the sick and warned of impending danger. They combated witchcraft and magic. Hence the medical practitioner was regarded as both healer and pastor. They took preventive measures. Although part of an underground network today, and referred to as "hoodoo" specialists, they continue to describe and explain problems encountered, and to perpetuate a course of action to deal with social concerns. Certain chants are uttered to call up good and to ward off evil spirits when practitioners dispense their potions. Patients purchasing a product may be privy to learning how to perform a certain chant.

Africans in New Orleans did not hesitate to look anew at themselves as skilled craftsmen. There was need for rice growers, indigo processors, blacksmiths, tailors, carpenters, and craftsmen who were masters of as many other professions as possible. Each sounded the music of their respective tool, the beating of the anvil by the blacksmith, the ringing of the hammer by the carpenter. Psychologically, they had to and did assess their inherent worth. The rhythm of their labor and the accompanying songs they sang to mark time and ease the burden reverberated throughout the land.

In "The Exchange Economy of the Lower Mississippi Valley," Daniel Usner informs how an exchange economy constituted the base of colonial Louisiana (Usner 1987: 166), and New Orleans was no exception. From historical records, one learns how particular negotiation with Africans set the schedule for their labor congruent with their demand relative to the worth of their service. MacDonald, Kemp and Haas echo this sense of reality:

> In city and countryside alike the organization of labor was determined by the demands of semi-tropical staple production, but the methods of work, the equipment, the pace at which it took place, and the workers' attitude towards their travail were all essentially products of the African past ... [and] produced the Africanization of the local culture. (McDonald 1979: 25)

Each tradesman placed his wares on center stage by singing of its value. For example, "Crawfish, I got crawfish, ten cents a pound." Sometimes little bells were shaken, or whistles were blown. Each sound announced a different ware for sale.

Maroon colonies established by runaway slaves amassed a body of knowledge beneficial to the whole community. They could sound messages performed on drums, which was outlawed on plantations. Key to survival was shared responsibility relative to the family, spiritual outlook, sex roles and attitude about warfare. Extensive ads about runaways during the territorial period in New Orleans from 1803-1812 confirm that in language, dress, tribal markings and peculiar habits, Africans understood that they were African. Continual transport of Africans to the United States until the eve of the Civil War helped to reinforce and to sustain this sense of understanding.

The proximity of the maroon colony in *la cipriere*—the cypress swamp to the rear of the plantation served as a check and balance system to forge an alternative lifestyle during slavery. *La cipriere* offered cypress logs for building, palmetto leaves for thatched roofs, spice for cooking, medicines to cure many ailments, and wildlife and fish for consumption. Maroons developed a superb system of espionage. They could show their kinsmen how to navigate a *pasajes* (passageway) between the swamps and the plantations to enjoy in an alternative lifestyle. These enclaves were vibrant institutions that keep orality in the forefront of ceremonial gatherings that taught new dances and song. The local color of language and tales about the maroon colonies remain a central feature of performance in New Orleans to this day.

The church is another central social setting that sounds the orality of New Orleans with English, Latin and jazz Mass, the Sunday brunch, concerts, and historical pageants on site and in cross-country traveling venues. One such enterprise is St. Augustine Church Parish, founded in 1841 on a former plantation at the edge of the French Quarter. The roots of the Catholic Church in Louisiana are African, French, Haitian and Spanish. Short pews arranged along the walls in St. Augustine were set aside for slaves. The gold-leaf French inscription over the antique marble altar reads—*"Si tusavais le don de Dieu"* ("If you knew the gift of God"). The polished cypress stump altar and the chest-high cypress rail encircling the pulpit in St. Augustine call to mind the cypress swamp maroon colonies inhabited by Africans who ran away from plantations. At St. Augustine Church pictures of black Mardi Gras Indians line the walls between the stations of the cross depicting the passion of Christ. After mass, enslaved and free Africans walked over to adjoining Congo Square, today renamed [Louis] Armstrong Park, to participate in drumming, bartering, making music, exchanging memories and recipes to fashion a culture, cuisine and sound that to this day uniquely characterizes New Orleans.

The lifeblood of African memory is veneration of the ancestors. In African culture, the ancestors form a continuous link with the living. In New Orleans the jazz funeral of a relative on their way to join the ancestors is a pronounced event, and the body is laid to rest in one of the majestic cemeteries that resemble a village. New Orleans sits below sea level. Hence the dead are buried above ground in elaborately designed tombs that rival some of the elaborately built homes of the living. The cemeteries are the scene of sounding the living and the dead, the sacred and the secular. Hence when someone dies the *first-line* of the funeral constitutes the grave and somber music of bearing a body to join the ancestors. Because the living must go on, the *second-line* of the funeral is one of the more spectacular performances that encapsulate the signature of sound that is New Orleans. With umbrellas open, white handkerchiefs waving in the air, the brass band blaring, and song and dance in synchronization to celebrate the life that the departed lived and all who will come after them, truly the performance is taken-to-the-street.

*Time* and *place,* which can be transported anywhere, can be embraced as constituting the social biography and collective memory of a people. *Spac*e can be regarded as accommodating the framing of time and place in a particular locale or when transported. To reflect on this premise relative to scattered populations, especially those who disavow what is socially constructed to control them, one can draw from commentary presented in *Against Race: Imagining Political Culture beyond the Color Line* by Paul Gilroy.

> The concept of space itself is transformed when it is seen in terms of the ex-centric communicative circuitry that has enabled disperse populations to converse, interact, and more recently even to synchronize significant elements of their social and cultural lives. (Gilroy 2001: 129)

Given the history and culture of New Orleans, it is not the space that is important. As the people say, the space simply is the bosom that stretches out its arms to keep them living out time and place.

In a world governed by Natural Law and Divine Order, not socially constructed law, life manifests as *object* and *subject.* A human being is both a body and a mind. Hence one must not live via one or the other extreme, but a fusion of both, which constitutes the commanding performance of total *Being,* the sacred and the secular. This is a way of life that has and continues to sign the signature that is New Orleans. Descendants of the inaugural inhabitants embrace that life is the one entity that goes against the direction of probability: one never knows what an individual will say or do next. This understanding rests on the premise/foundation that the measure of humans is humans. In New Orleans, due to its unique topography, it is said that one never looks down on the world because one must always look up to see the world. Like the *flambeau* bearers who carry the torches to light the way during the celebration and ritual of *Mardi Gras,* the flame of orality is the cultural and intellectual continuum that keeps New Orleans rooted in time and place as the people continually announce, *Laissez les bon tempts rouler*— let the good times roll!

# Bibliography

"Senate Debate on the Breckenridge Bill" (1917). in *American Historical Review* 22 (October 1916 to July 1917). London: The Macmillan Company.

Baudier, R. [s.n. 1939]. *The Catholic Church in Louisiana.*

Blanchard, O. (1940). trans. *The Black Codes*. Survey of Federal Archives in Louisiana.

Brandon, G. (1997). *Santeria from Africa to the New World: The Dead Sell Memories*. Bloomington: Indiana University Press.

Brown, A. (2002). "Performing 'Truth': Black Speech Arts" in *African American Review* 36.2, 213-225.

Chandler, S. (2005). "Oral History Across Generations: Age, Generational Identity and Oral Testimony" in *Oral History* 33.2, 48-56.

Gilroy, P. (2001). *Against Race: Imagining Political Culture beyond the Color Line*. Massachusetts: Harvard University Press.

Hall, G. M. (1992). *Africans in Colonial Louisiana*. Baton Rouge: LSU Press.

Hamer, P. M. and Arthur, S. C. *Code Noir* (1685) in Federal Archives of Louisiana (1940).

Lundy, D. (1974). "Role Adaptation: Traditional Curers Under the Impact of Western Medicine" 1, 103-127.

Mbiti, J. S. (1970). *African Religions and Philosophy*. New York: Doubleday and Company, Inc.

MacDonald, R. R., Kemp J. R., Haas, E. F. (1979). *Louisiana's Black Heritage*. New Orleans.

Ong, W. J. (2002). *Orality and Literacy: The Technologizing of the Word (New Accents)*. New York: Routledge.

Pollard, L. J. (1961). "Aging and Slavery: A Gerontological Perspective." *The Journal of Negro History* 66.3, 228-234.

Rosaldo, M. (1973). "I Have Nothing to Hide: The Language of Ilongot Oratory" in *Language in Society* 2.2, 193-223.

Usner, D. (1987). "The Frontier Exchange Economy of the Lower Mississippi Valley in the Eighteenth Century" in *The William and Mary Quarterly* 44, 166-192.

# CHAPTER FIFTEEN

# LANGUAGE AND LYRICAL VIOLENCE:
# A CRIMINALIZED ROMANTICISM
# OF THE GHETTO

## E. JERRY PERSAUD

Critical Media and Cultural Studies combined with Race and Cultural Criminology inform this methodological departure based on a critical Content Analysis of rap music lyrics and violence with the referent of the ghetto. This combination of theories and specific songs aims to bridge urban language and space. In addition, it also aims to explore if there is a prerequisite for the urban representation of what Frantz Fanon, in a different context, referenced as "the lived experience of blackness" (Fanon, *Black Skin White Mask*).

I argue that a form of organic intellectualism became prevalent with hip hop culture that lends a language through, and from, which those in the margins narrate and critique their own condition and the dominant social formations. Hip Hop culture provides the form and forum of imagery, lyrics, violence, and criminality that, in an ingenious play of linguistics, fabricates a criminalized romanticism of the very locus of this culture—the ghetto. Jon Michael Spencer helps ponder a particular style of blackness that contributes to the process of philosophizing the ghetto, a social space also endearingly referred to as the "hood."

Urban culture and history in the United States demand scholars and indeed rappers to contextualize language with some of the unique black experiences in order to address the politicization of identity as oppositional and even subversive to the official status quo. This is a battle of more than semantics and aesthetics; it is a resistance to the erasure and closure of self, imagination, creativity; a subversion of meaning through reversal; a reclamation with a politics of difference and repositioning; a "rhythm" of confidence. Thus "rhythmic confidence," according to Jon Michael Spencer, emerged out of the socio-political, historical, cultural, and economic struggles concomitant with the subjugation of black people. "Afro-rhythms give rise to Afro-culture," posits Spencer (1991, 1995: xi).

Following Spencer, the argument herein moves black aesthetics as a form of ghetto hermeneutics between what the historian Fernand Braudel (1980) calls the temporal rhythms of history: the Event or *événementielle* (short-term, everyday life) and the Structure or *longue durée* (long-term, customs, mentality, language, ecology). According to Spencer

> African-American of all walks of life observe black youths dancing to today's hip hop or see their dance movements concretizing the rhythms of the music, most of us doing the observing (if not also doing the dancing) cannot help but feel some kind of cultural kinship. (Spencer 1995: xviii)

Taking into account literary subversive techniques of African diasporic aesthetics such as comedy, signifying and trickery, Spencer describes two strategies by which the rhythmic traditions have been maintained. Drawing upon the works of literary theory and criticism from Huston Baker, Jr. and Henry Louis Gates, Jr., Spencer examines the "deformation of mastery" and the "mastery of form" (1991: x). Rhythm and rap have been linked to these strategies, just as any other aesthetic expressions from the African Diasporic culture, especially those with subversive textuality and language.

Spencer's work positions the *register* of the ghetto or the 'hood as a driving force behind hip hop music. Without the ghetto, one could argue that hip hop music would certainly not exist. It is this specific environment of predominantly black oppression and disenfranchisement that has spawned one of the most popular, contemporary music forms. The ghetto is both a matter of signification and representation as shared and contested space and memories in the bodies of Black and Latino folks. Is the ghetto black or Jewish? Is it ethnic or racial? Is it class or race or immigrant? Is it margin or center? Could it be all or none? These and many similar questions of being from and belonging to the ghetto are crucial for many contemporary debates on the streets as well as in academia in the context of hip hop culture.

But the ghetto does not breed a singular style of hip hop. In fact, as Christopher Holmes Smith insists, the ghetto is a "crucial signifier for blackness" (1997: 2) but it is not without representative contestation. According to Smith there is:

'Ghettocentric' hip hop, which is becoming more and more pervasive in the music industry, and there is 'Afrocentric' hip hop. The Afrocentric group Public Enemy made the ghetto visible to abolish it while Ghettocentric rappers make the ghetto visible in order to sell it and be sold. In rap's dominant marketing paradigm, blackness has become contingent, while the ghetto has become necessary. (Smith 1997: 2)

In this instance, hip hop has transformed from a racial to a socioeconomic movement. This is reflected in the lyrics, popularity, and profiteering of poverty, inverting the "moral economy" (E. P. Thompson, E. Hobsbawm) of the inner city ghettoes. Social marginalization is one of the reoccurring themes in hip hop and it is this social outcry that has made hip hop extremely popular, especially among the urban under-class. Social marginalization has also been the cohesive force that has allowed hip hop to move from the predominantly Black ghettoes in the United States to other disparate countries and cities, often with little to no Black population.

Hip hop's social statements, especially with reference to the urban-ghetto, inner-city, have included a variety of topics. Most predominant is the call against racial and economic injustices and police violence or maltreatment. Hip hop lyrics tell stories of inequalities experienced because of the race and place of the oppressed minorities, and harassment they have seen and/or experienced simply because of who they are or seem to be, economically, culturally, politically, and racially. Education, or the lack thereof, scarce economic opportunities, and young people becoming parents before they are ready, often take center stage in hip hop lyrics; housing in the ghetto and dependency on the ghetto lifestyle are recurrent themes as well. Black women rappers often include lyrics about their fears, pleasures and promises as a means of having their voices, that have too often been consigned to the margins, heard (Wahl 1999).

But hip hop lyrics are not always about social concerns. Many MCs prefer to focus on sex, the opposite sex, violence, gang life, partying, and making money. Some hip hop lyrics are simply self-indulgent and more concerned with expressing arrogance than social issues or discontents (Cawker 1994). Being a pimp and "pimpin'" and making money is often the focus of such lyrics. White youths were, and still are, the largest consumers of hip hop music and thus of this romanticization, sometimes referred to as "thugganomics" (Cena 2007). Initially, Whites preferred the apolitical and physically non-threatening lyrics of artists like Will Smith, also known as Fresh Prince; LL Cool J; and MC Hammer. However, recording market analysts began to notice a strange phenomenon. Consumers of hip hop music appeared to prefer harsher lyrics, and in turn the vulgarity and violence content increased (Armstrong 2004; Ro 1996). Interestingly, there appears to be a growing division in the hip hop community about the appropriateness of the glorifications of crime, violence, misogyny, and greed, often found in gangsta' rap (Rose 1994; hooks 1994; Dyson 1996; Ro 1996; Ice-T 1994).

According to rapper Heavy D., the term "gangster rap" was coined by the US mass media while the concept of OG ("original gangsta") emerged from within the hip hop nation, as rapper Ice-T, one of the pioneers of the OG style concurs. Gangsta' rap is primarily devoted to glorifying and extolling the virtues of the gangster lifestyle. Analyzing the lyrical content of hip hop music, and, in particular gangasta' rap, helps to understand the culture that has affected the artists as well as the effect they are having on urban lifestyle.

The sub-genre of gangsta' rap uses the ghetto as a means and site of its messages: the ghetto is lionized as some ideal lifestyle. Although male rappers dominate the sub-genre of gangsta rap, female gangsta rappers can be found engaging in a discourse not only about violence in general, but putting themselves in their "narratives and often at the heart of the violence" (Haugen 2003) as demonstrated in the song "Spend a Little Doe" by Lil' Kim:

Man: Mmmm, baby, I missed you—
Woman: [sexy laugh] I missed you too...
M: I waited a looong tiiime for this—
W: [coyly] So why you didn't come to see me, don't conversate me or nuthin'?
M: I ain't wanna see my bird in no cage but I'm ready to take care of you now...
W: [crescendo] huh-now? after three years? three motherfuckin' years, nigga?
M: well—
W: you know what?
[the sound of a gun cocking is heard, then the music starts, and the actual lyrics begin]
Hasta la vista, bye bye—
Kiss your kids, it's the gangstresses—
When in need I lied for you, cried for you—
You know this down-ass bitch would have died for you. (In Haugen 2003)

The lyrics of this song place the artist right in the epicenter of violence and having her as the perpetrator as well. Lil' Kim is not alone. Rappers Foxy Brown, Missy Elliot, DaBrat, Eve, and to a lesser extent Salt N' Pepa' all used a combination of sex, violence or thug love in their lyrics.

In gangsta' rap, the recurring themes are those of sex, drugs, crime, money, and violence. In one of his biggest hits, "Big Pimpin',"Jay-Z announces, "I'm a pimp in every sense of the word" (Waite 2001: 5). Rappers Snoop Dogg, Warren G, and Nate Dogg (the crew of *213*), in the song "Keep it Gangsta," on *The Hard Way* album, encompass all of these themes. Warren G's first verse starts off with:

I was raised in the church but spent more days raised in the turf
And crime pays so I spent my days on the search. ("Keep it Gangsta")

Nate Dogg follows the chorus with his flow,

We were so gangsta growing up
We got the girls excited
Sluts up front just give their bodies. ("Keep it Gangsta")

Snoop ends the song,

Real flow, this is steel-toed biscuits
213 yeah we on that pimp shit
Mix in with some Crip shit, that's how it's scripted it
Pop 'em and bleed 'em you niggaz better follow the leader. ("Keep it Gangsta")

Similarly, in his "Gangsta Move" song, Snoop gives us an insight as to how one can live two opposite lifestyles—the family and the gangsta' life—at the same time. Dogg sings:

For all my homies in the pen
It's back on
My backbone, my wife in my life & down wit a nigga
before my paper was tite.
Boo, you's a real bitch ... I swim under water and don't
get wet
Then bounce back to the hood and C-walk the set
I keep it gangsta all the time
An you can ask the Doug, Insanes, and One-9
Cuz I'm:

Hook continues:

Born gangsta, stays on the move (Keep it tru, dawgz)
Dogg Pound just for the fuck of it (Dogg Pound!)
Born gangsta, keepin it true
None of y'all can stop me now. ("Gangsta Move")

Snoop Dogg, in several other songs such as "Gangsta Luv" and "Keepin it Real" straddles the lines of flights and staying gangsta' while wanting to remain also family, legit', and true to his homies. The tension of existing in two worlds as two beings, is prevalent in the ghetto/gangsta' rap axis. It produces as much tension and anxiety as it does also play, fluidity of mind, self, and body, or what Jon Michael Spencer called "rhythmic confidence" and DuBois—"double consciousness."

Dr. Dre, like Snoop, Biggy, Ice-T, Ice Cube, Tupac, Lil' Kim and so many other gangsta' rappers, tells his version. He, too, moves between two worlds, so typical of the urban black experience, as is clear from his song "Bang Bang," from his *The Chronic 2001* album—another pronounced example of the vicious lyrical content of gangsta' rap in the inner city.

I'm just a lot smarter now
cause these niggaz is bangin ten times harder now…
Niggaz spray strays and shoot without looking …
Always tryin to play Rambo with they ammo
Make a nigga wanna stay in family mode. ("Bang Bang")

The song laments the unrelenting description of violence that surrounds Dre. He informs that he no longer goes to house parties because he has seen too many of his friends die. The final verse follows:

Now tell me—what the fuck is this man?
Niggaz doin brothers in worse than the Klan
Can't even stand, in front of your buildin and chill
I got my, life preserver
And I'll do my time for murder…
I'm the wrong nigga to plot on
Took him out on the spot before he even got on
my hitlist—retaliation sounds like this. ("Bang Bang")

Evidently, the mixed and complex message of "twoness," "two souls," as DuBois outlines in his concept of "double consciousness" (1961: 23), is at play with Dre. He desires peace but wants to remain gangsta'. For Dre and others in such communities writing and living this story, this chapter of US urbanization is real, surreal, and hyper-real, all at the same time.

Tupac Shakur has become one of the most infamous gangsta' rappers in hip hop history, due to his untimely, gang-related murder and scandal with fellow gangsta' rapper Notorious B.I.G. aka Biggy Smalls. He lived his lyrics, and died by his lyrics. His work, too, is a pronounced example of the violent nature of gangsta' rap. In his song, "2 of Amerikaz Most Wanted," Tupac teams up with Snoop Dogg and the two brag about how their gangsta' deeds have made them criminals and two of America's most wanted.

> (Tupac) Ahh shit …Ain't nuttin but a gangsta party
> you done put 2 of Amerikaz most wanted in the same muthafuckin' place
> at the same muthafuckin' time
> ya'll niggas about to feel this …
> my intention's to get richer
> with the S-N double-OP dogg
> to help my fuckin' homie…
> (Snoop) Shonuff I keep my hand on my gun
> cuz they got me on the run
> my dream is to own a fly casino
> like Bugsy Segal, and do it all illegal. ("2 of Amerikaz Most Wanted")

Gangsta rappers often express the contradiction in their image of the popular hero that evolved from street authenticity and gangster legacies (Dyson 1996). As Fields eloquently sums it up:

> From the authenticity of lyrics like "Six in the Morning" (Ice T) or "Fuck Tha Police" (N.W.A.), which presented life on the street as rough, unglamorous, and dangerous, to the myriad of songs that send up the life of the gangsta as romantic and powerful, the gangsta rapper revels in the outlaw role. And yet, even as they lionize the gangsta lifestyle, gangstas rap about the need to "Escape from the Killing Fields" (Ice T). There is a double-awareness that the very social conditions that have helped distinguish hardcore hip hop and the gangsta personae have resulted in genocide for a whole generation of inner city boys and men. The self-awareness of this feedback loop—playing the playa and romanticizing the gangsta with bravado—makes for a powerful and conflicted genre. (Fields 2004: 8)

Thus, it comes as no surprise that many hip hop artists also glorify loving a gangster—rapper Eve's "thug-love" is a case in point. In general, they do not seem to be afraid to express what they desire sexually either, judging from the lyrics of Snoop Dogg's "Doggy Style," R. Kelly's "bump and grind," and Beyonce's "bootylicious"—the backside is a perennial referent in hip hop. Almost every hip hop music video features this anatomical intrigue as a physiological essential and desire, of female adulation and men beholding. But the heterosexual trope is not without controversy, ranging from obscenity to misogyny.

Yet in a high density urban environment, the fluidity of this type of "language" is a premium and preamble to being cool and being accorded all that comes with coolness, epically for inner-city youth culture. In rapper 50 Cent's song, "Thug Love," which features Eminem and Beyonce, the benefits of being involved with a gangsta', for women, are extolled:

> (50 Cent) Fifth Av. shit baby, Fendi furs ...
> Hustle hard for cash so I can spoil that ass ...
> To the hood I introduced her ...
>
> (Beyonce) I treat you like you need to be treated like you're special
> Tie your hands to the bedpost when I caress you
> When I met you it was Guess and Gap
> Now it's Gucci and Prada. ("Thug Love")

The remainder of the lyrics tell a bit more of the sordid details of the twisted thug love relationship. But such denigrating lyrics are constantly heard among youth culture and so this type of "relationship" appears as "normal." This is further amplified by the often absent parenting models, poor education, and a reliance on television and rappers as apostles of the "cool," if not the "truth" (Giroux 2003: 1996). 50 Cent in one of his more recent songs, "Ghetto Like a Mother Fucker," put the ghetto and its trials at center-stage.

> Slim chance I'ma go back to killing roaches
> Be quite, you can hear the rats in the wall
> The dope bring the dough in ...
> The wolves out there hungry, they looking for a lick
> Sun down to sun up, they looking for a come up
> 10-30 in progress right in your projects
> N-ggas pissed on the staircase in an elevator
> (Hook)
> You can say I'm ghetto like a mother fucker
> Pack heat, heavy metal like mother fucker. ("Ghetto Like a Mother Fucker")

The language of hip hop culture in general and the lyrics of gangsta rap in particular, affected an urban lexicon reminiscent of Jive in the Jazz Age. Following is a very small sample of this subversion of spelling and grammar in Standard English:

*wazzup* for what's up
*muttafucka* for motherfucker
*'ho* for whore
*wanna* for want to
*yaknamasayin* for you know what I am saying
*yo* for you;
*shouldn'ta* for should not have,
*diss* for disrespect
*streetz* for streets

But it is also the arrangement of words to a very narrow experience (the ghetto, police, welfare, sex, home life, everyday life, crimes, infidelity, mistrust, power and powerlessness) and thus it is simultaneously spatial and temporal; a violent uprooting and relocating of experiences; as much cognition as it is addictions and inhibitions. The specificity of the language affords the narration of the interiority of this experience. So the resonance of what Ice-T sings in "Grand Larceny," for instance, is rather real:

I'm like a time bomb, but I'm a rhyme bomb
Spray the whole audience with napalm. ("Grand Larceny")

As it is in his song "High Rollers":

Cash flow extreme, dress code supreme, vocabulary obscene
Definition—street player, you know what I mean.

The high rollers.

People of the city, stop foolin' yourself,
crime rules the streets, who the hell else. ("High Rollers")

Yet what was originally seen and treated as ghetto illiteracy has lyrically globalized into a statement of the young and oppressed. The very title of one of Ice-T's song, "I'm Your Pusher" plays on a language that is understood by the authorities and others as drug dealing, but in actuality is about pushing good vibes, music and dealing LP as dope...

I'm sellin' dope in each and every record store
I'm the king pin when the wax spins
Crack or smack will take you to a sure end
You don't need it, just throw that stuff away
You wanna get high? Let the record play ... ("I'm Your Pusher")

This interplay of language is incredible at so many levels and for so many reasons, for example, record stores were, in many inner-city 'hoods a site for petty drug dealing. If we were then to connect this concept of time, space, and ghetto experience from Ice-T to Flavor Flav of Public Enemy wearing a huge clock as a medallion to remind people what time it is in this nation, as in their song "41:19," we begin to see a horizontal and cross pollination among the rappers, their messages, and their audience:

> I'm past thirty three
> Word is born, born is my word...
> I got you before my word fails
> Fuck whatcha heard
> I keep it real, you never catch me fakin'. ("41:19")

And it is precisely this horizontal and cross pollination among rappers, their messages, and their audience that makes hip hop what it is... "Black Peoples' CNN," says Chuck D!

## Bibliography

Alim, H. S. (2006). *Roc the Mic Right: The Language of Hip Hop Culture.* New York: Routledge Books.

ALIM, H. Samy (2005). "Do You Speak American. Words That Shouldn't Be? Sez Who?" http://www.pbs.org/speak/words/sezwho/hiphop

Armstrong, E. G. (2004). "Eminem's Construction of Authenticity." *Popular Music and Society* 27(3) October, 335-355.

Boyd, T. (2002). *Young Black Rich and Famous: The Rise of the NBA, The Hip Hop Invasion and the Transformation of American Culture.* New York: Doubleday.

Braudel, F. (1980). *On History.* Chicago: University of Chicago Press.

D., Chuck (2003) *There's a God on the Mic: The True 50 Greatest MCs.* New York: Avalon/Thunder Mouth Press.

Darden, J. T. (ed) (1981).*The Ghetto: Readings with Interpretations.* New York: Kennikat Press.

DuBois, W. E. B. (1996, 1903 o. p.) *The Souls of Black Folk.* New York: Modern Library.

Dyson, M. E. (2007/2010). *Know What I Mean: Reflections on Hip Hop* (Intro by Jay-Z/Outro by Naz). New York Civitas Books.

—. (1996).*Between God and Gangsta Rap: Bearing Witness to Black Culture.* Oxford: Oxford University Press.

Fanon, F. (1967). *Black Skin, White Masks.* New York: Grove Press.

Forman, M. (2002). *The 'Hood Comes First: Race, Space, and Place in Hip Hop*. Middletown, CA: Wesleyan University Press.

Gates, H. Louis, Jr., (1998). "The Two Nations of Black America." *Frontline*. PBS.

Giglioli, P. P. (Ed.) (1990). *Language and Social Context*. New York: Penguin Books.

George, N. (1998). *Hip Hop America*. New York: Viking Press.

Giroux, H. (1996). *Fugitive Cultures: Race, Violence and Youth*. New York: Routledge.

Haskins, J. (2000). *The Story of Hip Hop*. London: Penguin Books.

Haugen, J. D. (2003). "Unladylike Divas: Language, Gender, and Female Gangsta Rappers" in *Popular Music and Society* 26(4) December, 429-444.

Heaggans, R. (2003). "When the Oppressed Becomes the Oppressor: Willie Lynch and the Politics of Race and Racism in Hip-Hop Music" in *West Virginia University Philological Papers*. Vol. 50, Fall, 77-80.

Hobsbawm, E. (1963). *Bandits*. New York: Delacorte Press.

Hobson, J. (2003) "The 'Batty' Politic: Toward an Aesthetic of the Black Female Body." *Hypatia*. Vol. 18(4) Fall, 87-105.

hooks, b. (1994). *Outlaw Culture: Resisting Representations*. New York: Routledge.

Hoye, J. and ALI, Karolyn (2003) *Tupac: Resurrection*. New York: Atria Books, Simon & Schuster, Inc.

Huxley, M. (2000). *Eminem: Crossing the Line*. New York: St. Martin's.

Iceland, J.& Steinmetz, E. (2003.) *"Class Differences in African American Residential Patterns in U.S. Metropolitan Areas: 1990-2000."* *US Census Bureau*. May, 01.

Izrael, J. (2004). "Hip-Hop Needs More than a Good Beat to be a Political Force." *LA Times*. August 27.

Javors, I. R. (2004). "Hip-Hop Culture: Images of Gender and Gender Roles" in *Annals of the American Psychotherapy Association*. Vol. 7(2) Summer, 42.

Kenyatta, K. (2001). *You Forgot About Dre: The Unauthorized Biography of Dr. Dre and Eminem–From N.W.A. to Slim Shady A Tale of Gangsta Rap, Violence and Hit Records*. Amber/Busta Books.

Kitwana, B. (1994). *The Rap on Gansta Rap*. Chicago: Third World Press.

Kopano, B. N. (2002). "Rap Music as an Extension of the Black Rhetorical Tradition: 'Keepin' it Real'" in *The Western Journal of Black Studies*. Vol. 26(4) Winter, 204-214.

Light, A. (1999). *The Vibe History of Hip Hop*. New York: Three Rivers Press.

LL Cool J (1997) *I Make My Own Rules*. New York: St. Martin's Press.

Massey, D. S. and N. A. Denton (1993) *American Apartheid: Segregation and the Making of the Underclass*. Cambridge: Harvard University Press.

Miller, I. (1994). "Creolizing for Survival in the City" in *Cultural Critique*. Spring, 153-188.

Osumare, H. (2001, 1999) "Beat Streets in Global Hood: Connective Marginalities of the Hip Hop Globe" in *Journal of American & Comparative Cultures* 24 (1/2) Spring: 171-181.

Perkins, E. (1996). *Droppin' Science: Critical Essays on Rap Music and Hip Hop Culture*. Philadelphia: Temple University Press.

Peterson-Lewis, S. (1991). "A Feminist Analysis of the Defences of Obscene Rap Lyrics" in *The Emergency of Black and the Emergence of Rap*. A Special Issue of *Black Sacred Music: A Journal of Theomusicology*, ed. by Jon Michael Spencer.

Quinn, E. (2005). *Nuttin' but a "g" thang: The Culture and Commerce of Gangsta Rap*. New York: Columbia University Press.

Ro, R. (1996). *Gangsta: Merchandising the Rhymes of Violence*. New York: St. Martin's Press.

Rose, H. M. (1971). *The Black Ghetto: A Spatial Behavioural Perspective*. McGraw-Hill Problems Series in Geography. New York: McGraw-Hill.

Rose, T. (1994). *Black Noise: Rap Music and Black Culture in Contemporary America*. Hanover: Wesleyan/New England University Press.

Shakur, T. (1999). *The Rose that Grew from Concrete*. New York: Simon & Schuster, Inc.

Smith, D. (1996) "Ghetto Fabulous." *New Yorker*. April 29—May 6.

Smitherman, G. (2000). *Black Talk: Words and phrases from the 'Hood to the Amen Corner*. New York: Mariner Books (revised and updated edition).

Spencer, M. J. (1995). *The Rhythms of Black Folk: Race, Religion and Pan-Africanism*. New Jersey: Africa World Press.

—. (Ed.) (1991) *The Emergency of Black and the Emergence of Rap*. (A Special Issue of *Black Sacred Music: A Journal of Theomusicology*). Durham: Duke University Press.

Stanley, L. A. (Ed.) (1992) *Rap: The Lyrics*. New York: Penguin Books.

T-Ice (1994). *The Ice Opinion* (As told to H. Siegmund). New York: St Martin's Press.

Thompson, E. P. (1991). *Customs in Common: Studies in Traditional Popular Culture*. New York: The New Press.

Wahl, G. (1999). "'I Fought the Law (and I Cold Won!)': Hip-Hop in the Mainstream" in *College Literature*. Vol. 26 (1) January, 98-112.

Waite, A. (2001) "Hip-Hop: A Raging Business" in *World and I*. Vol. 16 (1) January, 73-81.

http://www.dr-dre.com/lrics/2001.

http//www.killerhiphop.com (2012). Hip-Hop Artists, Lyrics and News.

http://www.ohhla.com (2012). The Original Hip-Hop Lyrics Archive.

# CHAPTER SIXTEEN

# THE EDGE OF THE CITY: CREATIVE PRACTICES THAT TRANSFORM THE URBAN

## MATTHEW HAWKINS AND MARTA RABIKOWSKA

The argument below originates from our academic and professional experience in film, creative industries and cultural studies. While situating the project of urban regeneration at the cross-juncture of these fields, we operate mainly with the Deleuzian concept of rhizomatic multiplication of identities, which challenge the traditional positivist approach to urban regeneration as an outcome-oriented process. By looking at urban regeneration through the prism of creativity affected by the materiality and living concreteness of the place, we question both the concept of the spatial wholeness and the concept of community cohesion.

The creative community project, *Edge of the City*, partly funded by a London-based governmental organization, applied in a London suburban locale, started as our voluntary practice, and changed into our academic research, morphing into further collaborative artistic outputs. As such, it contributes to the understanding of both urban regeneration and creative practice in the city, while it also shows that academic practice as research within film and cultural studies takes on a fresh dimension when uprooted and relocated from a traditional academic environment and undertaken in an urban cityscape.

We launched the *Edge of the City* Film Festival in 2010 as part of our community project undertaken in Plumstead—a small suburb situated on the margin of London. The annual Festival comprises of one half-year season of educational workshops on film history and filmmaking, screenings of classical Hollywood films, World Cinema and short films, which culminate in a Gala event where new short films from the local area and further afield are projected in an old local theatre. The *Edge of the City* project was conceived in parallel to our other volunteer activities, which we started in the neighbourhood in 2005 in the aftermath of our relocation to London. While establishing a new life in Plumstead, we were also trying to establish new creative networks among the local people. In this way we hoped not only to find inspiration for our creative practice, but most importantly we were relying on securing the sense of home in that diverse area. Knowing about the critical reputation of Plumstead: infamous for its poverty, high unemployment, shortage of institutional culture, ethnic cacophony, detachment from any regenerative governmetal schemes, we found the place particularly challenging. Experiencing the shortage of creative opportunities in the area, we started informal meetings with the local people in the pub situated in the High Street. Thanks to the patience and generosity of its Irish owners, that pub has become an important meeting point for our group and creative hub for our activities, where we could screen films and hold film classes free of charge. In time, we were able to attract some funding to deliver *Edge of the City* Film Festival from governmental organisations interested in our work at the grassroots of this deprived area. Those organisations support social cohesion and integration in diverse urban environments, which suffer from social, economic and cultural deprivation—the problems Plumstead knows too well.

Located at the edge of London, Plumstead is a place in constant transition. The High Street (a central parade of shops and main road for traffic) serves as a gravitational centre for the area, attracting business and commerce, community groups, teenage hooligans, school children, and commuters (see Rabikowska 2010). The area is home to a high immigrant population that is made up of, amongst many others, Indians, Nigerians, Polish and Nepalese, although the national make-up of the area is constantly shifting. In 2006 the largest immigrant population in the area was Indian, as it had been for many years. This gave way to an influx of Nigerian immigrants, who were soon joined by a new wave of Eastern Europeans, especially Polish and Lithuanian migrants, arriving after the extension of the European Union in 2004. In 2012 Plumstead is home to one of the largest Nepalese populations in the United Kingdom. The diverse and fluid ethnic make-up of this particular area of southeast London results in a chaotic, impulsive, and centre-less diaspora. Oliver Gillham (2002) calls such urban creation a "limitless city", while Joel Garreau (1992) "edge city," where both terms signify the lack of control and the lack of pre-planned institutionalised investment.

Indeed, as soon as one begins to orientate oneself within the neighbourhood, things change, they mutate, they shape shift. To use a concept adapted from Gilles Deleuze and Felix Guattari, Plumstead is a "rhizomatic" formation (1987). As Deleuze and Guattari state in their opening of *A Thousand Plateaus: Capitalism and Schizophrenia*, in which they critique the concept of the center-dominating Western economy and imagination, "any point of a rhizome can be connected to anything other, and must be. This is very different from the tree or root, which plots a point, fixes an order" (1987: 7). From an urban studies perspective, Plumstead represents the edge of "postpolis" (Soja 2000), which materializes through paradoxes. There is an element of the anarchic and the volatile at the edge of the city, which reminds of the behavior of "metropolis unbound" debated by Engin Isin (1996), where the kaleidoscopic urban space unfolds in a multidirectional and multispatial manner. Although in our practice we claim to have a plan, we are often at the mercy of events outside of our control. As requested by the funding body, we started our workshops in a public space, which would connect our project with residents who have some interest in creativity and education. Thus we chose the local library, which offered us support and a free venue. However, the registered library readers did not approve of the disruption in their own routine and complained about the frenzied atmosphere of our workshops, which led to the cancellation of our initial agreement. Our argument that the library as a public space will extend its life and service to the local public through the support given to our project did not change the decision of the management. Thus, we had to move back to the pub where we started, hoping that such environment would not discourage the participants who the funding body wanted to embrace. Being driven by unpredictable forces, we have to be prepared for different collisions that may occur at any time. After Deleuze, we call these collisions "events." Cliff Stagoll describes Deleuze's understanding of the event as follows:

> The event is not a disruption of some continuous state, but rather the state is constituted by events 'underlying' it that, when actualised, mark every moment of the state as a transformation. (Stagoll 2010: 90)

Our workshops in the local pub transform the place but that does not mean that they add coherence to it. We claim it is not just the place that constitutes the identity of its community, but rather, as Bernard Tschumi argues, it is the event that produces the place (1994: 145). The point of departure for Tschumi's critique of urban space is that abstract ideas, imagination, ideological discourses and empirical experiences constitute events, which build into the materiality of the place and its social identity. In his theory, representation and experience have equal status, although they can contradict and challenge each other. Arjun Appadurai (1996: 31) expands on this equation when he states that in global cultural processes imagination becomes a social practice. Our implementation of film workshops, which aim at the creative regeneration of the place, is grounded on this conclusion; we also acknowledge that imagination contributes to the creation of the trans-cultural space of the city, where watching, shooting, screening, thinking, talking, experiencing the pub, or conflict with the library, re-organize traditional borders between city "scapes." According to Soja (2000), imagination defines the life of "postpolis" and should not be neutralised as "soft influence" in urban regeneration. Alongside social and cultural life, imagination plays an equal part in the re-organisation of the city-scape next to quantifiable "hard" attributes, such as housing (Massey 2005). In postpolis, hard and soft factors co-exist and collide while feeding a creature of many limbs, with Plumstead being just one. Although geographically Plumstead stays on the edge of the city, it connects on different levels with the transcultural tissue of postpolis.

The workshops formulate and operate within a new "transcultural city space" (Soja 2000), which opens up fresh interpretations of cohesion, locality, local participation, and creativity. That space is manifest in the visual interpretations of the place in films made by us and the participants of our workshops, in the spatio-temporal alternations the pub undergoes during our events, and importantly in the different motivations of the participants who decide in what form they want to engage. After advertising the project on the Internet, we realized that we face very different motivations, qualifications and experiences from the participants, who feel connected with different elements of our project, but not necessarily with the community or the place. The trajectory of participation in the project by different participants is an event on its own: their demographics and their reasons to join the project are diverse, from film-oriented, to locally and socially inspired to purely accidental.

Clark, an English man in his forties, does not live in the local area. Like a few other participants he had found out about the project through the website and decided to join the workshops in order to further his knowledge of filmmaking. He does not have any interest in Plumstead, but quickly makes friends with other participants, especially with Anush, who became his film-buddy during the workshops season. Anush, a single man in his twenties, moved to Plumstead from Nepal to undertake his degree. He had no specific interest in film, but he found out about the Festival and workshops through a family friend who had already been affiliated with project. Anush joined the workshops, as he wanted to meet new people and socialize locally. During the workshops, Clark and Anush developed their own film and decided to submit it to the festival. It had no direct relation to Plumstead, however, the local environment served as a setting in their articulation of human loneliness in one's own place against the vastness of the city. In the aftermath of the project, Clark and Anush were thinking about starting their own production company, but they could not secure sufficient means. Since then Clark left the country to find a new job, and Anush opened a tattoo salon in Plumstead.

A few other participants "from the outside" have developed similar collaborations with the local attendees. Their films resulted from their common encounter in the pub and undertaking a series of tasks together. Yet not all participants were so actively engaged, while some collaborations ended abruptly in the middle of the project. Diana, a British graphic designer living locally, entered the project to meet new people and further her professional skills. She made a film about "life on the city edge," to which she invited all workshop attendees. As a local volunteer and advocate for local creative regeneration, she applied her professional skills and designed a logo for the project free of charge. Having completed her final film, she left the project permanently. Others left us because they could not accommodate so much time on a regular basis, while some have become very diligent and brought new friends. Gaston, a mature local resident of Nigerian origin, has completed all workshops and produced a few small films about the local area. He joined the project in its first season and stayed for good. While working full time, he has become the engine of social networking among the participants; he involved his wife and his children in the festival and started learning the secrets of social media to stay in touch online with other participants. As a result of his involvement with *Edge of the City*, he produced his own film, which was a reflection of his personal encounters with people and spaces in the city of London and was to serve as a guide for those who live on the city margins. He has brought his own ideas of how the locality could be improved and he wants the *Edge of the City* to develop further, especially in connection with different ethnic groups. Angelie, an English social worker living locally, was looking for activities to take part in with her son. She discovered the workshops through our website and joined us even though she had little interest in filmmaking. They both became more and more engaged as the weeks went on, and they finished the Festival season with a short film that was directed, shot, edited by the mother and son team. The film captured both the vibrancy and struggle of living in an urban environment with Plumstead as the setting. The workshop experience led to Angelie getting a few small paid jobs as a freelance filmmaker promoting local businesses. She eventually quit filmmaking to concentrate on her day job, but she still stays in touch with the project online, and regularly sends us contacts to film festivals, funding, and local events. Clark, Anush, Gaston, Diana, Angelie, and others, would have probably never met if it had not been for this one call from *Edge of the City*. Although their collaborations did not continue outside of the project, their encounters have instigated several attempts at capturing the local neighborhood for cinematic purposes and as such contributed to the imagination of the place, which lives its own uncontrollable life now.

Through this encounter the people, the project, the films and the space have become uprooted, or, as Deleuze would say, deterritorialized, from their identities. Deleuze recognises such transformation (morphing) as the effect of the process of deterritorialization, which, we argue, is characteristic of the city space but also of social participation. The process of deterritorialization refers to people, imagination and places, which constantly collide in a series of displacements. Yet such displacements are not negative acts, as ontologically they are followed by reactions, which would not happen otherwise. To use another definition from Delezue, inspired by Bergson, they create a process of constant becoming. However, their epistemology cannot avoid ethics and subsequently, politics. Andrew, who did not approve that the funded workshops embraced people from outside of the local community, after completing our course and meeting likeminded people in the pub, decided to start his own creative group in Plumstead, devoted exclusively to the locals. Depending on what is expected by the stakeholders of urban regeneration, this kind of sequence can be regarded as a positive or negative type of impact (see Jones & Evans 2008). For example, justifying their decision with the gauge of locality understood geographically, our funding body did refuse an award for the best film granted by us to the participant of the Festival living abroad. "Chain-reactions" such as these are hard to trace, yet they can serve the objectives of governing bodies depending on their political agendas.

Through the project, we collide with, mix, and distort the pub-scape and thus create a milieu of the transformed pub/classroom/film set, which constantly transforms itself into new directions. Through this process the borders of the identity of the pub, the identity of the residents, and our own identity as academics are called into question. As these identities collide, another arbitrary event occurs, which, we argue, transforms the place.

The users of the pub who enter the premises whilst our Festival activities are occurring, instantaneously pose their concern, "what are you filming for?" or "what's going on here?" They cannot imagine what would attract a camera or a film screen to their dingy little watering hole. English men with wooden queues and pints of beer play pool and old Caribbean men sit in the corner playing dominos, and without further ado a camera and tripod are placed in the middle of the room and someone shouts, "action"! The men pause for a second, but soon return to their games as the filmmakers begin their own play. However, when the camera captures their image, the patrons become actors, and they joke that they are now movie stars. A film, which we started making in the pub as an educational tool, captures the regular visitors who want to be included.

After some time, they are so used to the cameras, that they complain if we do not film them. They do not mind being involved in our educational tasks which the participants perform using the pub's environment as a prop. At the same time we feel irresistible attraction to the cinematic appearance of the events unfolding in front us and we cannot help but film them. Thus our own film, separate from the project, becomes conceived by the place. Our film practice is shared between the workshop participants, pub visitors, and professional actors who we employ to play the parts of the local people. The film we create in parallel to the project is called "SE18," which is the postcode that designates the border of the neighborhood. It presents a story of two lonely people living in the area, a female Eastern European immigrant and a male English resident, who meet in "our" pub and build a relationship. While we capture the script-based scenes, Joe, the oldest customer of the pub, asks for his whisky as usual, oblivious to what we are doing. A small chat between him and Paul, the barman, is recorded by our cameras, while the participants of the workshop act the pub crowd. The borders between our film practice, the project, the space, and the people in the pub become eroded. We cannot state for sure who is playing whose role. We observe what we thought was a "project" with an identity conceptualized by the funding body, become its own living organism. It can be said that our practices unfurl in response to the place, whilst the place "morphs" through this influence and as such responds to us. In this reciprocal manner, new identities and social roles multiply, but they are still delineated, although not limited, by the "event" in that place. As Deleuze and Guattari state, "multiplicities are defined by the outside: by the abstract line, the line of flight or deterritorialization according to which they change in nature and connect with other multiplicities" (1987: 8).

Reciprocal influence, however, is not without collision. As the film crew, we are not so secure in our identity any more. The teaching in the pub is based on our academic knowledge, but the physical environment and the presence of the regular pub visitors challenge our knowledge and attitudes. We feel uprooted from the relative safety of our offices, and we uproot the pub from its established identity as well. We think that we know the film craft and that we know what we are doing, but the presence of seasoned visitors who make jokes at our expense from the safe ground of their own territory undermine our confidence. Meanwhile, Joe becomes a member of our project without him or us realizing, when he welcomes the new participants joining the workshops and offers them a drink and tells them about "our" film. Another participant calls over to Paul, the bar man and asks for the lights in the function room to be turned off for the screening. Paul is now used to this weekly ritual, but he can never completely disguise his amusement at this ridiculous charade. Chairs are arranged in rows and the screen erected. People take their seats as the projector starts and the film begins. Two young men order a beer from the bar and peer through the open door into the dark room that is illuminated by the neon lights of Martin Scorsese's New York, or Ridley Scott's Los Angeles. The familiar sound of pale ale filling a glass is ruptured by a chorus of galloping horses and explosions from Sergio Leone's *A Fistful of Dynamite*. The cinema audience is glued to the screen as Decker from *Blade Runner* stands on a rooftop, the pouring rain the only sound in that dark function room. At the same time a huge roar from the boys in the front bar pervade the moody sci-fi ambiance, as Manchester United score their third goal of the afternoon.

The rest of the day is spent routinely on film practice. One exercise involves asking the participants to adapt and interpret a scene from Romeo and Juliet in three basic. The aim of the task is to encourage these new filmmakers to use the camera subjectively in order to create their own unique view of the space. The participants are not allowed to include Shakespeare's dialogue or dialogue of their own design. They are charged with the challenge of recreating the scene using images only, and these images are to be created using things that could be found inside the pub: bottles, glasses, coats, billiard balls, their own bodies or the bodies of willing conspirators. At the end of the workshop, once the footage has been produced, the images are saved onto a computer and projected back into the room in which they were originated.

When the film is screened back in the function room of the pub, a rupture of an ontological and empirical kind occurs. The screen displays images of the place, but they are more than mimicry, more than a reflection of the materiality of the objects. The screen is not a mirror that reflects the local universe, yet it is not a window through which to look, either. Rather, the screen is a refraction, a splitting of the imagination, a tear in the materiality of the pub. For a certain time period the environment of the pub is disrupted. But this disruption does not end when the screen is dismounted, and the projector put back into its box. Both the landscape and the psyche of the place have acquired a new shape: it may not be visible or palpably recognizable at all, but it is there in the new relations between space and people. Although the regular visitors of the pub come back to their routine immediately after we leave, as Deleuze would say, a new rhizomatic "line of flight" has sprung forth. Something has changed in that space for a moment before it is "morphed," shifted, and displaced by a new altered rhizomatic formation of the next event. In the meantime, during a pool competition in the front bar, the regular visitors will be making jokes at our cinematic efforts at animating a glass of whisky in a "romance" with a fork, while an extension of this space appears through an online exchange between the participants of the projects who place their films and comments on social network sites, thus connecting globally with wider audiences from both personal and formal circles.

The digital representation of the pub-scape is another rhizome of the social space created through the "event." It adds to what Danah Boyd (2010) defines as "networked publics," where unrelated agents of the public meet and challenge the established social ties. When we see the recording from the workshop task that the participants have posted on YouTube, we know that the pub has acquired a parallel life, while the material objects, which belong to it, live their new "Shakespearean" drama through local and digital gossip. However, the marketing benefit from this rhizomatic extension, for which the owners of the pub hoped, is less than minimal, no one in the local street has noticed the difference. In fact, the life of the project is so fragile and so capricious, that it cannot be defined in terms of the structure or the outcome.

Our encounter opens up a new space, neither pub, nor creative workshop, but a hybrid space that has the potential to produce transformative forces. Homi Bhabha (1991) calls such hybridization "the third space," where new cultural meanings emerge from the collision between the centre and the margin, majority and minority, high and low culture, and thus destabilize the old "centers" with their values and norms. Bhabha's definition is politically saturated and reflects his interest in possible resistance against dominant powers, understood as the first space. In the same respect, but with less emphasis on conflict, Soja uses the term "third space" in the analysis of postpolis. Both conceptualizations problematize the binary character of the relation between the first space of the subordinating power and the second space, reserved for the subordinated. Most regenerative projects funded from public money in the UK (see Bishop 2012) build their philosophy on the conjuncture between "first and second" space, which they want to reconcile. Supporting regenerative activity located in the anarchically inclined "third space" would collide with the neo-liberal ethos of communal cohesion.

As Jeremy Gilbert (2008) argues, very much in Bhabha's spirit, that this ethos is based on conflicting values and as such is flawed from the outset. Yet providing the ideological foundation to the dominant discourse, it also has the organizing power, which governmental funding bodies and regenerative projects follow. "Collision" and unpredictable "morphing" goes against the requirements of funding bodies expecting a "commodifiable product" to be the outcome of urban transformation, whether it is through a material mark on the environment, numbers of volunteers involved, or numbers of integrative events (Bishop 2012). Yet, we argue, that the force of urban "events" cannot be predicted or channeled; its life cannot be stopped or controlled. In our project this was reflected not only through the deranged transformation of the pub-space, when it changed into a cinema, but also through the impulsive creativity and the volatile participation of the people. Although we are able to count the events, volunteers, and films, we cannot state definitely what kind of change took place in our participants' and community's lives.

From the perspective defined here as rhizomatic, the transformation process does not have a rational structure. Like in the post-metropolis described by Soja (2000), it is difficult, if not impossible, to measure the transformation of Plumstead in tangible terms. Perhaps it is not even desirable to produce such quantifiable data, which could be used to paint an arbitrary picture of the "vibrancy" of this deprived area of London. Projects like ours take form through momentary events, through the energy of people who come and go, through art being made, and that being abandoned, through exchanges with others, through paradoxes and contradictions. The spatiality and sociality of the postpolis is living simultaneously *in* and *between* representation, bricks and mortar, imagination and desire, projection and experience. Consequently, the life of the regenerative project cannot be defined with precision, as its transformations are too multifarious and contradictory to constrain in the rigid borders of identities, histories and universal concepts of locality.

# Bibliography

Appadurai, A. (1996). *Modernity at Large: Cultural Dimensions of Globalization*, Minneapolis, London: University of Minnesota Press.

Bhabha, H. (1991). "The Third Space" in *Identity, Community, Culture, Difference*, J. Rutheford (ed) London: Lawrence and Wishart.

Bishop, C. (2012). *Artificial Hells: Participatory Art and the Politics of Spectatorship*, London, New York: Verso.

Colebrook, C. (2010). "Rhizome" in *The Deleuze Dictionary; Revised Edition*, A. Parr (ed) Edinburgh: Edinburgh University Press.

Deleuze, G. and Guattari, F. (1987). *A Thousand Plateaus: Capitalism and Schizophrenia*, trans. by Massumi, B. London/New York: Continuum Press.

Garreau, J. (1992). *Edge City: Life on the New Frontier*, New York, London: Doubleday.

Gilbert, J. (2008). *Anticapitalism and Culture: Radical Theory and Popular Politics*,     Oxford, New York: Berg.

Gillham, O. (2002). *The Limitless City: A Primer On The Urban Sprawl Debate*, Washington, Covelo, London: Island Press.

Isin, E. (1996). "Metropolis Unbound: Legislators and Interpreters of Urban Form" in *City Lives and City Forms: Critical Urban Research and Canadian Urbanism*, Caufield, J. & Peake, L. (eds) Toronto: University of Toronto Press.

Jones, P. and Evans, J. (2008). *Urban Regeneration in the UK*, London: Sage.

Massey, D. B. (2005). *For Space*, London: Sage.

Rabikowska, M. (2010). "Whose Street Is It Anyway? Visual Ethnography and Self-reflection" in *Qualitative Market Research: An International Journal*, Vol. 13. (1).

Soja, E. W. (2000). *Postmetropolis: Critical Studies of Cities and Regions*, Oxford: Blackwell.

Stagoll, C. (2010). "Event" in *The Deleuze Dictionary, Revised Edition*, A. Parr (ed) Edinburgh: Edinburgh University Press.

Tschumi, B. (1994). *Architecture and Disjunction*, Cambridge, Mass., London: MIT Press.

# CHAPTER SEVENTEEN

# NEW WAVE GUERRILLA THEATER: THE CAPER CRUSADE

## MELANIE SOVERN

Living in any city is an inherently performative act; the streets and structures are the stage, and the men and women, as Shakespeare would say, "merely its players." The daily performance of citizens of cities, if considered as such, is infinite. Performance Studies examines how actions along every spot on the performative spectrum manifest in, depict, and influence daily life.

This essay examines the history, inspirations and context of guerilla theater in New York City through a case study of the improvisation theater troupe Improv Everywhere. It argues that because all performance is a reflection of the social, cultural, and political milieu, all performance is inherently social, cultural *and* political. These guerrilla theater troupes improve their city by turning even the most unlikely places into stages. But they can only do so because of the unique contexts cities provide.

You're hurtling through Grand Central Terminal, frantically searching for your train track. All around you, families and couples and businesspeople collide and trip and dash from every direction. A child totters into your path, and as you swerve out of your way to avoid trampling her, suddenly—every person in Grand Central Terminal freezes. In mid-step, mid-word, mid-breath, everyone has suddenly stopped moving.

As you peer around the palatial concourse, you realize that no, not everyone is frozen. Some people are still walking around, as bewildered as you. Even the frozen are still breathing and blinking slowly, almost imperceptibly. You weave among the frozen, reassuring yourself that you are not crazy, because those still walking around look as concerned as you do. For five full minutes you forget about the work you have to do tonight, dismiss the possibility that this is a terrorist attack, and just wander through the train station that has transformed into a wax museum.

When was the last time you looked up at the vast, arching ceiling of delicate constellations? The shops bustling in the distance that normally irritate you with the bumbling foot traffic they produce now seem so quaint. Even the mobs of people towards whom you usually shoot death glares are now comprised of individual humans who seem so fragile in their stillness.

In an instant, Grand Central Terminal whizzes into motion again. A man and woman who were stuck in the middle of a heated argument have thrown themselves back into their fervent anger as though no time has passed. When you ask a man who had frozen while biting into a sandwich what happened, he smiles faintly and says, "I don't know what you're talking about." You hurry to catch your train, and everything else in your day is exactly the same, except that it isn't.

There are several names for what you just experienced: Guerilla Theater, a prank, a mission, or an example of the urban playground movement (Cohen-Cruz 1998; Todd 2009: xiv, 106, 141; Newmindspace 2011). In the last decade, these moments have punctuated with increasing visibility and intensity the din of one of the most urban locations on the planet: New York City. In these guerrilla performances, many kinds of actors, professional or amateur, stage many kinds of theater in many kinds of places: on the street, in a restaurant, in a store—virtually anywhere. And because the audience, that is, the general public, does not expect the performance, or even necessarily understand what happened by the end of it, these performances are often referred to as guerrilla theater troupes.

This Caper Crusade has just begun, but the origins of such performances are far-reaching and always the result of or reaction to their particular political, social, and cultural contexts. Flash mobs, peaceful protests, violent riots, the Occupy movement—all of these public acts are in the some way performative. While many performance theorists offer their own definition of performance or performativity, perhaps the most influential is that of Richard Schechner, the American theater director and theorist. In his seminal survey of world performance, *Between Theater and Anthropology*, Schechner identifies various lenses and systems through which theater can be understood. Schechner emphasizes that the performative nature of a practice depends upon the perspective of either performer or spectator. During a performance, "a 'presence' is manifest, something has 'happened,'" as he explains, "the performers have touched or moved the audience, and some kind of collaboration, collective special theatrical life, is born" (Schechner 1985: 10-11). Once either party considers an act a performance, choosing to view the behavior through the lens of a performance, it automatically becomes—one, regardless of where or when it occurs. A performance may transpire, therefore, without performer or, alternatively, audience member, understanding it to be a performance at all.

The applications and implications of this phenomenon have influenced history. During the dramatic sit-ins of the 1960s civil rights movement, for example, blacks used their bodies, which had been involuntarily politicized, to fight the racist and unjust politics of the time. Sitting was an inherently peaceful act that demonstrated the non-threatening possibilities of racial integration, and yet refusing to leave forbidden areas was still a physical confrontation of the absurd racism of the time. And so many remember the image of the lone man of Tiananmen Square standing before the monstrous machinery of the Chinese tanks that became the iconic embodiment, a very vulnerable and human embodiment, of a people oppressed by the government.

Jan Cohen-Cruz, a creator of socially-relevant theater, and the editor of *Radical Street Performance: An International Anthology*, offers a multitude of such performative social movements. She includes an essay by the Brazilian social activist and theater practitioner Augusto Boal from his manifesto *The Theatre of the Oppressed*, in which Boal explains his "invisible theater," as just one of the many types of theater that serves as a "weapon" for the people to wield (Boal 1985: 122). Boal describes a scenario where a man, a secret actor, eats at a real restaurant, but admits at the end of the meal that he cannot afford to pay for it. Other secret actors in the audience provoke a discussion among the patrons and wait staff about the outrageous food prices in the poor community. They rally the unknowing public into taking a collection for the protagonist, highlighting the injustices of food prices all the while (144-147). Boal favors the kind of "invisible theater" that this scenario illustrates because of its liberating potential for action. Unlike in a traditional theater setting, the audience member of invisible theater can "act freely and fully, as if he were living in a real situation—and, after all, it is a real situation!" (147). The audience is thus free to participate (or not) and contribute to social change (or not). What matters here is the provocation.

The difference between invisible theater and a typical rebellion is merely a subtle distinction; after all, the "audience members" are behaving as they would in real life because, as Boal notes, they don't know this is an "artificial" set-up. Neither actor nor audience agree upon (or, in the case of the audience, are even fully aware of) the performativity of the act. Indeed, these particular actors participate because they believe they are doing more than simply entertaining; their location, however secretive, among their peers and townspeople, is crucial. Their performance may be their best means of addressing their societal issues.

Guerilla Theater continues to exist today in its explicitly political incarnation; one need only take the train downtown to Occupy Wall Street to see how the body continues to be a weapon (albeit of contested effectiveness) in the political sphere. The bodies of the Occupyers obstruct or, at the very least, disrupt the routes and patterns of the bankers they abhor. The protestors are physical manifestations of the anger, desperation, and resolve of those who the banks fooled and failed. As gender studies critic Judith Butler proclaimed in a speech,

> It matters that as bodies we arrive together in public ... this is a politics of the public body, the requirements of the body, its movement and its voice. We would not be here if electoral politics were representing the will of the people. We sit and stand and move as the popular will, the one that electoral politics has forgotten and abandoned. (Butler: 2011)

Yet a more recent variation of Guerilla Theater—one that coexists with the original, political form—denies any overt political ambitions. Indeed, their main ambition appears to be fun, plain and simple. Flash mobs that burst out of the crowds in malls or town squares to sing and dance for the bewildered people not "in" on the joke have found increasing popularity. In fact, flash mobs are now so popular that the commercial world has co-opted them as a public relations method. Flash Mob America is one company that specializes in such faux-spontaneous PR. The Union Square Silent Rave, during which people dance in silence while each person rocks out to different music playing on their headphones, has many vocal advocates. And public pillow fights occur annually in several cities across

America (Todd 2009: 141). At least for some, the city of strangers is becoming a city of neighbors eager to good-naturedly beat each other with their couch cushions. But without the context and contrast of the city, these pranks, though perhaps still odd, would not be nearly as funny or joyful.

And we now have the economics to prove it. The ideas and culture that lead to such novel humor arise from "knowledge spillovers,"[1] or "the exchange of ideas among individuals," that in turn correlate positively to the diversity and density of cities (Carlino 2001: 17). Economist Gerald A. Carlino describes Alfred Marshall's 1890 theory that the denser the concentration of members of a common industry (say, humor), the greater the chance that they will exchange ideas that lead to innovation; Carlino then demonstrates how urban studies theorist Jane Jacobs expounded upon Marshall's idea by proposing that "an industrially diverse urban environment encourages innovation because it encompasses people with varied background and interests, thereby facilitating the exchange of ideas among individuals with different perspectives. This exchange can lead to the development of new ideas," jokes among them (18). Noted economists Paul M. Romer and Charles I. Jones also have added that density and diversity may be complimented by "laws supporting intellectual property rights," that is, laws that do not penalize the exchange of ideas but rather encourage such exchange and creativity (Jones and Romer 2009: 7).

While New York laws governing arts or public assembly are not drastically different from other American cities, the diversity and density of the city certainly contributes to its creative freedom and output. New York's economic prosperity after WWII, its former status as doorway to America for immigrants, and countless other factors have also contributed to the creative overflow that gushes out of New York City. Unfortunately, as Nobel Prize-winning economist Paul Krugman observed in *Geography and Trade*, "knowledge flows are invisible; they leave no paper trail by which they may be measured and studied" (Krugman 1991: 53). Indeed, without patents, consistently reliable written accounts or data, the social or political inspirations of guerrilla street theater today can be equally difficult to recognize.

---

[1] Much of the impetus for this particular idea derives from Jonah Lehrer's book *Imagine: How Creativity Works*. Though news that Jonah Lehrer fabricated elements of *Imagine* have both disappointed me and forced me to question the validity of his ideas about cities, my own independent research into his primary sources and other sources confirm this particular thesis, if not other elements of the book (Bosman 2012).

The political inspirations of Improv Everywhere, perhaps the most famous organization of this new guerilla theater scene in New York City, are certainly difficult to recognize; the group eschews all social commentary or analysis, even as it recognizes other improvisation groups that preceded it (Todd 2009: 133, 139-40). Charlie Todd, an improvisation actor, founded Improv Everywhere as a way to give himself acting jobs. As he says in *Causing a Scene,* his how-to guide and account of Improv Everywhere's success, his goal was "to make people look up from their newspapers and turn off their iPods for a minute or two" (Ibid.: 206). But what may initially appear to be just fun and games is actually a result and reflection of the precise social, political, and cultural circumstances of New York City, or any city where these pranks occur.

Charlie Todd's internationally renowned organization grew from a harmless prank in a bar when Todd decided to impersonate alternative rock star Ben Folds (xii-xiii). It was, as he considers most of his pranks today, a prank "that didn't need a victim" (xiv). Todd gradually escalated his pranks to more public and pre-meditated stunts, such as convincing a fake U2 band to perform a free concert on the roof of a building in midtown (1-22). Some might contest the argument that these pranks are indeed victimless; if the U2 performance were poorly received, for example, the artists' reputations and sales could suffer. Or perhaps some audience members might never attend another U2 performance because they had already seen one for free. Identity theft, even of the silly kind, can be damaging.

But for the majority of participants, Improv Everywhere is an organized merriment machine. This is largely because of the Internet; almost all missions are secretly recorded with hidden cameras to share with joy with the World Wide Web without exposing the nature of the prank to those experiencing it first-hand. The smaller missions include only Todd's closest friends and coworkers, and often involve more clearly defined "plots" with specific characters and naturalistic acting. One mission, for example, included an agent impersonating the long-deceased playwright Anton Chekhov giving a reading of his work at the Union Square Barnes and Noble (Todd 2009: 75-87). Larger-scale missions include anyone on their mailing list, and entail simpler but more obvious activities like the No Pants! Subway Ride, during which thousands of New Yorkers ride the subway one winter afternoon each year wearing no pants, just very inspired underwear (161-188). All participants are instructed never to admit that anything is amiss. They are to disappear into the crowd, leaving the "audience" with a typically bizarre New York experience.

In the vast majority of Todd's pranks, what makes New York "New York" is also what makes Improv Everywhere funny. His prank in which he designated an express lane on the sidewalk for New Yorkers and a slower lane for tourists alludes to the universally acknowledged fact that New Yorkers are in a hurry and you'd better get the hell out of their way (Improv Everywhere 2011). And yet he also staged a dance performance in the windows of the Filene's Basement in Union Square that featured large signs compelling the busy New Yorkers to "LOOK UP MORE" (Todd 2009: 205-215). This, perhaps, is the closest Todd comes to openly admitting to social action and relevance, as he firmly believes that "Not only do New Yorkers live life at a frenzied pace, but they also tend to be a bit removed from their surroundings" (206). But how can Todd escape social commentary if he wants to be social?

In addition to providing the fodder for Improv Everywhere's jokes, New York City, eclectic urban insanity that it is, provides the necessary logistics to enact such missions; the context is truly crucial. The first boon the city affords is anonymity. Even as Todd appears on national television and all over the Internet, he remains anonymous to many of the eight million people of New York City, and can therefore continue to participate in pranks. Whether he's the (fake) MC for a (fake) sadistic hypnotist in Union Square or the (fake) coach for the (fake) Olympic synchronized swimming team that wades through the filthy waters of the Washington Square Park fountain, Todd and his agents can continue their missions without revealing their identities or the truth (217-233; 119-134).

Yet another advantage of city life is Todd's large quantities of agents in reserve ready to prank at the drop of an email. The magnitude of the freeze in Grand Central Station derived from the sheer number of participants contrasting the number of people who pass through Grand Central every day. The joy of the Mp3 experiment, in which people simultaneously follow ridiculous instructions downloaded to their Mp3 players, such as launching balloons or joining a conga line, depends on large crowds (135-142). If all the world's a stage, New York has more than enough willing ensemble players.

New York also has, of course, an audience both willing and tolerant of the strange or even the crazy. Todd remembers how when he and his friends first attempted the No Pants! Subway ride in 2002, one woman in the audience turned to her perplexed husband, "rolled her eyes at him and explained, 'Honey, it's *New York*,'" (164). She knew that practically anything goes in New York City. And though Todd has had a few run-ins with the police (apparently dressing in uniforms almost identical to those of Best Buy employees is enough to prompt employees to call the police, but not enough to get arrested), even his wildest pranks are within the juridical, if not always social, laws, of the city (39-62).

Charlie Todd has emphasized repeatedly that he does not create his missions "to make any kind of social or political statement;" rather, he just wants "to capture the attention of people walking on the street" (206). Yet so much of humor, indeed, of all art, depends upon social norms of the cities that the Improv Everywhere pranksters defy. Indeed, Pulitzer Prize-winning playwright and social activist Tony Kushner, in Thinking About the Longstanding Problems of Virtue: Essays, A Play, Two Poems and a Prayer, his collection of essays and plays about his life, politics, and art, beautifully articulates the notion that culture (and, we can extrapolate, the art or humor of that culture) is necessarily a product of a particular political atmosphere, and is, therefore, inherently political. Kushner writes, "How much sense does it make to separate Culture and Politics as distinct categories? If culture can be thought of as both the exalted and the quotidian expressions of a people's life, then all culture is ideological, political, rooted in history and informed by present circumstance. And art has to reflect this, as well as reflect the artist's desires for society and social change which will, whether revolutionary or reactionary, find expression in the work he or she creates" (Kushner 1995: 44).

Though Charlie Todd may not aspire to convince all of New York City to abandon their pants forever, he nonetheless relies on the social norms of what we consider appropriate clothing for the basis of his jokes. If everyone in New York City walked around exposing their underpants every day, then the No Pants! Subway ride wouldn't be funny. Moreover, this prank would not be possible in a city like Riyadh, Saudi Arabia, which maintains much more conservative clothing norms and laws. Todd relies on the politics and culture of New York City—or wherever he is—as the basis of his humor.

Many of Todd's missions poke fun at more complex or insidious social constructs, provoking two main questions: why the joke works, and what it means. While at a comedy festival in Aspen, for example, Todd and his friends noticed that the city had practically no black people, so they set up a "Meet a Black person booth." As Todd describes it, they simply "threw up our sign inviting Aspen residents to meet an actual black person. People stopped and shook Agent Dunn's hand, and more than a few asked if they could pose for a photo" (Todd 2009: 116).

This prank, obviously dependent on the precise racial demographics of Aspen, makes an uncomfortable commentary on the lack of diversity in Aspen. First, that black people are so rare in Aspen that some white residents had never met a black person before raises all sorts of issues about urban population trends, diversity, and exposure to different cultures in America. This stunt certainly dissolves the myth of the melting pot, and highlights how far America still has to go in increasing diversity and awareness of other cultures or ethnicities.

Second, the use of a stall and photography calls to mind a freak show or animal exhibit, which would objectify and further alienate Agent Dunn, the "black person" in the booth, from the audience, even as he poses with them and shakes their hands. If this prank was funny in Aspen, it is probably because everyone is aware of and possibly troubled by the highly white population. But if Todd were to pull this prank on the Upper East Side of Manhattan, doing so would be a rather strong statement about gentrification and the relationship between race and socio-economics in New York. Todd, a resident of New York, has never, so far as I know, attempted this prank in New York.

But another one of Todd's "pranks that didn't need a victim" that did take place in New York did, in a way, target the socio-economic discrepancies of the city, and worked largely because it occurred in New York: that of the bathroom attendant in the Forty-Second Street McDonald's (Ibid.: xiv). In *Causing a Scene*, Todd recounts how one agent threw together a high-class bathroom attendant service in the McDonald's men's room, complete with mints, condoms, cologne, and more, all displayed on silver trays and a lace tablecloth lain across the diaper changing panel. As men entered the less-than-luxurious bathroom, Agent Todd Simmons offered them his high-class services and amenities. The victimless prank continued until the manager of the McDonald's stumbled in. Simmons bought enough time to escape by convincing the manager he was sent from the corporate offices to test this new service, but admitted that maybe he wound up at the wrong McDonald's.

The absurdity of Agent Simmons with his dapper tuxedo offering baby powder in a not-quite-immaculate McDonald's restroom is clear from the photos and videos posted online. The juxtaposition of such a swanky (and unnecessary) service with the cheapest of restaurants certainly speaks to the prickly coexistence of the rich and poor in New York City. When Todd explains the mission, he jokes, "After all, don't the loyal customers of McDonald's deserve the same amenities as, say, the diners at an exclusive restaurant?" and, in doing so, highlights the socio-economic disparities upon which the joke is dependent (144).

Like many of the Improv Everywhere missions, this prank could have taken place in any number of cities of comparable density and diversity to New York, but it somehow seems perfectly suited to the Big Apple. Because there are McDonald's restaurants in almost every neighborhood,

Simmons' exit strategy to play a man confused about the McDonald's to which he was assigned is perfectly plausible. The sheer size of the Forty-Second Street McDonald's also helped keep the employees from noticing the bathroom shenanigans. And the prevalence of tourists heightened the joke, as they understood New York culture less, and therefore were less likely to see through the ruse. Todd also notes that because the employees were immigrants with poor English—certainly not an anomaly in New York—they may not have understood as quickly as a native speaker might have that Simmons was lying.

Though such a comment does not necessarily constitute taking advantage of an immigrant in an exploitative way, the socio-political undercurrents can certainly be felt. Indeed, that a significant product of these interactions is a bunch of people "having fun" does not preclude these interactions from being political. Much of what we would claim to be apolitical is, in fact, a phenomenon that is permissible within its specific legal and political framework. If I were to poll the American public today, inquiring which of two activities is the political one, canvassing for votes or attending a play by Shakespeare, chances are the majority of people would contend that canvassing for votes is the political act. But the question itself, like the question Todd has posed for himself, is flawed. Because all acts are inherently a reflection of their political (and social, and cultural…) milieu, all acts are political. It is not a question whether or not an act is political in the first place, because that is a given.

The question, rather, is *in what way* is the act political, and *to what degree* that act emphasizes a particular issue. After all, as the 19th century American theater producer and historian William Dunlap explains in his *A History of the American Theatre*, theater in Puritan Boston was illegal during the 1790s (Dunlap 2005: 129). The moral corruption of the characters within the plays, it was thought, would infect the audiences with sinfulness. To attend a Shakespearean play was therefore an overt and public political act against the cultural values and restrictions of the state. But in New York or Boston today, few would consider attending Shakespeare in the Park an act of rebellion.

The contrast of censorship or other forms of oppression with the carefree pranks of Charlie Todd or any other guerrilla performers is not intended as a criticism of the ideas Todd chooses to emphasize. New Yorkers could certainly use a day in their underwear now and then. But an acknowledgement of the influence of that context, whether physical, cultural, social, or political, is crucial to understanding the reasoning behind each performance's purpose—and sense of humor.

We will never know whether Improv Everywhere would have flourished as it has without the immense size, level of tolerance, and level of crazy in New York City. What we do know is Todd has been pulling pranks his entire life, but his Improv Everywhere missions only started in New York. What we do know is Grand Central Station is one hell of a place to stage a freeze. What we do know is thousands of New Yorkers have embraced the No Pants! Subway Ride, even in the January chill. What we do know is, for years to come, New Yorkers will shrug at their spouses and say, "Honey, it's *New York*."

Many New Yorkers have their city to thank for Charlie Todd. But Charlie Todd has New York City to thank, too.

## Bibliography

Boal, A. (1985). *Theatre of the Oppressed.* New York: Theatre Communications Group.

Bosman, J. (2012). "Jonah Lehrer Resigns From The New Yorker After Making Up Dylan Quotes for his Book" in Media Decoder, *The New York Times.* 30 July. http://mediadecoder.blogs.nytimes.com/2012/07/30/jonah-lehrer-resigns-from-new-yorker-after-making-up-dylan-quotes-for-his-book/

Bracken, K. and L. Kufner (2011). "Newmindspace." *Newmindspace.* http://www.newmindspace.com

Brooks, C. and S. Lawrence. (2012). "Flash Mob America" in *Flash Mob America.* Decosta, Web. 24 June 2012. http://www.flashmobamerica.com/who-we-are

Butler, J. (2011). Washington Square Park, New York City. Oct. Speech.

Carlino, G. A. "Knowledge Spillovers: Cities' Role in the New Economy" in *Business Review, Federal Reserve Bank of Philadelphia.* http://www.philadelphiafed.org/.../business-*review*/2001/q4/brq401gc.pdf

Chan, S. (2007). "Name America's Most Liberal City" in *The New York Times.* 21 Nov. http://cityroom.blogs.nytimes.com/ 2007/11/21/ name-americas-most-liberal-city

Cohen-Cruz, J. (1998). *Radical Street Performance: an International Anthology.* London: Routledge.

"The Dark Lights of Home." (2012). *The Economist—Prospero,* 13 June. http://www.economist.com/blogs/prospero/2012/06/belarus-free-theatre

Dunlap, W. (2005). *A History of American Theater from Its Origins to 1832.* Urbana: University of Illinois Press.

Goldman, F. (2012). "Children of the Dirty War" in *The New Yorker*. 19 March. Electronic.

Hagen, J. J. (2011). "And Then Judith Butler Showed up at Occupy Wall Street. *Autostraddle*. 25 Oct. http://www.autostraddle.com/ and-then-judith-butler-showed-up-at-occupy-wall-street-in-solidarity117911

"Improv Everywhere." (2011). *Improv Everywhere: We Cause Scenes*. 24 April. http://improveverywhere.com

Jones, C. I. and Paul M. Romer. (2009). "The New Kaldor Facts: Ideas, Institutions, Population, And Human Capital" in *National Bureau of Economic Research*. June. http://ww.nber.org/papers/w15094

Krugman, P. (1991). *Geography and Trade*. Cambridge: M.I.T. Press.

Kushner, T. (1995). *Thinking about the Longstanding Problems of Virtue and Happiness: Essays, a Play, Two Poems, and a Prayer*. New York: Theatre Communications Group.

Lehrer, J. (2012). *Imagine: How Creativity Works*. New York: Houghton Mifflin Harcourt.

Schechner, R. (1985). *Between Theater and Anthropology*. Philadelphia: University of Pennsylvania Press.

Todd, C. (2009). *Causing a Scene: Extraordinary Pranks in Ordinary Places with Improv Everywhere*. New York: William Morrow.

—. "Charlie Todd on the Today Show." Interview by Al Roker. *The Today Show*. NBC. New York City, NY. Television.

# CHAPTER EIGHTEEN

# PIECES OF LEMON AND OTHER BLACK LATINA STORIES

# RAFAELA SANTOS

Sociology allows us to understand, wonder about, and question who we are in this world, as well as how the world both frees us and imprisons us. Here, I entertain C. Wright Mill's seminal text from 1959, *The Sociological Imagination,* and its main concept: that the "sociological imagination" is a critical quality of the mind, which is crucial in understanding the dynamics between self and society, private and public, personal experience and history. Folkloric stories help illuminate moments when the "sociological imagination" is provoked, and eventually, awakens.

As the folkloric snippets here show, the "sociological imagination" awakens when self and society do not line up. For instance, what does it mean to be a "Black" Latina in New York City? However painful some of these realizations may be, another notion resurfaces as well: true, the self is shaped by society, but the self also helps shape and re-shape the society that she is living in.

Chapter Eighteen

# Cantitos de Limon (Pieces of Lemon)

By definition I am an American but my English is heavily accented because Spanish is my first language and unlike many of my friends' parents, my parents don't speak English. Born in Manhattan, bred in the Bronx, *Una Boricua Negra*, a Black Puerto Rican who eats rice and beans almost every day, a true Puertorriqueña, I live in a vast urban environment with public schools, mass transit, and graffiti; heroin use is stylish, pot fills duffel bags, and $1 joints are all the rage.

First generation in every respect, I dream of distant places. Cute, color *caramelo*, curly brown hair, athletic and petite, a dark Latina—I only want to find a way to feel that I belong in this urban world.

This is an exciting year for me because every 4th grade class in my school is taken on a yearly trip to the Poconos in November and this year it is our turn. The classroom feels electric and buzzes with contained excitement as we fidget in our chairs anxiously. We can't wait to get to lunch so that we can talk about the trip. We share our daydreams about the trip in hushed whispers and boast about potential escapades. Most of us haven't been anywhere except to places in New York like the Empire State Building and the Statute of Liberty. Some of us have been to Puerto Rico and I don't mention that I lived in Pennsylvania for a short time because I don't remember much of it.

*Mami* is buying my sister and I (she always buys us the same things at the same time so that neither of us feels neglected) more winter clothes because she heard that it is colder in the Poconos than it is in The Bronx.

Everything is going great in school. Our teacher speaks Spanish and makes us feel special. She is the only teacher who listens to kids and smiles when we ask questions. It is great to have friends in school and it is even better to have your best friend live in the same building where you live. Life is perfect.

It is a quiet weekday afternoon in early fall and despite the sun there is a nip in the air. If you listen closely, you can hear rustling as the leaves fall through the air. The fall, my favorite season, puts me closer to our trip to the Poconos. From my window, I see the people rushing home; the sun is setting and casts a long quiet shadow across the sidewalk in front of the building. I quickly finish my homework, and go downstairs to hang out at my friend's apartment for a little while.

We sit on her bed talking. I like her room a lot. It is pink and white with curtains that match the *colcha* (bedspread). She has teddy bears all over her room! She is the only person I know that wears a nightgown and a robe on top of it; both of them are hanging on a hook behind the door waiting to be used again. We talk about the trip to the Poconos, when my friend's mother walks into the room and reminds her that it is time for her bath. "Oh" she says, "And don't forget to use lemon on your elbows because you don't want black elbows." As I leave, I can feel that my eyes get all scrunched up and I ask myself, "What _are_ black elbows?" I shrug and walk back upstairs to my apartment. I go to bed, having forgotten about that question.

The trip to the Poconos is only a few weeks away. I don't remember how but one day I notice that I have "black elbows." And I hear my friend's mother's voice again, "... you don't want black elbows." Are black elbows bad? Why do I have them and my friend does not? Mami uses lemon to clean the meat and fish. Why did my friend's mother tell her to use lemon on her elbows? I don't know what lemons have to do with black elbows. Would lemons get my black elbows cleaner, less black? How about my knees? My friend and her whole family look like vanilla ice cream, like my sister and *Papi* but *Mami* and I are caramel color with black elbows. How do I ask my friend about the lemons? I don't know how to ask my *Mami* about it either. I look at the bed and see all the stuff that *Mami* has bought us for the trip. She even bought us these itchy winter blankets in grey and blue pea coats; I begin to try on my clothes and soon forget the lemons again.

The day has come and we are on our way to the Poconos. Everyone is quiet on the bus. I guess we are all nervous (at least I am) about this new experience. We sleep in a big house called a "Lodge"; it has a big fireplace that makes the living room feel warm and toasty. The house is so big and has a lot of windows; the biggest window is shaped like a triangle and the living room is almost the size of our gym in school.

We do all sorts of wonderful things, learn about nature and drink the best hot chocolate that melts in your mouth and warms you from the tip of your head all the way down to your toes. It is the last day and we say goodbye to everyone, I am so sad because I feel so at home here and fear that I will never see this place again. As we sit on the bus getting ready for the drive back to The Bronx, I take one last look out the window and memorize everything that is within sight: will I ever experience something like this again?

This is my best school year ever. It ends and there are rumors that the 5th grade class will go to the Poconos again next year! I beg *Mami* to let me go next year; "*Vamos a ver,*" she says, "We shall see."

I get to go to the Poconos the following year and at the end of the summer Mami and Papi decide to move to another part of the Bronx. I settle into the new neighborhood, lemons being the furthest thing from my mind. I wonder if I will never see my friend again.

Hennessey Place is a hill of a street, nestled between 179$^{th}$ Street and Burnside Avenue and extending for only one block. There is a lot of life and activity here. People are always coming in and out of the Bodega, *los Viejos* (the old folks) play dominoes in front of the building, kids play stickball, babies cry. Most people do not know of the existence of this block, so I usually tell them I live on Burnside Avenue. Burnside Avenue's clothing stores are perfect for shopping and the subway makes it a perfect place to live. Everything is nearby to everything, yet not that close—it is my favorite place to live.

My first summer here is exciting and fun. I love playing softball with my friends in the middle of the street. I go to the pool every day at Roberto Clemente State Park. It costs 50 cents to get into the pool and you get a quarter back when you return your locker key—the right amount of money for me to buy a snack—I am always so hungry after going to the pool! On my short walk home, I stop at the bodega for some lemon cookies, my favorite after pool snack, sweet but tangy at the same time, they satisfy my hunger until I get home.

## Que Negra Bella! (What a Beautiful Black Woman!)

I climb fences, play stickball with my friends and don't care how I look. But then the summer of 1977 arrives, and changes everything. "Canto El Gallo"—I get my period for the first time! And I realize that everything Mami has been teaching me has been about how to become a *Senorita,* a young lady. I am being groomed to be a wife! Soon I will learn how to cook rice and meat, go "food shopping," iron, sew, do laundry, care for the sick, change a diaper and yes, do my own *rolos,* hair rollers.

I am thinking that my life is over. Chin in hand, I am annoyed with the cramping in my stomach; my friends yell from up the street, "hey girl, come and play ball," "Come on," and I respond "Maybe later," "I can't right now," *A hora no puedo,* but I know that later would never come again. Soon, the boys no longer want me on their team; they begin to treat me differently. My body starts to change: hips, chest, and butt become distorted, stretched, and fuller but all I want to do is play stickball.

It's dinner time. I am sitting on the window sill, looking out into the street. My neighbors, who have to run errands, hurriedly walk to and fro on Burnside Avenue, stopping by the Bodega to get the last items needed for dinner or just to buy a pack of cigarettes before the place closes. I begin to stay upstairs more often, looking out the window—I enjoy that—

or listening to the radio—I listen to Pop, and Rock & Roll—or reading books. The book that I am reading right now describes distant places with names like Switzerland, Paris, and England. I dream of being someplace else, the Poconos, or places in the book, somewhere away from all the concrete and boxed in feeling in this city; a place just for me.

One day I'm lying across Mami's bed facing the dresser. She has all this make-up and perfume on it. I don't remember where she is going but she is getting ready to put on her make-up and get dressed. She walks around the house all day in her *rolos* until it is time to get dressed and style her hair. How easily she transforms from a housewife with a flowery *Bata*, house-gown, to a movie star! Mami starts getting ready and I am fascinated as I watch her grab a bottle of Ultra Sheen hairspray and start mummifying her hairdo so that by the time she finishes, her hair looks like a still life perched on her head. She sprays so much of that stuff that a white cloud of hairspray fumes hover in front of the dresser.

The make-up comes next. Her skin looks like a dark caramel color because of her suntan, smooth like cream that has been whipped a thousand times, *que negra bella*. Her full lips and rounded cheeks stand at attention when she smiles and make her expressive brown eyes glisten with suppressed laughter. She uses only the best make-up and perfume, Max Factor and Chanel #5, which she buys somewhere in *Ma'hatan*.

Stickball becomes a distant memory as pencil eyeliner and lip gloss are my new obsession. I greedily read fashion and Right-On magazines and one day I am reading a beauty magazine and discover an article that awakens something in me that has been buried long ago. The article has beauty tips:

1). Use cucumber slices to reduce eye puffiness;
2). When applied monthly, olive oil will add sheen to your hair;
3). Use lemon slices on elbows and knees to lighten unwanted darkened
   areas of your skin.

"Unwanted darkened areas of your skin ..."

I push the magazine to the side as I absorb this information and remember the pieces of lemon. I finally understand why my friend's mother told her daughter to use them and suddenly I am sad. A question pops into my head, "What does a Puertorriqueña look like?"

## Rompiendo Las Barreras (Breaking the Barriers)

When I am 19 years of age, I decide to go to college but it will not be easy. I am already a mother twice over, with my own apartment. I have an interview at the Empire Business School, a stepping-stone for now. I hear that this is the best place to get your GED and get a business certificate. I am excited to embark on this new journey.

I feel nervous as I get dressed, a pair of slacks and a collar shirt. *Mami*, ever supportive, is watching the kids for me while I go on this interview. I arrive early so I sit in an outer office for a while before I am called in. A Latino man calls me into his office—he looks so tall—he shakes my hand and introduces himself, and I'm so scared that the blood rushing in my ears doesn't allow me to hear him. He is large and seems to dwarf the desk and chair.

"So, tell me why you want to attend the Empire State Business School?" he asks. "Well, I want to get my GED so I can go to college, get off of welfare, and get a bank account," I answer. He has this smile on his face … then he puts his hands together and puts them both on his desk, leans forward, and asks, "Is your mother on welfare?" and I say, "Yes, she is, why?" He leans in a little closer and asks, "Have you been on welfare all of your life?" I whisper, "Yes." And he says, "Well, I doubt you will ever get off welfare because you are probably used to the money and wouldn't know how to balance a check book." There is nothing else to say so I leave, not understanding why I had tears streaming down my face.

Two months later I go to another business school, one that has an accounting course. I am studying for my GED and taking typing and accounting courses. A few weeks into the first semester, I beg the director to allow me to take the GED and I pass it with high marks. He is surprised by the results and sends me to my first job interview at a law firm. I am so nervous but the interview goes well. The lawyer calls me and tells me I got the job and asks me when can I start working. I cannot wait to get my first paycheck so that I can open my first bank account. When I do, I make a silent vow that I will have this bank account forever so that I can prove to him, the guy at the business school (although he will never know, but I will) and to myself that I can change my life and make it better.

## An Urbanite in the Country

It has been a busy two months for me, and the Christmas of 2011 is almost upon me; it may well end up being the most historic because I have done only 20 percent of my shopping, half-hearted attempts here and there. Work deadlines almost every day, mommy and wifely duties can fill the space that is reserved for excuses, but for this year, this is not the case. It seems as though Christmas has taken on an obligatory flair, what do I HAVE to buy for so and so and what will SATISFY the rule for a "friends" gift? Sifting through the archives of my mind, I try to remember what gifts I meted out last year; I am frustrated at my lack of recall. Finally, I have a few days off for the holiday.

I head to my house in the country, a few hours away from the City. I bought this house a few years ago; it is my sanctuary, a place for me to escape the chaos of the city, where I don't have to worry about who I am. Every time I am there, but especially in the winter, I am reminded of my first visit to the Poconos, back in fourth grade: the cold and crisp air, the serenity, the clarity, the simplicity of things... Here I enjoy the opportunity to spend time with my family, re-group, re-charge, and re-assess my life. Unlike the City with its constant noise and distractions, the cold country air is good for reflection and peace; I certainly need some of that! It is also the place where I can lose myself doing something I love to do, which is painting. When I am on the deck painting, with the mountains in the distance and the sun setting behind them, I am suddenly transported to different places, all at once, with my worldly concerns far behind me.

It is midday, there is a grocery list to complete, wine to buy, and so we decide to stop at the local strip mall that we go to on the weekends. The "strip mall" is small in comparison to the ones you find in larger towns. It has a supermarket, drug store, pizza shop, discount store, a tractor country store and the only clothing store within 20 miles. Hey, we have been coming here for over 7 years; it is on the way to the house.

Just like other retailers in the Country, the clothing store has their annual Christmas sale. Designer labels for less, how can I go wrong? As I enter the store, I decide almost immediately that EVERYONE is getting a sweater or some article of clothing for Christmas; that will take the guesswork out of everything! A few gift bags at the discount store next door and my shopping will be complete in a matter of hours. I should have I thought of this before.

After years of shopping at this store, I feel perfectly at home here. I am a curvy short black Latina with short blond hair and walking in behind me is my teenage daughter—a beautiful girl who people often ask if she is the product of white and black parents—who jauntily walks in as if she owns the place, head flicking left and right looking at all the cool clothes and very ready to spend my money.

I set to my task, as my daughter becomes my shopping assistant as I unload my ever-increasing burden of clothing onto those reluctant arms.

Most teenagers don't feel the need to help out, but with the promise of a few articles of clothing, voila, the protests cease! The load becomes so heavy that we carry the clothing to the counter and ask that they be set aside until our shopping spree is complete.

It appears that we are not the only ones getting those last minute gifts; people wander in and out of the store at a steady pace. After about two hours, and after going over the list of names who need gifts in my head countless times, to make sure that I haven't forgotten someone, we make our way to the counter.

I have a smile on my face because I realize that at some point during the shopping spree I got into the "Christmas" spirit. My bank account, the same one I've had for twenty years, is about to take a big hit but who cares; the thought of friends and loved ones warm my heart. I notice that the cashier is tight-lipped and the older woman who is helping her jerkily folds my clothes.

The cashier scans the items and I ask if the discount is automatically taken off the original price; I receive a curt reply. While at the register, I decide to try on a blazer one last time to be sure I want to buy it. The older woman behind the counter exclaims in a loud voice "She has that blazer; don't forget to charge her for it!" I look over at my daughter who is as perplexed by the woman's behavior as I am. I smile and inform the cashier as I take off the blazer and hand it to her, "yes," I am also purchasing this piece.

The older woman, in the same loud voice begins to ask the cashier if she counted all of the items and if she charged me for everything. I begin to flush and feel embarrassed that this woman is speaking of me in such a loud manner. Customers standing on line behind me whisper, "Why is she talking so loud?" "Why is she acting like that?" I steal a glance at my daughter and see anger clearly registered on that youthful face, her lips barely visible as she grimaces.

Throughout the whole exchange, I remain polite, thank both women, and carry my purchases from the store, yet I am in a haze. As we walk out of the store, my husband comes out a few minutes after us. You can tell he witnessed the whole exchange because he is livid.

He is telling us that he lingered in the store after we left to see if she, the older woman, treated anyone else that way. He says that the bizarre behavior by this woman was reserved solely for me. Although I am a Black Latina, all I am reminded of is my "blackness." All I can think about is this: she is racist, she is ignorant, she is this, she is that … but it doesn't matter what she is because for the first time I feel out of my element, that this is not my environment. I am not in the City, my true home, dealing with some rude store employee who I can call to task and speak to the manager about his or her lack of professionalism.

My family wants to file a complaint, blog, send emails and have someone, anyone, acknowledge this injustice: it is just not right! The only explanation I can come up with is that the woman's behavior is ignorant, and yet I have this inexplicable desire to run … We are reminded that despite volunteering our time for this community, despite baking pies year after year, despite embracing our neighbors and their concerns, we are still outsiders, and we always will be. My multicolored Latino "urban family" is in a country store with country people, and we are made to feel that we simply don't belong here.

My heart is beating fast and the sense of wanting to run does not abate. For the first time in all my years I understand why innocent people run. I reassure everyone that everything is fine. I am proud of my composure in front of my daughter and family but inside I feel something very different. If you ask me why I feel this way, I will not be able to answer that question because in this instant all I want to do is run: outrun the shame that I feel and wait until the danger is over.

Today, I am reminded of who I am, and of how I do not fit in because of that… I add this experience to my memory box, right next to the pieces of lemon, and remember a promise I made to myself long ago: that I will leave my mark on this society as a "Black Latina."

Fig. 18-1. An Urban Woman, By Rafaela Santos, February 2012

# CONTRIBUTORS

**Keisha-Gaye Anderson** is a Jamaican-born poet, writer, and multimedia producer living in Brooklyn, New York. She is a past recipient of a fellowship from the North Country Institute for Writers of Color and was short listed for the Small Axe Literary Competition in 2010. She is a 2013 candidate for a Master's of Fine Arts in Creative Writing from The City College, The City University of New York, and a long standing member of the Harlem Arts Alliance Screenwriting Workshop, led by noted screenwriters Jamal Joseph and Zach Sklar.

**Lois Ascher** is a Professor in the Humanities Department at Wentworth Institute of Technology, Boston, MA. Her area of professional interest is urban studies, which has grown out of teaching a course on Boston, titled "Boston Voyages." Currently she is a member of the Board of Directors of the West End Museum.

**Nathalie Boucher** holds a Master's in Anthropology from Laval University and a PhD in Urban Studies from the Institute of National Scientific Research in Montreal, Canada. After studying social interactions in the public spaces of Downtown Los Angeles public spaces, she now focuses on interactions in aquatic public spaces, such as public baths and pools, as a post-doctoral scholar at the University of Western Australia's Center of Excellence in Natural Resource Management. She is a board member of the Canadian Society of Anthropology Society since 2011.

**Michelle Lee Dent** is a Senior Language Lecturer in the Expository Writing Program at NYU where she teaches creative non-fiction, persuasive essay writing, and research analysis. She holds a PhD in Performance Studies from NYU, a MA in Cultural Anthropology from Columbia, and a BFA in Dance from Cornish College in Seattle, Washington. Her research interests are typically located at the intersection of the Arts & Humanities and the Social Sciences; she is currently working on a book about women in Alaska during the early 1900s.

**Ronald Dorris** holds the Alumni Class of '58 Professorship in Liberal Arts in African American Studies and English at Xavier University of Louisiana. He is a lifelong resident of Garyville, LA, a small sugarcane town thirty-five miles west of New Orleans. He has traveled to Africa, Canada, Europe and the Caribbean.

**Matthew Hawkins** is a lecturer in Media Production at Coventry University, UK. **Marta Rabikowska** is a senior lecturer in Media and Advertising at the University of East London. Rabikowska and Hawkins are actively engaged in community-based creative research and local collaborations at the outskirts of London. Their visual research has received funding from the Leverhulme Trust and charity organizations and their ethnographic documentaries made in Plumstead received jury prizes at film festivals in Milan and San Francisco.

**Margarita Kompelmakher** is a PhD student in Theater Historiography at the University of Minnesota. Her areas of research are in migration and performance and Eastern European Theater and Film.

**David Michalski** is the editor of the journal *Streetnotes* and the author of *Cosmos and Damian: a World Trade Center Collage.* (Bootstrap Press 2005) He has written a number of essays on cities including, "Cities Culture Memory Collage" in *Art and the Performance of Memory.* (Routledge Press 2002) and "Portals to Metropolis: 19th-century guidebooks and the assemblage of urban experience" in the journal *Tourist Studies.* David Michalski earned his Ph.D. in Cultural Studies and Critical Theory at the University of California, Davis in 2010, where he serves as the Social and Cultural Studies Librarian.

**Tara H. Milbrandt** is an assistant professor of sociology at the University of Alberta's liberal arts and sciences campus, Augustana. She works in the areas of classical theory, interpretive theory, and contemporary culture. Her current work explores the intersections of urban, public and visual culture.

**Samuel Neural** is currently pursing a doctorate in Anthropology at the Université Lyon II Louis Lumière. His study centers on First Nation cultures in Canada (James Bay Cree, Mohawks) and contemporary issues such as cultural ecology, native media, and native urban culture. His prior research includes the pastoral societies in Chile, contemporary Hunting and Gathering societies in Argentina and Australia, and fishing in Oceania.

**E. Jerry Persaud** is an assistant professor in the department of Media and Communication at the State University of New York at New Paltz. He has also taught in the Black Studies and Sociology departments. His doctorate work was completed at York University in Toronto, Canada.

**Matthew A. Postal** is an historian at the New York City Landmarks Preservation Commission. He holds degrees from Vassar College, New York University, and the Graduate Center of the City University of New York. Matt teaches in the graduate program of the New York School of Interior Design, as well as at Lewis & Clark College. In addition to writing essays on the history of American architecture and urbanism, he recently co-authored two books on New York City, the *Guide to New York City Landmarks* and *Ten Architectural Walks in Manhattan*, both published in 2009.

**Inés Rae** is currently Lecturer in Media Arts (Photography) at Plymouth University, UK. Her research explores the photographic image in terms of the vernacular, cultural anthropology and material culture. Recent publications include *Kurl up n Dye*, a monograph published by Wild Pansy Press incorporating photographs and typography investigating the vernacular in British high street culture. Current work in progress is *The Grammar of Glamour: Shooting the High Street* — an investigation into the materiality of photographic media, social space and the street.

**J. Emmanuel Raymundo** is an Assistant Professor at Tulane University. He has held fellowships at the Max Planck Institute for the History of Science, the Chemical Heritage Foundation, the University of Pennsylvania and Princeton University. He received his PhD from Yale University.

**Rafaela Santos** is currently employed as a Project Coordinator for a federally funded mental health program in the Bronx. She is a product of that borough who was educated on the streets and went on to earn a BA in Urban Legal Studies and a Master's in Sociology at City College of New York. A poet, an artist and a sociologist, she continues to nurture her family, teach crotchet, salsa, and expressive urban art.

**Melanie Sovern** is a 2012 Fulbright Finalist, Lewis Rudin Scholar, and recent graduate of New York University Gallatin School of Individualized Study, where she received her BA in Performance Theory and Administration, with a minor in French. As she pursues a career in theater management and producing, Melanie continues to write essays that consider how performance interacts with other aspects of life. She currently works at the Manhattan Theatre Club, one of the premiere not-for-profit theaters on and Off-Broadway.

**Tolonda M. Tolbert** has worked as a diversity consultant and independent researcher in New York City for the past fifteen years, founding *Diversity Speaks NYC*. She teaches graduate classes on diversity, racism, oppression and privilege at New York University, and is a national facilitator on social justice issues for the Anti- Defamation League's A WORLD OF DIFFERENCE Institute®, GLSEN (Gay, Lesbian and Straight Education Network), and Morningside Center for Teaching Social Responsibility. Dr. Tolbert is a community organizer and public advocate in Brooklyn, New York, where she lives with her family.

**Joe Trotta** is an associate professor of English linguistics in the Department of Languages and Literatures at the University of Gothenburg, Sweden. The focus of much of Trotta's research has been on modern grammar/syntax, but Joe is a scholar with many interests and eclectic tastes, which include, among other things, semantics, sociolinguistics, urban dialectology, semiotics, computer-mediated communication and Popular Culture. Most of Joe's most recent publications deal with issues of identity and linguistic representation in different Popular Culture channels such as TV dialogs, music lyrics, ads, social media, etc.